Praise for
THE BODIES OF OTHERS

"Naomi Wolf is one of the bravest, clearest-thinking people I know. The reason you hear the forces of repression so desperately trying to dismiss her is because she is right."

—Tucker Carlson

"Dr. Naomi Wolf's book stands apart in a world of groupthink. It is an impeccable, thought-provoking compilation of the troubling and distressing consequences of the COVID-19 pandemic, including censorship and the suppression of alternatives to the mainstream narrative."

—Dr. Paul Alexander, former WHO COVID
pandemic evidence-synthesis advisor

"Naomi Wolf warned America and the world at the start of this 'pandemic' that it would be used to eviscerate the Constitution and civil liberties. It is uncanny how right she was, how she predicted the tyranny that was to come via the lockdowns and mask and vaccine mandates. In *The Bodies of Others,* she takes you on a journey through a modern day Dante's *Inferno.* This is a book that will shake you to your core, a warning of the struggle ahead and what you can do to resist it."

—Steve Bannon

"Naomi Wolf's courage is a gift to us all. Her work in this brilliant book is groundbreaking and inescapably important for anyone who cares about freedom and human dignity."

—Eric Metaxas, #1 *New York Times* bestselling
author and host of the nationally syndicated
Eric Metaxas Radio Show

T0034936

THE
BODIES
OF
OTHERS

THE
BODIES
OF
OTHERS

The New Authoritarians,
COVID-19, and
The War Against the Human

NAOMI WOLF

Bestselling author of *The End of America* and *Give Me Liberty*

New York, New York

All Seasons Press books may be purchased in bulk at special discounts for sales
promotion, corporate gifts, fund-raising, or educational purposes. Special
editions can also be created to specifications. For details, contact the Special
Sales Department, All Seasons Press, 307 West 36th Street, 11th Floor,
New York, NY 10018.

All Seasons Press® is a registered trademark of Skyhorse Publishing, Inc.®,
a Delaware corporation.

Visit our website at skyhorsepublishing.com.

10 9 8 7 6 5 4 3 2 1

Library of Congress Cataloging-in-Publication Data is available on file.

Cover design by Brian Peterson
Front Cover image: 1218154152/uchar/istock.com. Stock photo.
Posed by model.

Print ISBN: 978-1-951934-42-2
Ebook ISBN: 978-1-64821-079-2

Printed in the United States of America

"And that stirring sent a wave of emotion over him: a
simple and reverent sympathy with his heart,
his human heart, with its questions and riddles,
beating all alone up here in the icy void."

—Thomas Mann, The Magic Mountain, 1924

For the 2049 Generation

ACKNOWLEDGMENTS

I owe great thanks to many remarkable mentors, friends, colleagues and subjects whose work, guidance and examples led me to write this book. Jeffrey A. Tucker supported my research by inviting me to be a Fellow at the American Institute for Economic Research in Great Barrington, Massachusetts. He, Dr. Edward Stringham, then-President of AIER, and my other colleagues at the Institute demonstrated daily commitment to the highest levels of intellectual achievement devoted to the service of liberty in a darkening time. Mr. Tucker is a beacon of leadership in the liberty movement in general and his example of adhering relentlessly to the defense of civilized norms was a source of inspiration. Phillip Magness shared insights about economics and liberty that helped me to evolve my own perspectives on these issues. Dr. Jay Bhattacharya and Dr. Martin Kulldorff gave me interviews with valuable public health information that changed my thinking, as did Dr. Paul Alexander, Dr. Harvey Risch, Dr. Howard Tenenbaum and Dr. Peter McCullough.

Steven K. Bannon exemplified what should be American ideals for civic life, for investigative reporting and for open debate, by regularly welcoming me to bring these arguments and findings to his podcast platform *WarRoom*. I am grateful too for the millions of patriotic listeners in "the *WarRoom* Posse" who supported and engaged with my updates about the current crisis. Other conservative or libertarian interlocutors, including my former Yale classmate Eric Metaxas, and Scott Morefield, gave amplification to my warnings about losses of rights. Dr. Drew Pinsky and Sharon Pinsky, Dinesh D'Souza, Jamie Glazov and the Independent Institute all hosted conversations that helped me to develop and communicate the themes in this book.

My colleagues at DailyClout.io, especially CSO Craig Klein, made our advocacy work protecting our rights possible, and lessons from this work also informed my analysis. Russ Stratton edited skillfully the video interviews I did with heroes of our era; he and Johanna Baldwin sustained me with friendship and sound advice.

I thank Jenin Younes for many important conversations at AIER as we both faced the painful fact that the contemporary Left had institutionally abandoned its historic role as defender of human rights and personal freedoms. She is a fierce advocate for liberty, and I learned a great deal about the legal aspects of "lockdown" harms and medical discrimination, from watching her work at NCRA. Lori Roman of ACRU tirelessly helped me field emails and contacts from people facing medical discrimination and modelled the way people should be able to form productive friendships and intellectual alliances across ideological divides.

Tucker Carlson invited me on his show to share information about harms to women's health and harms to personal freedoms, when my usual media contacts and platforms were refusing to look at these issues. Leslie Manookian of HFDF kept me informed about her groundbreaking legal work, which helped me develop an intellectual framework the harms of "lockdowns" and mandates within the law. State Rep. Melissa Blasek (R-NH) educated me about emergency law, and State Rep. Heidi Sampson (R-ME) brought me to the Maine Capitol to address her fellow legislators, informed me about harms to small businesses from "lockdowns," and broke a major news story about money flows to schools to enforce abusive policies.

Activist and producer Jennifer Sey, and Tiffany Justice of Moms 4 Liberty, both influenced my thinking about how children are harmed by the policy about which I write here. Wendy Ractliffe is a stellar activist for health freedom, whose work on pharmaceutical companies' influence was vital to my understanding of the corporate forces in play. I could not have done without her friendship, strategic guidance, and encouragement. Steve Berger frequently helped me understand issues at hand via sending important research links, shared impactful analyses of his own, and read the manuscript. Charlotte Walker was also a valued expert reader. Stephanie Locricchio, Aimee Villella, Mary Holland and Robert F. Kennedy, Jr., informed me continually in their roles as courageous advocates and commentators on the front lines of medical tyranny.

Jane Dystel, Miriam Goderich and the team at Dystel and Goderich are the kind of agents that a writer is fortunate to have. I appreciate their sterling support. Elaine Lafferty made thoughtful connections and shared with me responses that helped me bring the book to readers. I am very grateful for the energies, dedication and skills of the team at All Seasons Press, my publisher, who brought this work across the finish line.

My best reader and most reliable champion is, as always, my mother Dr. Deborah Wolf. I thank also my wonderful children Rosa and Joe Shipley, as well as my wonderful stepchildren Ayla O'Shea and Alex O'Shea, for their love, support, wit and patience. No writer/ mom/stepmom could be more fortunate in being inspired by four extraordinary young people, whose generations' future is the subject of this book.

Above all I thank my husband, Brian O'Shea. Daily he wrestled with these issues along with me; for two years he fought this battle practically, alongside me; and in the process he taught me a great deal about how to fight for freedom. I am grateful to him as an expert reader, as a rigorous interlocutor, as an ally, and as a partner in arms.

INTRODUCTION to the PAPERBACK EDITION of *THE BODIES OF OTHERS*

This book was published in 2022; it was among the very first of what became a torrent of books that sought to elucidate the darkness and chaos that descended upon the world—and especially upon the West—around March 11, 2020.

The subject of this book is and was the encroach of tyranny upon free societies in the West—and especially upon the United States—using the rubric of "public health" as its stalking horse.

This theme, of how societies lose their freedoms, was not a new subject for me.

I was prepared to notice the benchmarks of descending tyranny in 2020–2022, as I had published a book titled *The End of America* in 2007, which examined how fragile democracies can be subverted or overrun by authoritarian leaders—whether those authoritarians hailed from the left or from the right. Because of my previous work researching times and places in history where the levers of free societies were crushed, I could quickly tell that "coronavirus" and the narrative around it, was being deployed to take on the same role—that of frightening, intimidating, and coercing into compliance, formerly free citizens—that had been attempted in similar ways in 2001–2007, under the guise of "GWOT"—"The Global War on Terror."

Sadly, as this new edition of *The Bodies of Others* prepares to go to press, I must somberly conclude that all of the warnings I provided readers two years ago in this book, have come true—in flamboyantly awful scale and detail.

The entities that I identified in the first edition as spearheading a global coup—the World Health Organization, the World Economic Forum, the Bill and Melinda Gates Foundation, and the Chinese Communist Party—have proven indeed to have been spearheading a global coup.

It turns out that I was right in the nature of my warnings to the world. The "Opposition" did indeed want to target humanity itself. It turns out that they did indeed wish to do so by isolating us, making us sicker, and destroying human connection, so that they can more fully control us.

Since the hardback edition of this book was published, the WHO has revealed its plans for what I warned would be a goal of meta-national governance. It is doing so in the form of a Pandemic Treaty that would drain signatory nations of their sovereignty, that would allow the WHO to declare a global pandemic at will, and also to deploy enforcers of their public health diktats around the world.

I warned in this book about the role of China in manufacturing MRNA injections; now we see that Fosun Pharmaceutical, the CCP's flagship pharma company, has produced a billion doses of the mRNA injection for export, and opened a dozen offices in the US alone, with two manufacturing plants here. Since the publication of the hardcover, my team of 3,250 doctors and scientists who joined the volunteer effort to read through the 450,000 Pfizer documents released via court order, the WarRoom/DailyClout Pfizer Documents Analysis Volunteers, have revealed via the Pfizer documents thousands of deaths, six-figure levels of disability, a focus on destroying reproductive health in women and in men, a causal relationship between the mRNA injections for pregnant women and the loss of babies in utero, and catastrophic levels of strokes, heart damage, blood clots, neurological conditions and other diseases, caused by the mRNA formulations. Birth rates in the West are down by 13–20 percent, according to government databases. The mRNA vaccines have led to a surge in excess deaths; a scaling-up of "turbo-cancers" a phrase that did not even exist in wide use before the mRNA vaccine rollout; and they resulted in permanently weakened immune systems among the populations as a whole. Those who follow our work know that I have concluded that the mRNA injections are bioweapons and part of the war against the West.

I warned that masks did not work to stop COVID, and that they were being deployed to alienate humans from one another and from ourselves. Indeed, peer-reviewed studies have since confirmed that masks don't work to stop COVID.

Masks do work, though, to torture children, just as "lockdowns" worked to delay children's socialization and learning. The effect of the school closures of 2020–2021, as well as the abusive "masking" of children, will set us back educationally at least a generation, with low-income children hurt hardest. Critical thinking skills have understandably declined among the rising generations—which in turn will in the future make it even easier for nefarious elites to control us.

I warned in this book that what was being imposed upon the cultures of the West, was a wholesale revision down to the very level of language, to re-align advanced-Capitalist and individualistic societies, along classical Marxist and communitarian lines. Since the first edition was published, we have seen the deployment of AI to align news outlets in attacking dissident voices and even opposition leaders; we have seen the weaponization of children's curricula to create more and more lawyers of State intervention between kids and their parents; we have seen concerned parents targeted by the State as "terrorists"; we have had revealed by successful lawsuits, the efforts of our own White House, CDC and NIH, to put pressure on social media companies to censor and de-platform dissidents. The Governor of New York State continues to fight for the right to establish quarantine camps that would barely provide judicial review for those unfortunate enough to be taken there; in Australia, since this book first came out, quarantine camps have in fact been established, and public figures have in fact been held there. Ireland has been targeted with new laws policing speech and turning opinions into crimes; our border at the South is open and millions of military-age men are pouring in. The realignment of our so recently free societies with a neo-Marxist totalitarianism is well under way.

The big-picture plans of the global elites, to seize full-spectrum control, are moving on apace. They have left the shadows, where they could be dismissed as the result of "conspiracy theories," and are visible on the legacy media news sites now, for all to see. AI? Done. Digital currency? Announced. Elimination of cash? Stated as a near-term goal. The Internet of Things? Fifteen-minute cities? Check, and check. Biometrics monitoring? Unrolled. Social credit scores? One small developer step past Digital ID. Aerosolized vaccines, that make a mockery of informed consent? Announced. MRNA platforms in everything, including livestock, RSV shots, flu shots? Done and done.

It is very painful to put together these pieces. It is staggering to process the fact that evil people in positions of power wish to strip humanity as a whole of its dignity and autonomy and reduce us to the status, in effect, of cattle. It is scary to consider that AI can now complete for the "Opposition," what the most sophisticated human coordination cannot manage.

How will we emerge from this dystopia that has been prepared for us?

The first step to fighting back is understanding what the nature of the battle is. I am proud to have sounded the alarm in *The Bodies of Others*, and to have helped early to inform the resistance that has been growing for the last few years. These efforts to inform and awaken the world, are also happening globally, almost keeping pace with the destructive plans continually mounted against us. I see protests in Spain and France; I see calls for COVID investigations and for criminal accountability in Europe. I see Poland refusing to take more mRNA injections, and nation after nation decline to join the WHO pandemic treaty. I see a massive activity in creating an alternative set of systems to replace the corrupt media, corrupt financial system and corrupt universities and hospital networks, that have so badly failed in their missions and in their basic ethics. As fast as this handful of demonic leaders are targeting humanity, I see humanity trying to build a newer, freer, more transparent, more ethical world.

Who will win in the end? As in 1775, we do not yet know the outcome. As in 1775, the answer is up to us.

Will we be winter soldiers?

I trust that the answer must be Yes. And I trust that *The Bodies of Others* can continue to inform, warn, inspire, and fortify those now, and in the near future, who are willing to defend the survival of a free humanity itself.

CONTENTS

INTRODUCTION

On February 14, 2022, as protesting Canadian truckers filled Parliament Square in Ottawa, giving joyous hope to all those worldwide who were done with pandemic totalitarianism, it was Chrystia Freeland, as Prime Minister Justin Trudeau's Deputy Prime Minister, who gave chilling proof of how far the global elites would go to enforce absolute compliance to their diktats by the citizenry. "As of today, a bank or other financial service provider will be able to immediately freeze or suspend an account without a court order," she announced. "In doing so, they will be protected against civil liability for actions taken in good faith . . . If your truck is being used in these illegal blockades, your corporate accounts will be frozen. The insurance on your vehicle will be suspended."[1] Police shattered truck windows, arrested a hundred protesters, including the demonstration's leaders, and Prime Minister Justin Trudeau invoked an emergency order.[2] For a time, representative government was suspended in the nation of Canada.

It would be an overstatement to say that Chrystia Freeland was ever a friend, but for a while we were in the same circle of hardworking, underpaid reporters and editors, all just trying to earn a living. I'd seen her around at social events in Manhattan, and one day when we were both adjusting our makeup — she after a television appearance, me in preparation for an interview — she mentioned, happily and with absolute confidence, that she was shortly to run for Parliament in Canada. At the time her humble title was as Reuters' "Managing Director and Editor, Consumer News." I remember looking at her with astonishment at this out-of-the-blue leapfrogging of many career levels. She must have powerful friends, I thought.

It turned out to be a good guess.

Ms. Freeland was part of a small cadre of "influentials" connected to the World Economic Forum; indeed, she is now on the WEF Board of Trustees.[3] She and her peers, along with allied elites in other fields, eventually masterminded a crime against humanity unprecedented in our times — a crime that involves the theft of assets and the destruction of cultures, as well as untold deaths.

This book is about how we came to this harrowing civilizational crossroads — engaged in a war against vast impersonal forces with limitless power over our lives for the freedoms we have taken for granted; how those forces seized upon two years of COVID-19 panic in sinister new ways; and how, yet, against overwhelming odds, we still might win.

Others have looked at this war from a biomedical perspective, or from a strictly political one. My focus is on how this ongoing war against us is far more basic, aimed at nothing less than dissolving the meaning of humanity itself and undoing of the rich cultural legacy we in the West have long treasured and passed on to succeeding generations.

In those two years, the COVID-19 pandemic, which began unfolding with the unprecedented global "lockdown" in March 2020, has fundamentally remade human relations, capitalism, and culture in the West. No matter that in the past we had lived through far graver medical crises without even passing thought to stopping all congregation, suspending the production of all culture, or compelling all healthy people to cover their faces and close their businesses and keep apart — this time, our elites used the "crisis" to shut down Western norms of liberty, the human-centered world, and civilization itself.

But what is our culture, which we once thought durable, to be replaced by? A world managed by machines and mediated via digital interfaces; a world predicated on cruelty, without human empathy as an organizing principle; a world in which national boundaries, cultures, and languages are drained of meaning, in which institutions embody only the goals of distant meta-national oligarchs, a world organized for the benefit of massive pharmaceutical companies, a few global tech giants and technocrats, and a tyrannical superpower that is our deadly adversary. In short: a world redesigned to ensure the dominance forever of these distant elites, both geopolitically and via market share.

In 2020–22, we entered a time in which the post–World War II organizing principle of human affairs, the democratic nation-state, was being intentionally diluted in power and undermined in the interest of constructing a replacement meta-structure of unaccountable loosely aligned global nonprofits, Big Tech corporations, the WEF, and the Chinese Communist Party (CCP).

Their aim was to construct engines of history designed to dissolve human culture, closeness and community. United in an alliance of convenience, these forces see human beings and the troublesome individualistic West, with its stubborn insistence on human rights, on joy, on spontaneity, on quirkiness, acceptance, and tolerance, as obstacles to be managed, drained of power and resources, and sidelined. Their goal is to subvert Western cultural norms and ultimately to alienate Western children from their families' influence and from Western history and freedoms generally. The war against "the virus" has really been a war waged via technologies and their masters to dissolve human culture and disempower human beings. It is a war on free thought and free speech — a war against our most fundamental beliefs.

These oligarchical elites are supported in this vast project to remake humanity by massive, opaque nonprofits through which pour billions of dollars aimed at transformational social change. Behind benign-sounding "pro-human" mottoes — such as "We are a nonprofit fighting poverty, disease and inequity around the world" (The Bill & Melinda Gates Foundation) or "Who Stands Between YOU and the Next Pandemic?" (EcoHealth Alliance) or "Using the Power of Epidemiology to Fight the Spread of COVID-19," (Council of State and Territorial Epidemiologists) — these groups have used their power to advance the most malign anti-human ends.[4]

The pandemic gave them pretext and opportunity on an unprecedented scale, and they have taken full advantage.

The faces of some of those who have visited this evil upon us are all-too-familiar — the power-besotted political figures, the domineering healthcare "experts," the bought-off media talking heads, the titans of tech and social media, the unapologetically tyrannical leader of Communist-ruled China, Xi Jinping. We know others, such as the super-elites of the World Economic Forum mentioned above, by reputation, by their pronouncements from their gatherings in Davos, Switzerland, or via their books. But collectively, during the pandemic, they have come to wield power over even the smallest particulars of human existence. And that is because this is a war aimed at undoing humanity itself.

This claim is hard to process, but we need to do so.

Since the end of the Middle Ages, and into the Renaissance, and up until the near-present, we in the West have taken for granted that it is human perspectives that drive history.

No more. Machines have, in the past, served us, but we are at the point in history in which we are being reoriented to serve machines and their masters.

For all their public proclamations about building a "better world" some of the most powerful leaders arrayed against us do not even bother to obscure that this is their real goal. Klaus Schwab, the founder and executive chairman of the World Economic Forum, could hardly have been more direct about his intent, invoking the need to provoke a worldwide "Great Reset" in the wake of the pandemic. The COVID-19 crisis has shown us, Schwab argued, that our old systems are not fit anymore for the twenty-first century. On June 3, 2020, when we still did not know if the pandemic would be perhaps in the rearview mirror a week hence, Schwab declared, "[T]he world must act jointly and swiftly to revamp all aspects of our societies and economies, from education to social contracts and working conditions. Every country, from the United States to China, must participate, and every industry, from oil and gas to tech, must be transformed. In short, we need a 'Great Reset' of capitalism."[5]

I remember reading this and thinking, "What? Why?" and also noting the megalomaniacal, dictatorial tone: "We must . . . "

"Our old systems" — privacy, paper and metal money, the ability to drive a car without being tracked, the nation-state, human expression, human touch, cultural activities, churches, mosques, and synagogues, town halls, theaters and concert halls, democratic governance, a free press, schools and universities, books and libraries, and the right to decide what happens to one's own body, property and family —

none of these suit the WEF leadership and their tech- and pharmaceutical-industry and CCP allies.

"Many of us are pondering when things will return to normal. The short response is: never. The world as we knew it in the early months of 2020 is no more," declared Schwab in his eerily early book *The Great Reset*.[6] As early as July 2020, Schwab expected that we would soon see "a lot of anger": "we have to prepare for a more angry world . . . how to prepare? It means to take the necessary action." Again, he called for "a Great Reset."[7] He asked for "full global citizenship." He confidently predicted winners and losers economically: "We know that certainly the health industries, the digital industry, will go out of this crisis strengthened, but we know that many industries that rely on physical interaction will have difficulties to survive."[8] He did not say "physical labor," he said "physical interaction."

In 2022, as resistance to his plans was in full force worldwide, in remarks that are no longer easy to locate online, Schwab irritably reiterated that the "good old world" of pre-2020 was never to return and that believing that it could do so was a fiction.

Davos 2022 shows clearly the intentions for humanity still ahead from this group of elites: from planning for endless pandemics and "variants" in the future, leading to endless social control; to the digitization of identities and currency; to the intervention in free markets by a "stakeholder capitalism" that chooses winners and losers in the world of commerce via the fig leaf of ideology; to "global cooperation" that seeks to dissolve nation states and national boundaries, the Davos cadre, with a gathering headlined yet again by Chinese Communist Party General Secretary Xi Jinping, has plans for our subjugation that are being implemented, now into the third year of this pandemic, at full throttle.[9]

But the people of the world did not vote to abandon "our old systems" and destroy our old ways.

The attacks on organized religion have been particularly telling, as these attacks are characteristic of Communist policies, especially in China. From the Orthodox Jewish community in New York, to Christian churches in California, since 2020 the religious were often singled out for punishment for not following "official" COVID rules. One synagogue in Brooklyn was threatened with an investigation, and New York's then-governor spoke out against it with hostile language when its community dared to hold a secret wedding celebration in November 2020.[10] The Supreme Court had to make an affirmative ruling against the governor of California to allow people to worship at church in person.[11] Churches and synagogues by the thousands were forcibly closed. The Martha's Vineyard Hebrew Center in Massachusetts was still, as of the first week of March 2022, "Zoom only" two years after the start of the pandemic.[12]

Policies that weaken the bonds between human beings and weaken the family were similarly introduced and policed. Shaming and ostracism, "struggle sessions" characteristic of CCP-style communism, replaced American-style civil debate and tolerance for different points of view. Hyper-empowered boards of health harassed members of formerly free institutions. These unelected board-of-health functionaries hounded professors at universities and demanded that houses of worship, historic sites, and community gathering spaces remain closed, long after any epidemiological danger had passed.

School boards with broad new powers and heavy-handed, seemingly centralized scripts and policies have bullied parents and tormented children, turning formerly safe and supportive schools into terrifying and hostile authoritarian battlegrounds. Concerned parents were even tagged as "domestic terrorists" by the FBI — just as dissident parents are targeted in Communist China or were in the former Soviet Union.[13]

None of this is accidental. Nor does it have anything to do with "science." The data were soon widely available, and even in 2020 studies showed the "lockdowns" and restrictions did not stop disease and often made health outcomes far worse.[14]

But the draconian measures did not stop.

The agents of destructive change also have psychological targets. Under the "fog of war" the pandemic was from the start terrifyingly narrated in the direst of terms, thereby enabling the systematized global attack against traditionally human physical spaces, traditionally human speech and communications, and other traditionally human norms of Western civilization.

Simultaneously there was a systematic attack on what might be called "humane spaces" and "analog products" — the spaces, activities, and objects that are especially supportive of human enlightenment, social cohesion, and cultural continuity and especially resistant to being surveilled and tracked digitally.

Indeed, one of the reasons our current crisis feels so strange and disorienting to us humans, especially to us Western humans, is that it was in some ways modeled by machines and by programmers and may well have been continually modified via machine learning. We are not living through organic human history as it has unfolded in the past. Since April 2020, computer "models," whether their assumptions turned out to be right or wrong, have driven policy.[15] The other reason for its bizarre, uncanny quality is that it is aimed at translating and transitioning Western cultures and instincts into the language and instincts of CCP-type civic subjugation.

If you asked a computer program to define a human being or what supports human culture, it would likely spit out a list of all the relationships, attributes, and spaces that were targeted by the policies of 2020–22. The machine program might respond: smiling, touching, hugging, praying, and speaking; the ability to read and to communicate via speech and facial expressions and touch; the ability to cooperate and to form bonds. If you asked a machine program, "What makes people free?" It might respond with: "Their ability to gather in spaces where they generate representative government." If you asked a machine program, "What are the building blocks of human culture?" It might spit out: "Dancing, listening to music, watching concerts and theatrical productions, holy days and rituals, teaching children in a school, singing, and worship."

So it is not for nothing that the bad actors have intentionally targeted the "analog/humane world" of: physical books; physical bookstores; human-populated lecture halls; physical libraries; physical currency; physical maps; paper and metal money; human employees and human workplaces; concert halls and theaters; pubs, bars, and restaurants; in-person classrooms; churches, synagogues, mosques; dinner parties; summer camp; recess; Boy Scouts and Girl Scouts; playgrounds; team sports; non-electric cars; holy days and rituals. They have taken aim at representative in-person democracy, at state capitals, in-person parliaments, and congressional assemblies, local town halls and in-person town hall meetings, and at the museums and statues and historical sites that give humans a sense of meaning and an origin story.

When two human beings are in contact with one another, they produce communication, culture and maybe plans. This is simply what humans do face-to-face. A facilitator of communication and alliance between humans is touch.

How do you dissolve human civilization? One way a machine program could target human beings is by attacking and undoing the magical power of touch. One of the strangest diktats from the start of the pandemic was the demand for "distancing," that inorganic, awkward verb that was introduced in a new context, and redefined, early in the pandemic.

The implications of this war on touch, more than two years on, are beyond tragic. Physical closeness is not an "extra" for human beings. Without it, we suffer from mental illnesses ranging from depression to anxiety and are even vulnerable to hallucinations and other forms of psychosis, as many studies have demonstrated. As the Prison Policy Initiative warned, "The Research is Clear: Solitary Confinement Causes Long-lasting Harm."[16]

Indeed, one reason that solitary confinement has been seen as torture by prison-policy networks is that isolation can cause permanent changes to the human brain that result in madness. First identified by psychiatrist Dr. Stuart Grassian, the ailment manifests along several lines, including "a progressive inability to tolerate ordinary things . . . hallucinations and illusions; severe panic attacks; difficulties with thinking, concentration, and memory; obsessive, sometimes harmful thoughts that won't go away . . . and delirium."[17] Indeed, premature deaths — by suicide, homicide or opioid overdoses — are more likely for those who have been released from prison *if they spent even a single day in solitary confinement.* Loneliness, even a little loneliness, causes humans trauma.[18]

As those versed in addiction and mental-health issues well know, humans don't simply want touch and close relationships; we need them. In the absence of positive human touch and social support, we can develop a condition called touch deprivation, leading to numerous additional negative psychological and even physiological effects. "Touch starvation" causes anxiety, depression and *greater vulnerability to infection.* Individuals who go without positive physical touch for a long period can even suffer from post-traumatic stress disorder.[19] From a hug to a high-five, positive moments of human touch can calm the nervous system, boost mood and release endorphins, *strengthen the immune system, and improve healing.*

Little wonder that the distancing requirements put in place allegedly to eliminate "the spread" of COVID-19 have led many people to experience profound sadness and an overwhelming sense of isolation. They could have also worsened illnesses. Love is indeed a drug — and a good one.

Unsurprisingly, group singing — from the start, weirdly singled out by pandemic policies — has likewise been shown to work magic on human beings in relieving pain and sustaining mental health.[20]

The same near-magical advantages are inherent in "analog/humane," non-digital spaces and products that humans have long used. Though advertised (by digital companies) as being second-rate these days in comparison to digital alternatives, these "analog/humane" products and experiences retain advantages that digital competitors cannot begin to approach.

Humans in human space create sophisticated outcomes unmatchable in many ways by technology. A human being in a lecture hall, speaking directly to five hundred people, can reach all of them equally without an algorithm mediating or censoring him or her; a human being walking alongside a physical bookshelf or speaking to a human bookseller can find a little-known book, or one out of print, or a controversial book or pamphlet that an Amazon algorithm will bury. A human being reading in a library of physical books cannot be hacked or surveilled or tracked. Indeed a physical book itself, like the physical pamphlets that launched many revolutions, is a miracle of cyber-secure technology. When you carry a book in your pocket or shoulder bag, no one can track it; when you read print on paper, no one can put tracking cookies on what you are reading. Your human brain is still private.

As a political force, humans in "analog/humane" spaces have unmatchable superpowers. A group of humans in a local town hall, or a statehouse, or Congress, or Parliament have powers that they lose when driven to digital alternatives. In person, they can privately caucus and form alliances. They can lobby one another in confidence. They can review paper documents together. They can point things out to one another free from censorship and surveillance.

A speech is a radical technology. A smile is a radical technology. It boosts endorphins better than a hundred smiley emojis. A physical classroom is a radical technology. A community of human beings is a radical technology.

They are miraculously sophisticated technologies, the human body and mind, human touch and faces and verbal communication, especially within a group of fellow humans, in a classroom, a library, a statehouse, a church. Digital technology simply cannot touch these advantages. And Big Tech knows and hates that fact.

These human advantages over technology are precisely what the world of Big Tech, supported by powerful globalist allies, longs to annihilate. For these "analog/humane" spaces and analog products are far more empowering to human beings than is the digital alternative world.

Indeed, these enemies of the human advantage seek to erase it all — physical flirtation, physical play, physical expressions of love, physical worship, physical teamwork.

By isolating us for more than a year and a half, leaving us terrified in our homes, and bombarding our minds with messages that activate the amygdala, where fear is processed and reason cannot enter — and then re-allowing humans only to reconnect in restricted, muffled, silenced, and surveilled ways — our elites have stifled troublesome

Western cultural norms and effectively made us far more manageable and more completely controlled within their own digital matrices.

Again it was left to the WEF's shameless Klaus Schwab to openly envisage the future he sees via technology. Quoting Eric Schmidt, the then-executive chairman of Google's parent company, Alphabet, Schwab observed: "The coming decade would be a battle between robots and humans, and to win that battle we would have to know what makes us human."[21]

What did not have to be said was that the WEF and its Big Tech allies have indeed examined the question of what makes us human, only to use that analysis in alliance with the machines *against* the humans.

And the obvious first step in that process is the obliteration of free assembly, of community.

As pandemic panic took hold, "restrictions" poured out in waves around the formerly free world, echoing one another, but continually shifting and changing their flavor, endlessly assaulting a disoriented, increasingly fragmented, and psychologically fragile set of formerly free nations. (Remember: AI models can tweak simultaneous soundbites and input global outcomes to alter them in real time, in a "cat's cradle" type of dynamic.)

It is no exaggeration to say that these coordinated offenses, orchestrated by government in lockstep alliance with tech and pharmaceutical companies and the dominant media, represent an evil we had never seen before in human history.

Worldwide, as well as state by US state, we heard the same soundbites and the same charges aimed at those who dared speak up against these plans; we saw the same novel methods of bypassing legislatures and laws to empower boards of health to restrict rights and liberties. Later we saw the same vaccination goals in nation after nation, and the same abuse heaped upon the recalcitrant. Finally we observed the same punishments, from the denial of access to restaurants to the denial of the right to work — even the same lures of free donuts[22] or McDonald's coupons[23] to cajole "the hesitant" to fall into line.

———————

The end goal is something much darker than simply a dark-enough world in which everyone is coercively vaccinated, whether they are at risk or not, whether they have natural immunity or not, a world in which "boosters" for seven billion people annually are guaranteed forever.

The end goal, rather, is to ensure that our pre–March 2020 world disappears forever. Irretrievable. To be replaced with a world in which all human endeavor is behind a digital paywall, and a world in which all of us ask the permission of technology to gain access to the physical world, access to culture and access to other human beings.

The data presented in 2020 about the uselessness and harms of "lockdown" were reconfirmed again and again. The Great Barrington Declaration had warned, in October 2020, that this would be the case.[24] In 2021, *The Wall Street Journal* reached that conclusion again, after tens of thousands of businesses had permanently closed.[25] Eight months after that, a study in Johns Hopkins University's *Studies in Applied Economics* series reached that conclusion yet again.[26] But it was not until February 2022, that tanking poll numbers, an internal memo from a campaign advisor,[27] and a court decision to lay bare 55,000 pages of Pfizer internal documents[28] led US governors and the US presidential administration to pull back on "masking," "mandates," and "restrictions."

The real goal had nothing to do with public health.

The real goal is to dissolve and destroy Western and human culture, and to replace it with a techno-fascistic culture — a culture in which we have forgotten what free human beings can do.

The crime that was perpetrated during the pandemic years of 2020–22 was perhaps the greatest ever committed against humanity. And it is being perpetrated still.

CHAPTER ONE

MARCH 2020: "LOCKDOWN"

On March 8, 2020, I was sitting backstage at the Southbank Centre in London. I'd been invited there as a speaker in connection with the celebration of International Women's Day.[29] I was excited to join many other female writers, speakers, and activists. I was seeing old friends, as I'd appeared there before, and I was enjoying the bustle and excitement of the typical festival crowds.

Parents and children, single people, babies in strollers, visitors from every background — wealthy and low-income and middle class; streams of retired folks: all this rich, peaceful array of humanity thronged the facility.

For decades, the Centre had been a dynamic, beloved destination on the banks of the Thames. It was a delectable smorgasbord, and a pride of London: with plays, lectures, films, dance troupes, comedians, debates, cafés, restaurants, a library, even an outdoor food court with food from all kinds of cuisines, the Southbank Centre represented the finest Western cultural and civic delights. It gathered people who wanted to learn and absorb culture at little or no cost to them. It supported people in the making of culture. It sustained a peaceful, complex, advanced community in which people from all different viewpoints and backgrounds moved freely, associated freely, and shared their thoughts and stories and ideas freely.

This jewel adorned what had been for over two thousand years a great city on a mighty river, where the crush of people who for centuries had been seeking — and at critical points attaining — always more inclusive and institutionalized levels of freedom of association and movement and expression. This civilization had brought about many of the glories of liberty, including Magna Carta;[30] the principle of habeas corpus, which ensured that people could not be locked up in prison forever without trial; John Milton's paean to free speech, the *Aeropagitica*; parliamentary processes and traditions that were admired and emulated worldwide; increasingly humane innovations in incarceration; free primary education for children of all backgrounds; the work of the Enlightenment-era advocate for women's rights, Mary Wollstonecraft; the marches of the Suffragists and the securing of the vote for women; and the Human Rights Act of 1998.

Unsurprisingly, this tradition of ever-developing laws and institutions was centered on the Western ideals of liberty and democracy and led to cultural glories that were also admired worldwide, inspiring readers in less free nations with a vision of nearly complete liberty and, over the centuries, a movement toward a relatively robust democracy and an accountable rule of law. Britain gave us cultural glories from Shakespeare to Milton, Jane Austen to Blake to the Brontës, Dickens to Auden, Thomas Paine to John Stuart Mill, and riches in music, theater, fiction, and philosophy too extensive to name.

At the Southbank Centre I was seated on a low platform next to a young Italian intern. We were chatting as we waited for the post-lecture wine and snacks backstage.

She was preoccupied, though, and explained that she was worried because she could not reach her mother in Milan. She said the region had been "put under lockdown."[31]

I remember the sense of vertigo I felt when she said that. What? That could not happen in Italy — in a free, modern nation. I understood that "lockdown," the holding of citizens against their wishes in one area, the restrictions of their liberty to assemble freely — only happened under totalitarian systems. I remember a kind of shudder going through me as I tried not to let the young women see how concerned her words had made me feel.

I knew what it meant. The flower of Europe was being struck at the root.

All around us continued the bustle and conversations and laughter. The excited crowds were lining up for the next events and chatting about the themes of the evening; attendees were making new friends in line or adding dimension to their existing friendships.

Our own event began and ended. It was a success.

As the crowds streamed out, you could hear the buzz of human culture being generated: this was human politics organically evolving. You could feel the power and potential of the living crowd, the energetic froth of a new set of ideas rippling through the audiences, new conversations to be explored at scale. People were talking, talking, talking.

As a writer who had spoken to many audiences, I'd seen and felt time and again the hard-to-describe power of this creature — the wave of energy that is new, like a wave in an ocean that can encircle the world in a moment, when hundreds of people assemble in person to hear ideas as a community and to discuss them with one another freely. Crowds even walk differently after such events, as I'd seen before. Heads that had been bowed were held higher. People approach each other more

confidently. Strangers, even shy strangers, could be beautiful warriors
-in-arms once they had convened like this.

There must have been six hundred women in the crowd that night.
They streamed out of the theater, seeming euphoric.

The sense of possibility and, yes — empowerment — among them,
acted on their moods like champagne. A massive crowd had entered a
vast shared space tentative and hopeful and left it more optimistic, with
barriers ripped away in their minds.

The women streamed out of the auditorium with old or new
friends, heading toward drinks or a nighttime walk, or to the Tube
together, in the endlessly exciting, inviting city.

I still have a picture from that last day of the old world.

Eight or ten of us, the activists and writers who had just addressed
this audience, grouped ourselves together for a photo in the comfortable greenroom backstage. We were together in a line, women of all
ages and backgrounds facing the camera, arms around one another.
You could sense the proud new friendships, sparked in our brief discussions before and after the event, and the new possibilities for alliance:
the exciting new possibilities that human gathering always brings to
free people.

That is, until that very moment.

I can't forget that feeling of those women in that picture right
before the world came crashing down.

Back at the hotel, I called my husband, Brian. I told him about
Italy having closed down.

Other countries were also "closing down" or "locking down,"
whatever that meant. I had planned to head north to visit a mentor at
a university.

"Come home," he said. "They are going to close down flights."

I made it home to New York just before flights shut down from Europe.

The city I left behind was effectively destroyed in many ways. London has never been the same again.

———————

On March 9, 2020, *I was back home in the South Bronx, where we were living at that time. We had moved to the borough a few months previously.*

Mott Haven, a neighborhood in the South Bronx, had been going through a period of renewal and efflorescence.

Though it is one of the poorest neighborhoods in greater New York City, and had long endured the serious problems that very low income areas often do, it also boasted tremendous cultural richness. It had strong communities and impressive human capital.

And lately opportunities had been everywhere. New projects and institutions were rapidly being imagined. Investment was secured for them, and they were being built.

A block away from our apartment, two entrepreneurs had started up a workspace for South Bronx–based creative artists and professionals and small business owners. The project had reclaimed what had been a rundown, disused red-brick industrial factory building. The Bronx is the birthplace of hip-hop music and culture; a gifted hip-hop artist had been commissioned to do a majestic mural on an exterior wall. A range of hip-hop visual artists also displayed their work to gallery owners on the walls of the facility. Entrepreneurs with just enough capital could rent out spaces affordably, or start an innovative T-shirt line, or hire a corner of a shared room in which to create an animated TV series. The proprietors of the neighborhood incubator were building out an elegant café.

Cultural offerings were everywhere. A Latino ballet company was housed a few blocks further north. The city had allocated funds to build what was sure to be a huge tourist draw — a museum of hip-hop.

The South Bronx was becoming more powerful politically, as well. A talented up and comer, Bronx Borough President Rubén Díaz Jr., had been securing millions for investment in the cultural institutions of the neighborhood. Affordable housing was being built, and local talented community advocates were being groomed to run for office.

Three blocks away from us, a young woman from the area had opened LitHub — thus establishing the only bookstore in the South Bronx. This had become a welcoming destination, offering a sweeping range of novels, histories, political-science volumes and biographies, most of them related to communities of color. A café drew in young people from all backgrounds, older people who had lived in the area for decades, and newcomers.

We'd only been living there for a few months, but we were making friends, putting down roots, happy to be part of a creative, diverse, innovative community.

Even before all the new investment and new institution-building poured in, the South Bronx had boasted massive entrepreneurial energy. Hundreds of small business owners were running their enterprises effectively, in the great tradition of American waves of immigrants.

Conditions in America, as usual, let hardworking small business owners and workers who were new arrivals to the nation thrive.

Side streets and boulevards were dense with tiny cafés and res-
taurants that served Dominican, Nigerian, Mexican, Ethiopian,
Cuban, and many other kinds of cuisine. Some were so small that
they were only a few tables and a bar. Some had been started by
talented home cooks and had developed a devoted following. Small
business owners ran their shops without large inventories but with
regular customers. Small florists, small bakeries, small clothing and
handbag boutiques abounded. When I stood in line at the neigh-
borhood bank, a significant number of customers waiting to make
deposits were the local small businessowners.

Importantly, too, up to March 2020, the Bronx had many vibrant
faith communities, whose centers were scattered throughout our
neighborhood. This was a complex network of old nineteenth-cen-
tury stone Catholic churches, convents, new storefront evangelical
churches, Baptist churches, venerable synagogues, elegant mosques,
mosques tucked into empty office spaces, mosques devoted to
members of the Nation of Islam, mosques filled with families who
had left Palestine two and three generations before, mosques that
catered to Moroccan or Somali immigrants; yeshivas, a Chabad
House and a Black Jewish congregation. Every Friday, Saturday,
or Sunday people poured in and out of these houses of worship.
Children in white dresses awaited First Communion as parents
proudly took pictures. Families thronged newlyweds, and traffic
stopped to admire bridesmaids and brides and flower girls. Men
finished long shifts and came home and showered, then dressed
again, but in elegant white shirts and black slacks to join their
equally beautifully dressed families to pray in the mosques on
Friday, to hear the Imam's sermon, and to celebrate Ramadan or
Eid or other festive times in the calendar. Black-clad Orthodox

Jewish men shook hands on the sidewalk outside the synagogue after the ten o'clock Shabbat service, while their wives chatted in groups, keeping an eye on the girls in modest dresses and the boys in side-curls, as they scampered and played.

Everyone who wanted one could have a community or many communities, and have a rich culture, or be part of many rich cultures.

The South Bronx had areas of great beauty, too. From the front of our building, you could see across industrial warehouses to the Harlem River, its steel-gray depths glittering flatly in sunlight and its gray-white ripples flowing in moonlight. Great steel bridges spanned the river; trains hurtled across them, creating a fantastic industrial urban sculpture. You could see the spires of City College in Harlem, like a castle on a distant hill. You could see the vast towers of midtown faint and clustered like giants, like the towers of Oz from the perspective of faraway Dorothy. A waterpark was being constructed along the Harlem River, and though it was not yet complete, the people of the South Bronx walked down to the riverside on summer evenings to admire the sunset, the flowing river, and the astonishing view of the city that at times a trick of the light made seem close enough to touch. The sun was on their faces.

Everywhere there were crowds: buying and selling, or flirting, or scrambling to get to the next opportunity, or rushing to school or college.

Everywhere you looked, something was happening. Everywhere were the diverse, excited, energized, impatient crowds of greater New York — that is, of greater New York until March 2020.

Despite the serious problems so many faced, there was a sense of possibility in the neighborhood. No matter how hard times might be, people could act in regard to their own lives.

Because this was America.

————————

Primary among The Bronx's systemic problems was that people's health suffered disproportionately here; the borough's inhabitants dealt with the many illnesses of poverty, and the suffering from these illnesses and medical shortcomings was visible everywhere. The Bronx had the highest rate of childhood asthma in the city. Obesity and poor nutrition were chronic. We lived in a "food desert" and a physical-recreation desert; fresh, nutritious food was expensive and hard to get, and there were few green or open spaces for exercise.

Almost no one had good medical care. As the Institute for Family Health notes, "In the South Bronx, the poorest urban congressional district in the country, the population suffers high rates of diabetes, obesity, heart disease, asthma, HIV/AIDS, and infant mortality."[32] There was a black market for diabetes strips and insulin. Aspirin and antacids were sold in two-pill packets at the bodegas. In no other borough did I see so many underattended mobility issues such as people who needed wheelchairs leaning on ill-sized walkers and people who needed walkers struggling with old wooden crutches and people with neither, who were forced to lean for support on friends or relatives.

Once I had to go to the emergency room, and we all faced a five-hour wait. I saw a homeless man whose frostbitten foot was being tended to. In the depth of winter, he wore only socks; and complained that the nurses were cutting away his sock, because socks were expensive. People had terrible respiratory illnesses; antibiotics were expensive. People suffered from tuberculosis. There were gurneys with people lying on them in the ER hallways; the patients lay still for hours. When I went to the ER in 2019, there had been a body on a gurney in the ER hallway, its face covered.

This was the day-to-day reality. It had been so for years. The health of the poor was expendable.

Almost no one at the state, let alone the federal, level cared much, if at all, about the health of my neighbors, the poorest inhabitants of the five boroughs, or about the terrible deaths that they suffered.

———————

On March 11, 2020, as Brian and I were in his SUV running an errand, an announcement was broadcast on his car radio.

Because of this mysterious virus from China, Broadway was closing.[33]

All of Broadway. Not just one theater or ten theaters, as in a free society in which business owners make choices based on individual risk. All of Broadway, in one iconic, sweeping, Soviet-style, top-down gesture.

We had both been in conflict areas and we had both lived in closed societies — we recognized their movements. We both knew something very bad was on its way; whether natural or political, or both, we could not yet tell. But from our time in conflict areas we both knew what checkpoints and forced closures inevitably meant, so we both knew that whatever was coming, it would be very bad.

"We have to get out of here," we agreed.

We barely packed and we drove north.

I'd bought a little cottage in the Hudson Valley many years ago, just before the crisis days of 9/11. I'd been haunted since that time by how easy it could be to target or control populations densely packed on an island with no way in or out but bridges and tunnels. I'd brought my small children to the cottage when the city was assailed with smoke and catastrophe, and I had been grateful for it then and as they were growing up, and now, too, though they had left home.

We moved to the Hudson Valley on March 12, 2020. At first it was just for a few days.

At that time, the United States was not yet discussing a Milan-type COVID "lockdown" in America — it was inconceivable! Nor was there much talk yet of the faraway infections that would ravage our own nation.

I'd been renting out the little cottage on Airbnb for income. On about March 13, we got a booking inquiry from an Apple executive. She wanted to move her entire family, including two small children, from their home in Brooklyn into our cottage in the woods, right away, "for a work project."

"For how loog would the booking be?" I asked her via message on the rental platform.

"For a few weeks to start out with," she said. "But it could be for months."

When something bad is on the way, a few elites tend to know it first. They know to flee it in advance.

I told her the house was unavailable, took the listing off the platform immediately, and called a moving van. We let go our rented home in the city, along with a security deposit, but there was no way around it.

We both recognized the straws in the wind: massive instability was on the way. Whatever the Apple executive may have been describing, Brian and I were both alarmed.

That very night, we moved to the little cottage in the woods full time. We moved to a tiny town that had a Methodist church and a Catholic church right in town and a synagogue a half hour away. It had a diner, a grocery store, a town hall, and a library. Most local people had enjoyed years or even decades of networks of neighborliness and professional relationships and friendships. Our tiny town was in an area dense with cultural and other kinds of history, and it was ringed by dozens of richly meaningful historical sites.

As of this writing, the close-knit and productive South Bronx community we left on March 11, 2020, was never to be the same.

As of this writing, the close-knit and productive small Hudson Valley towns among which we arrived on March 11, 2020, were never to recover either.

Both went from having been part of America to being coerced into another culture, having been forced over the next two years into another dimension of human experience, with another political system and a completely different, grotesquely lesser, set of options for human life and community.

In March 2020, human beings were still at the center of culture, and the culture was America. Two years later, machines and technology and "public health" were the centers of culture, and the culture was something altogether new in the West.

More like Cuba or Beijing than like Mott Haven, South Bronx, or Copake, New York. More like "Meta" or Google or Apple than like human community and contact.

More like the dicta and norms of the CCP than like the culture and beliefs of the United States of America.

CHAPTER TWO

"UNIFORM SAFETY
FOR EVERYONE"

In New York State, where we lived, Governor Andrew Cuomo declared emergency law on March 7, 2020 — before anyone really knew the extent of what would become the pandemic — and on June 23, 2021, he promised to end it by the next day.[34]

I knew about emergency laws from studying the decline of democracies, and I knew by the middle of March of 2020 that something catastrophic had happened.

Nearly two years later, we were *still* under emergency law in New York State.

By Governor Cuomo's initial March 2020 regulation (A mandate? An edict? We didn't even have legal language for declarations under emergency law, since the emergency-law declaration supersedes actual law) Main Street stores and restaurants would close, but "essential businesses" could stay open. This executive order was just that — an "order." It did not go through the legislature. This would be among the first of many "edicts" and "mandates" and "orders," acts whose very linguistic structure seemed designed to habituate citizens of a representative democracy to top-down, unquestioned "order-following."

The "executive order" put everyone in the state "on pause," for everyone's "safety."[35]

To many, this sounded like leadership for an emergency — like the "war footing" language with which George W. Bush launched the "Global War on Terror." Many people in the safe, affluent nations of Canada, the United States, and the United Kingdom, who were not used to crises, were cowed by this language. Also, who could object to a "pause"?

But my husband and I were not reassured by the Nurse Ratched–type comforting language, and we were astonished at Governor Cuomo's dicta. Since we had both lived in war zones and conflict areas, we knew that commerce was *never* closed, even in the worst crises. People needed to keep making their livings in order to survive the crisis, and the economy needed to be sustained in order for the *community* to survive the crisis. We both knew from the history of warfare that when populations are forbidden to buy and sell, they can't fight back. It is the death of their economy that kills them off or leads to their eventual enslavement or occupation.

Even in 1997, when there were sequential terrorist attacks on Mahane Yehuda, the open-air market in Jerusalem, in which sixteen people were killed and 178 injured, a national point of pride was that the market stayed open.[36] The same was the case in 2002, when six people were killed and eighty-four were injured.[37] People who are huddled in refugee camps around the world still buy and sell, and even when there is a war or terrorist attacks, children still try to go to school.

But for us in America in 2020? With a serious respiratory illness underway? *"100% Closure of Non-Essential Businesses Statewide, Effective*

8pm Sunday — Exceptions Made for Essential Services Such as Groceries and Healthcare."[38]

Governor Cuomo provided a series of directives that were bizarre and new at the time, phrased in CCP-style prose with a CCP-style concept: "Uniform Safety for Everyone." This CCP-style language and concept took the place of what had been our American assumption that individuals are sovereign and cannot be "put on pause" by a ruler, and that it was citizens' own responsibilities to deal with their own decisions about personal risk. But now:

- 10-Point Policy that Assures Uniform Safety for Everyone

- 100% Closure of Non-Essential Businesses Statewide, Effective 8pm Sunday — Exceptions Made for Essential Services Such as Groceries and Healthcare

- "Matilda's Law" Will Provide New Protections for Most Vulnerable Populations — New Yorkers Age 70 and Older, People with Compromised Immune Systems and Those With Underlying Illnesses

- Directs 90-Day Moratorium on Any Residential or Commercial Evictions

- Asks PPE Product Providers to Sell Non-Essential Products to the State and Encourages Companies to Begin Manufacturing PPE Products

- Confirms 2,950 Additional Coronavirus Cases in New York State — Bringing Statewide Total to 7,102; New Cases in 23 Counties[39]

What were the essential businesses, according to Governor Cuomo? Who had to be "on pause"?

The Walmart in nearby Hudson was open. The McDonald's was open. Target was open.

But the Millerton library — that haven for kids from abusive homes, or from homes with no books — was closed.[40] The Roeliff Jansen Community Library up on Route 22 was also closed. Indeed, many of New York's libraries were forced to close.[41]

But Amazon stayed open. Not only that, when its workers were getting sick from COVID-19, the behemoth told them, against California law, that they could not take paid sick leave to stay home. Workers said that this drove them to come to work while ill.[42] Their illnesses were unsurprising: these were big box stores or factories with no windows, in which hundreds congregated at once, forced into even greater proximity by the closure of all smaller competition.

The beloved Hudson, New York, independent bookstore, The Spotted Dog, had to close when a worker tested positive for COVID-19.

(Indeed, New York State was not alone in this; independent bookstores across the country were forced to close.)[43]

Forced to close in New York State: Broadway plays, off-Broadway plays, local theaters; movie theaters; concert halls; houses of worship. Thus: no galas or symphonies, no concerts, no weddings or baptisms, bar mitzvahs or funerals.

Small restaurants were forced to close. Dad's Copake Diner, not far from us up on Route 22, a beloved 50's style diner that was built and run by a local family, was forced to close, and four waitresses lost their incomes, along with two cooks. All the small businesses that supplied the diner — their income dried up, too. One waitress, an upbeat, energetic single mother who had been working three or four jobs, had a son in college. Her income was suppressed too, through no actions of her own. Her son was compelled to come home for the duration.

Somehow corporate chain restaurants were "essential" and by logic germ-free, but owner-operated restaurants were cesspits of disease to be forcibly shuttered.

Open: tech companies. Open: telecoms. Open: chain drugstores such as CVS. Open: liquor stores.[44]

Pot stores stayed open in many states.[45] These were deemed to be "essential" services.

In England the news was even stranger. At first, they had an "essential services" list similar to ours.[46] But then there were ostentatious displays that just seemed cruel — in which shoppers could go to big box stores or stores on the "High Street" (main street) and buy food and alcohol, but could only gaze sadly at the retail products that they wanted to buy for their kids — retail products that could have kept small businesses alive. These would-be shoppers saw displays of model trains, dolls that could drink from bottles, Legos. These physical toys were all visible to the customers but roped off. The only items for sale were groceries and medicine.

In Britain you could see a product in the odd roped-off display then go home and order it from Amazon.

Schools in state after state were suddenly, systematically, forced to close. Overnight, to my astonishment, "distance-learning" platforms appeared in school districts and were launched into use. I knew that these products took months or years to develop and took a year in advance at least to contract to school districts. But quickly they were ubiquitous and all ready to go, at all levels, for all subjects: a monumental and actually chronologically hard-to-fathom feat of curriculum development, engineering, and contracting.

And suddenly no one but parents and kids were alarmed at the prospect of millions of children directed onto screens, alone, as a replacement for "school." Teachers were not alarmed, or if they were, their voices went unheard. Unions and school districts were definitely not alarmed. Teachers' spokespeople vocally spread the message, using canned talking points, that teachers were living in mortal fear of children and saw them as little death bombs, and that it was *they* who refused to come to school to teach.

This bizarre situation overall immediately became "the new normal" — that buzzy phrase popping up in news articles about our state of suspended animation — with nowhere to debate it. Of course you couldn't debate it: you too were forcibly "on pause." All of this was happening whether you liked it or not, and no matter how much your child suffered and fell behind.

College students were sent home. Colleges were shuttered.

———————

Playgrounds were roped off with tape like the tape at a crime scene. In California, hiking trails, state parks, and beaches were closed off, with a "regional stay-at-home order" that would not lift until January 2021; for millions, the miles of open, windswept beaches were inaccessible.[47]

As in a communist regime, people were told what they could and could not buy, and where they could and could not go, and indeed how close they were permitted to be to one another. Scared and confused, they complied.

It was not as if we could easily escape all these bizarre "emergency measures." In Massachusetts, right across the border from us upstate, on March 10, 2020, Governor Baker had also declared emergency law.[48]

In a sweep, Governor Cuomo replaced a vibrant, free, capitalist system with, in essence, an oligarchical economic system. By using the Stalinist taxonomy of "essential" and "non-essential," he selected those businesses that would die and those businesses that would not only survive but thrive, eating up the market share that others less fortunate had been forced to abandon.

Advanced capitalism had taken five hundred years to develop in the West. Modern capitalism had built up delicate norms and regulations to allow reasonably fair competition. Banks had developed sensitive metrics to choose businesses likely to succeed over businesses with flaws. A relatively level playing field in North America and Western Europe, and easy access to capital, had led to a seventy-year stretch of innovation and growth and prosperity. With all its flaws, advanced Western capitalism was the fairest system, and the one most likely to support human development, that the world had yet seen.

Advanced Western capitalism shuddered, and came to an almost complete stop at the gesture of state governors wielding emergency powers, and, globally, at the pronouncements of prime ministers seizing emergency powers; in the blink of an eye, massive economies, businesses, and business owners were forced to freeze in time like the inhabitants of Sleeping Beauty's castle.

What happened in New York State happened in similar language across the nation and throughout the formerly free nations of the world.

Legislation was passed federally in the United States "to address the crisis." Emergency measures were passed in most states. A welter of regulations descended on schools, restaurants, shops, warehouses. Boards of health are not elected, so these were creating a situation that bypassed the will of the people. Millions of businesses were forcibly closed.

Massive bills were passed with little debate — everyone was at home, after all, including legislators. These bills carried names that suggested that they were about a medical crisis: in the United Kingdom it was "The Coronavirus Act."[49] I read that bill in April of 2020 and was astounded. I could not understand from where it had emerged or why it took the shape it did. At that point, we had no idea if this "pause" was for a week or two and when all would return to the way it had been. But the UK "Coronavirus Act" was dozens of pages long, and in the version I read it suspended elections until 2021 in the UK. Why? What did these people know that the rest of us did not yet know? Why could the people of the UK not vote in 2020?

In the United States it was "The CARES Act," [50] "The HEROES Act."[51] Later came "The American Rescue Plan," doling out millions of dollars to states for individual schools.[52] But there were strings attached — the Treasury threatened to claw back funds from Arizona, for instance, if it continued awarding grants to school districts that didn't support the government line on masking, distancing and vaccines.[53] In Canada, according to Jay Cameron of the Justice Centre for Constitutional Freedoms, the health agencies were similarly empowered by emergency regulations to impose "edicts" and "mandates" on the population while bypassing and essentially emasculating the Canadian Parliament and its processes.[54] In democracy after democracy, the COVID-19 "emergency" was used to create an emergency governance structure that hyper-empowered health ministers and agencies, simultaneously draining decision-making powers from congresses and parliaments. It was the softest, sneakiest coup in history.

As the CEO of a website devoted to legislation, I followed the laws closely. I had never before seen bills that were structured to facilitate the wholesale bribery and thus the corruption of so many individuals and civil institutions.

In just two years, five hundred years of ever-developing capitalism — which since the Glass-Steagall Act gave opportunity to millions of middle class and working class investors and entrepreneurs and landlords — was replaced with a bleak, coercive, Marxist-style crony oligarchy. And when the dust settled, billions of dollars in value were seen to have been essentially stolen from one group, the middle and working class people of the West, and handed to another, the globalist oligarchs.

At the end of April 2020, I looked at the sky in the Hudson Valley. It was so cerulean, so trackless a blue.

By now we were fully "locked down," and seemingly overnight "lockdown" had become part of the lexicon, along with the culturally alien notion of "social distancing."

The first time I heard this phrase — one that, thanks to AI, was suddenly everywhere in both legacy and social media — I was alarmed by it. "Social distancing" sounded so . . . Chinese Communist. Obviously, from a Western point of view, if it is "distancing," it is not at all "social."

Embedded in the phrase was a Marxist assumption: that you serve the community by obeying, even to the level of how you moved your body in relation to the bodies of others, even against your own individual instincts or inclinations. Where you went, how you went there, how you assembled, how you congregated were, per this alien phrase, soon defined as being a "community" concern. Whereas previously, in actual America, per our very Constitution, where you went and how you assembled, had, up till now, been your choice.

One day I went shopping across the state border at a supermarket in Salem, Massachusetts, and was startled to see big, bright, stylized circles pasted onto the floor, indicating exactly where you were supposed to stand. Soon they too would be "normal," but I remember my dismay. The circles were like the colored tags on your kindergarten cubby with your name written on them IN BIG LETTERS when you were five. Instead of the Western/American cultural approach, which would be to remind adults that a severe respiratory disease was around and it was recommended to try to keep our distance, someone had planned, designed, printed and installed these circles, then measured six feet from six feet from six feet throughout the whole big box store, then placed arrows pointing up one aisle and down another to propel people in only one direction. It made my heart sink. I understood what I was seeing. I was seeing the totalitarianizing, which has to be a word now if it is not yet, of Western habits of thought and Western patterns of movement.

The circles said to shoppers: You are children. We — the forces who impose and set the circles — are the adults. You are the powerless. We decide.

They said it in bright, cheery letters and colors: You can't be trusted to behave sensibly and make your own decisions.

The arrows said: You can't turn backward if you forgot a jar of strawberry jam or just want to wander back to the rice and grains sections to idly gaze at a package of arborio rice and think about whether you might try to make risotto for what might be a special meal.

These circles and arrows on the floor were not trivial. They symbolically slashed away your positioning in society as an adult who can be trusted to make choices — and at your dreaming: the dreaming that might lead you in another direction altogether than the ones indicated on the floor.

It wasn't just about the distance.

It was about the infantilization.

CHAPTER THREE

UNDERSTANDING THE CRIMINALS

S o in 2020–22 a blueprint was put into action to crush Western people, crush Western economies, and steal the assets of the working and middle classes. Added to this was the strategy of utilizing mass vaccination of an incompletely tested substance, as a pretext for imposing a digital identity system that could create a CCP-style surveillance society and generate untold riches in data harvesting for a very few.

The minds of many will likely reel at such an assertion. A crime of this scale is too massive for most of us to grasp as fact or even to entertain as a hypothetical.

How can one imagine such criminals?

You probably would not commit any serious crime, let alone one of an immensity and scale of destruction that it would rightly be seen as an act of absolute evil. But that's because you probably empathize with other people, believe in basic human rights, and believe that human society, for all its flaws and the shortcomings of this or that human leader, is essentially organized for the well-being of human beings.

So you cannot conceive that a movement directed against humanity, a veritable "hack of humanity," would be conceived or executed by others. Surely you would have to be a demon or a sociopath to execute such a monumental crime.

But to understand what has happened to us, I must ask you to suspend for a while a thought process that investigators call "mirror imaging." This is when we assume others think as we do. Because most of us are decent people, and not sociopaths or psychopaths, we tend to assume that others are also driven by basic human motivations such as empathy, altruism, and kindness — or even just by the basic notion that other human beings are also deserving of life, self-determination, and dignity.

This "mirror imaging," though, is more than simply a flaw in analysis — it is a fatal error that leads us to miss important conclusions. For others do not always think as we do.

To understand such an immense crime, it is essential to grasp the thought processes of many political elites, of financial oligarchs, and of tech elites.

This understanding is fundamental to how otherwise nice people — and indeed Western people who grew up with post-Enlightenment norms about human rights and the rule of law — can be committing evil now with whole hearts. There are lessons from history that we have to learn, or re-learn, quickly.

To understand this moment, in which a brutal tyranny is being enacted upon us in lockstep globally by many otherwise familiar and formerly benign-seeming Western leaders and philanthropists and investors, we have to begin to "think like a tyrant."

I am not talking about anything arcane or occult. I am not talking about a QAnon fantasy of a few elites running the world.

I am talking here, rather, about the global elites whom I know and among whom I have lived for forty years.

I am describing what the German-Jewish philosopher of totalitarianism Hannah Arendt called "the banality of evil."

To understand what is happening in the current global lockstep of tyranny, we must understand that certain subcultures, certain leaders, and certain ideologies simply don't have our core values at heart; and we must face the fact that these monsters are not just Nazis long dead or members of the CCP far away. Some monsters are very near to us. Some monsters wear lovely suits and chat away about their kids at dinner parties. And some kinds of monstrosity and sociopathy are actively cultivated by the norms and within networks that are all around us, albeit half-hidden at elite levels and systematized and accepted at very high levels.

One source of the kind of global cruelty we see in medical fascism today derives from a post-war stratum of power.

Paradoxically, meta-national organizations founded after the carnage of the Second World War, such as the World Trade Organization and the United Nations, agreements such as the Regional Comprehensive Economic Partnership, and global corporate and investment communities have served to create a global elite of policymakers, nonprofit leaders, and bureaucrats, who are able to engage in cruel and oppressive policymaking precisely because they are no longer part of the communities whose lives are affected by what they impose on others.

All these meta-national organizations purport to foster a more peaceful, cooperative world — one that would blunt enmity between historical adversaries (such as France and Germany). They make the case that this meta-national organizational structure will far more greatly benefit ordinary men and women in the street than did the poor, battered, dysfunctional nation-state, with its rotten history and its bloody impulses.

The first half of the twentieth century, with its two catastrophic world wars, seemed indeed to reveal conclusively to the world the dark side of nationalism and the tragic limits of the nation-state; the period seemed like a textbook lesson in how decision-making at the level of nation-states seemingly leads inexorably to bloodshed and to racist, cruel jingoism.

The problem, though, as it turned out, is that you can't have accountability to citizens or a real democracy if you do not have a democratic nation-state. In fact, the alternative, a world of transnational entities, spawns a class of distant, unaccountable deciders.

As faulty and limited as the post-1848 secular, parliamentary nation-state doubtless is, it is the most perfect form of government yet created, owing to its accountability to a set group of people — that is, to the citizenry of a constitutional democracy bounded by clear national borders.

Meta-national organizations, by contrast, rapidly created super-structures that made decisions above the heads of citizens of nation-states. Quickly, the unelected decisionmakers of the EU became more important and powerful in many ways than were the parliamentary leaders at the national level in Greece or Portugal or Spain. Quickly, in turn, citizens of various European countries began losing the skills to understand how their local and national levers of power worked, as citizens were encouraged to leave it all to the bureaucrats at a level high above that of national parliaments.

But nationalism within a bounded nation-state, excessive or perverted to the dark side though it can surely be, also has constructive and protective aspects. Positive nationalism, within an accountable, constitutional nation-state, allows people to care about and act on their own futures. It allows them to be motivated by allegiance to their own families, their own communities, their own landscapes, their own histories, and their own cultures. And its leaders have to face their citizenry.

But a discourse was propagated — by global elites, who benefited from this discourse — that shamed well-intended people, especially in the West, for being in the least bit proud of or loyal to their own nation-state or national culture. It was a discourse that scolded and belittled any member of any nation-state in the West for worrying about what might happen if there were any limits at all on national borders.

Yet seeing the positive aspects of a nation-state is not by definition negative. If one is French, it is not by definition racist to celebrate what is brightest about French culture and history. If the terms "French" or "Dutch" or "Moroccan" or "American" are defined as by citizenship rather than by race, then cultures expand and welcome the new, and what is "French" or "Dutch" or "Moroccan" or "American" simply evolves.

But just as you cannot have a constitutional democracy unless you have a discrete citizenry, of whatever background, race or faith, consisting of people initiated into that nation's culture, language, history, rights, and responsibilities, so you cannot have a functioning, accountable representative democracy if you have open borders and voting by non-citizens. You have something nebulous, but it is no longer a representative democracy within a nation-state, and it dissolves the ever-more-distant leaders' accountability to the people.

The recent handing-over of voting rights to nearly a million non-citizens in New York City[55] may sound to most readers of *The New York Times* like a right-on blow for "equity" and anti-racism, but it is actually a tyrant's dream, as are the fully open borders presided over by President Biden in 2021–22.[56] The effect, and the intention, is to dilute the power of citizens within the formerly discrete boundaries of a specific nation-state.

The democratic nation-state is by necessity accountable to its people in a way that meta-national organizations simply are not. The people in a nation-state can vote out corrupt leaders. They can change course when it comes to bad policies. Indeed, they can put corrupt leaders on trial and in prison, or in the case of the United States, can execute those who have been found guilty of espionage, or of having committed treason.

The leaders of such citizens must, whether they wish to or not, deal with their people and worry about their reactions. There are natural limits to the cruelty and oppression with which an elected leader in a constitutional nation-state can get away.

Not so with leaders in the post-war world of meta-national organizations, global nonprofits, and increasingly porous borders. Once these leaders go bad, nothing need constrain their cruelty. The same is true for economic global elites, once national allegiances and national accountability have been left behind.

What happened in the almost eighty years since the end of the Second World War is the development of an elite international class of technocrats, EU bureaucrats, global nonprofit leaders and international investors for whom the nation-state — even one's own nation-state of origin — is an artifact, a secondary concern, a sentimental add-on. What really matters are other global elites in one's social circle and business network and the valuable relationships one can create with them. One's "ordinary" countrymen and women recede and become theoretical. And the constant message one receives from one's peers and from the elite meta-national culture is that those "ordinary" men and women simply are not as smart or well-educated, and so it would be a disaster to let them make their own decisions. Indeed, deciding for them saves them from their own fecklessness, ignorance, and shortsightedness.

What does this have to do with the escalating global cruelty of 2020–22 and "The Great Reset"?

Experiments done by the social psychologist Stanley Milgram at Yale University not only affirmed the lamentable truth that ordinary humans are capable of great cruelty, but showed that the greater the remove from the victim — and the more authoritative the directive insisting on the harm — the more readily "normal" people become monsters and abusers.[57]

Dr. Milgram found that sixty-five percent of participants were willing to shock their purported subjects ("learners") to the highest voltage level possible on the insistence of an authority figure. "Participants demonstrated a range of negative emotions about continuing," he noted. "Some participants thought they had killed the learner. Nevertheless, participants continued to obey, discharging the full shock to learners. One man who wanted to abandon the experiment was told the experiment must continue. Instead of challenging the decision of the experimenter, he proceeded, repeating to himself, 'It's got to go on, it's got to go on.'"[58]

In a sense, this experiment was replicated on a mass scale over the two years of the pandemic. A great many people instinctively felt something was terribly wrong; that what they were being told did not accord with their own experience. But at the same time, they were being subjected to a massive propaganda campaign invoking authority and superior understanding; a campaign, aligned with unthinkably lucrative direct incentives in some cases, led by a network of global elites, who, lovely as they might be one on one, and as nice as most doubtless were to their own kids, unhesitatingly executed vast cruelties and inflicted untold damage.

How do I know about the value assigned to the holy grail of gaming the system, and the potential for cruelty, shared by certain global elites? I have seen them up close.

I will never forget being in a company car in 2015, heading to the BBC's flagship political show. It was driven by the BBC's longtime driver. As a reporter, I always talk to drivers in these circumstances, because the elite men and women often do not "see" drivers, waitstaff, cleaners, and other mere mortals. So drivers and waitstaff and cleaners tend to hear everything and know everything.

It was an important week, in which the people of Greece, distraught at having had policies of "austerity" forced upon them by the European Union, were about to engage in a referendum. The papers were full of elderly Greek men and women weeping and in despair because the proposed policies would wipe away their retirement savings. As is common, the European newspapers were portraying the people of Greece, in opposing austerity, as spendthrifts, as ignorant, as having brought their economic disaster upon themselves, and as needing to be rescued by the policies of those wiser heads above the level of their national leaders' decision-making.

I couldn't help thinking that maybe it will be the case that rejecting "austerity" policies will turn out to be an economic mistake for the people of Greece. But I knew about referenda: and if there is a majority vote in a referendum, it is by law the will of the people. In a democracy, their decision must be enacted. So you can have your opinion about whether austerity would be smart or not in this context, but since the people have a real nation-state, their referendum would determine what happened in their country. And if the people's decision turned out to be a mistake, well, it was their mistake to make, with their own country, in their own parliament.

"Oh no," explained the driver. "EU officials were in this car before you. The referendum is purely cosmetic. It will be ignored. Whatever happens, they are going ahead with austerity."

I was dumbfounded.

But as it turned out, the BBC driver was exactly right. The people of Greece voted against austerity. But they were not to get their chosen outcome.[59]

Later that week, back in New York City, I was at a dinner party. It was hosted by a major hedge fund manager. His clients were Chinese, Russian, Ukrainian, and other international investment funds. At the party were his colleagues: British, Swedish, Chinese, French, and Belgian hedge fund managers and investors.

My host, an otherwise lovely guy, trained of course in the Ivy League, was apoplectic — *furious* — at the rank-and-file men and women of Greece. He did not yet know what the EU officials knew. He knew that the people of Greece had rejected austerity in their referendum.[60] But he had positioned in the opposite direction. Now he was enraged at those grandmas and grandpas, and at their resistant, stubborn sons and daughters, for having temporarily messed up his bet on austerity. He was literally pale with rage. His fists clenched as he spoke about the Greek referendum. How dare they, was his attitude. The *fools.*

The mansion where we were gathered that night had been built by a robber baron at the end of the nineteenth century. The dining room was staffed by beautiful actors/waiters and actresses/waitresses in black pants and spotless white shirts. They charmingly served us a gorgeous *plaice velouté* dinner, with sides of grilled asparagus and heirloom beets. The ceilings were twenty feet high and wreathed in shadows. The walls were adorned with a mélange of works of art: Italian Renaissance princelings, luscious still lifes from the sixteenth-century Netherlands, and portraits of late-nineteenth-century American society doyennes.

The conversation was sprightly. To my right, a Norwegian investor spoke about the latest avant-garde theatrical sensation on Broadway. To my left, an artist friend of the host and hostess described escalations in the New York City art market. Everyone was educated, pleasant, and cultured. The money guys were all agreeing with the host about the perfidy and "bad behavior" of the stubborn people of Greece. The wine flowed, red and white; it was beyond excellent. No one at that table was visibly evil. There were no secret signs or shadowy conversations. If this were a movie, you could not identify a villain. No one was part of a cabal.

But the point was that these people did not need to gather in the shadows or to be part of a cabal. Why would this group need a secret sign or a secret meeting? They simply owned the global stratum in which they operated, and they were accountable only to one another.

Neither did anyone there, expressing his or her views about the events of the weeks, think for an instant there was anything wrong with ignoring and overriding the democratically expressed will of an entire nation of citizens who had articulated their wishes lawfully. No one there had to say aloud to anyone else, "Let's be sure to suppress the eruptions of popular sentiments in nation-states, going forward" to know what kind of unmanageable future events were bad for business.

Thus, the whole nation, all the people of Greece, were being treated with extraordinary cruelty and contempt by these distant non-Greek men and women. This cruelty was possible in part because these men and women would never see them or have to face them or ever answer to them.

At the end of the evening, I was introduced to a brilliant young woman, a protégée of my host's. She was from a small, poor, fairly recent democracy in the global South, and educated as well in the Ivy League. My host showed off the young lady's knowledge and acumen about financial markets in the context of a discussion about the "reckless" behavior of the Greeks, and their nonsensical referendum.

Did she think her own fellow countrymen and women should have a say in outcomes about their economic futures? I asked her gently. I truly wondered what her views would be.

"No; the ordinary people of any given country don't have the skills to make the right economic decisions for themselves or their nations. We should be deciding for them," she calmly explained, with all the confidence and certainty of a now-privileged twentysomething.

"That's right," my host confirmed proudly.

So the Greeks never got their referendum outcome. There was a famous U-turn, and austerity was imposed against their wishes.[61] Many elderly Greek men and women were driven into abject poverty in their retirement. Many small and medium-sized businesses were lost.

Not much later, I was at another dinner hosted by the same man and mostly attended by the same group of people. But among the guests now was someone new: a former Greek politician who until very recently had been at the center, first, of the fight to reject austerity, and then of the abrupt U-turn.

He looked flushed, proud and ashamed at once, and he was being introduced around like a captured prize.

Who knows what promises had been made, what arrangements attended this outcome, this new alliance? But that former leader must have seen a level of influence and wealth far above what mere allegiance to his fellow citizens, mere decency, could have gotten him.

And my host, well, he and his colleagues got, in the end, the outcome on which they had placed such a big, big bet.

That night the wine continued to flow — and a new constellation was part of the social mix.

Too bad about the hundreds of thousands of "ordinary" Greeks, many of them elderly, now ruined for the rest of their lives. Too bad about the wreckage of the small businesses.

But of course this is just one example of how great evil — evil at a national level, and now evil at the coordinated global level of "The Great Reset" — is achieved: by distance and by condescension and by the creation of a meta-national community who see and hear and are answerable only to each other; but who do not see, or in any way respect, the rights of nations; or of self-determination of elders, of voters, of property; of you or of me.

To understand 2020–22, it is essential to grasp that great evil need not arrive in the guise of a goose-stepping soldier, or an official knocking at your door wearing jackboots. To understand how COVID-19 policy can be so coordinated and so cruel and so neo-fascistic, we need to understand that evil can come in the form of a well-dressed man or woman far removed from any traditional human or national loyalties or decencies but pleasantly passing the sherry.

———————

A final factor to understand when we look at who committed the great crimes of 2020–22, and how these crimes were executed, has to do with understanding the extent of Communist China's infiltration of the institutions of the United States and Western Europe. Sinologists such as Michael P. Senger, Peter Schweizer, and the longtime presidential China advisor Michael Pillsbury understand that China does not use military might as the primary weapon in its fight against its targeted nations and especially against us, the other superpower. Rather, its strategy is to use "a set of asymmetric weapons that allow an inferior power to defeat a seemingly superior adversary by striking at an enemy's weakest point." Pillsbury, like other sinologists raising the alarm, sees "a 100-year-long effort to overtake the US as the world's superpower" with deception as the essential tactic. By China's encouraging the United States to view it as weak and in need of Western guidance, he writes: "For decades . . . the US government has freely handed over sensitive information, technology, military know-how, intelligence and expert advice to the Chinese . . . and what we haven't given the Chinese, they've stolen." He and other sinologists believe that the CCP is intent on a plan in place since the time of Mao Zedong to become the world's hegemon by 2049, the Communist revolution's hundredth anniversary. He and others warn that thousands of CCP-aligned academics, foreign students who are bound by CCP law to report intel back to the CCP, and businesspeople, are embedded in strategic institutions in US and Western culture, economics, and politics. And these sinologists warn, too, that while for years China's scholars have denied the goal of "a Chinese-led world order," the tone from the CCP has recently changed. Since 2020, CCP spokespeople have used insulting and confrontational language to their US counterparts, and the goal of being the world's hegemon is now stated overtly by the CCP. "The hard truth," warns Pillsbury, "is that China's leaders see America as an enemy in the global struggle they plan on winning."[62]

Among those tasked with our national security, these fears have long been prevalent. As far back as 2009, a US Senate hearing was titled: "China's Propaganda and Influence Operations, Its Intelligence Activities that Target the United States, and the Resulting Impacts on US National Security."[63]

Eight years later, in May 2017, Sarah Cook, a Senior Research Analyst for East Asia, Freedom House, gave testimony at the Senate's "US-China Economic and Security Review Commission Hearing on China's Information Controls, Global Media Influence, and Cyber Warfare Strategy." Her report was titled "Chinese Government Influence on the US Media Landscape."[64] That report was updated in January 2020 under the title: "Chinese Communist Party's Media Influence Expands Worldwide: Report Finds Global Rise in Propaganda, Censorship, and Control of Content-Delivery Systems."[65] These reports found widespread influence operations aimed by the CCP at affecting staff, content and messaging in Western media and social media.

Almost redundantly, a global influence campaign aimed at the world's media was uncovered in 2020 by the International Federation of Journalists. They called their report "The China Story: Reshaping the World's Media."[66]

What does all the well-established CCP influence on Western media and social media — and Western academics and sports stars and influencers — have to do specifically with the great crime of 2020–22?

Most obviously, it long kept under wraps the fundamental fact of the pandemic's origins, ensuring that the Wuhan lab-leak premise would be everywhere derided as "conspiracy theory." In this regard the CCP even now continues to get away with murder.

More, Communist China's vast influence over global media benefits it immeasurably in suppressing Western heroes, Western history, Western ideals such as freedoms of speech and assembly, and Western instincts of spontaneity and individualism. Indeed, even as China daily works to undermine Western values and fan discord among the warring elements of traditionally democratic societies, its interests (including in becoming the main global force in biotech and in DNA databases) align neatly with the goals of the WEF and the bottom-line drivers of Big Tech; they readily work toward allied goals, if not in coordination. All favor like policies, aiming to intimidate citizens and break communities and to surveil citizens in a lucrative and controlling digital grid. These policies especially target freedom of speech, and aim to cripple the mastery by Western children — whom we could call the 2049 generation — of free thought and expression.

April slid into May and June 2020:

Children were of course now indoors all day, staring at screens — with the media approvingly noting it was no longer safe for children to be sent to school.

Distance learning magically picked up there too, without missing a beat. Software to check attendance, software to give tests, software to grade tests.

Under ordinary circumstances, each school would have found its own solution to the pandemic as a matter of choice and circumstance — outdoor classes with heaters, open windows, etc. — or else they would simply have carried on as before. Or private schools would have made their own decisions while public schools perhaps made different ones. But no — everyone everywhere suddenly was to "distance learn," that awkward, heartless neologism.

College students, who had worked hard their whole teenage years for the college experience at Princeton or Yale or the University of Texas, were instead back home, living with their parents again. This exodus from campus didn't seem to make much sense, since as far as I knew there was not yet any clear data on how this illness affected healthy young adults.

SUNY and CUNY colleges closed; hardworking kids from all walks of life, who were working while studying, whose futures depended on these public universities, hastily packed up their dorm rooms and returned home. Foreign students were abruptly sent packing.

State colleges across the country closed. So did community colleges. The dreams of millions of young adults — and the skills acquisition during the precious early adult years when training takes place — were suddenly on hold, and for an indeterminate period of time. Millions of young adults who had looked forward to four years of college, to being young, to learning in classrooms, to forming friendships with their peers that might last for lifetimes, sat in their parents' living rooms, sad, isolated, and stunned as the days passed.

Their passivity was not innate; it was enforced upon them by the "pandemic." They were forced into a psychological state of "external locus," that is, of being dependent for success on outside conditions, which is not a mind-state that successful people use. But there was nothing they could do to retake their lives and plans.

College students who needed labs for their science majors were shut out of labs. College students who needed theaters for their theater majors could not perform. Music students could not practice in a concert setting.

Instead, they could message each other on Microsoft Teams.[67]

CHAPTER FOUR

"STANDING TOGETHER BY STAYING APART"

B y June, a meme appeared on social media: "Humans are the virus."
Were we?

"Mask" very soon debuted as a positive verb. It had been, in English, until that very moment, a negative verb — facts were "masked," true intentions were "masked."

But now everywhere in media and social media were instructions to don masks. Any masks! "Mask up!" became a catch phrase, like "Wheels up!" or "Bottoms up!" The phrase seemed

focus-grouped in the way that it was made to sound almost jolly; there was nothing in the language to indicate that "Mask up!" might connote "suffocate" or "inhibit speech and breathing."

Newspapers showed you how to make masks out of any random fabric. They even offered patterns to cut out. I thought that sounded pretty old-school and unscientific.

But *The New York Times* showed dramatic schematics about why you must "mask up."[68] They penned front-page stories about aerosol-transmission studies that concluded that virtually no situation in which other humans were breathing, indoors or out, was not potentially fatal.[69] They represented the "virus" embedded in human breath as a ghostly-white cloud of particulates in diagrams that showed the lurid clouds raining death and disease on a hapless recipient who thereby became a victim of that fatal viral stream.

I was puzzled by this emerging narrative about "masks" and "distancing," about staying home indoors and not venturing outside.

Mostly I was puzzled because, even as a layperson, I was aware of long-held understandings regarding airborne respiratory pathogens. As a student of English literature and British history, I'd read the famous novels and knew of the great operas whose protagonists suffered from a dangerous, potentially fatal, airborne, respiratory disease, that, as yet, had no cure. The heroines Violetta in Giuseppe Verdi's opera *La Traviata*, Antonia in Jacques Offenbach's *Les Contes d'Hoffmann*, and Mimi in Giacomo Puccini's *La Bohème* all suffered from tuberculosis. Hans Castorp, in Thomas Mann's novel *The Magic Mountain*, suffered from tuberculosis.

The New Zealand novelist and short-story writer Katherine Mansfield had herself suffered from tuberculosis. The British novelists D. H. Lawrence and George Orwell had suffered from tuberculosis.

So I knew that, though this predicament in which we found ourselves was being relentlessly messaged as "novel" and unprecedented, the conducting of human civilization while dealing with an untreatable serious, potentially fatal, respiratory illness was hardly novel for human beings.

"Masking" and "distancing" would be iconic human experiences. Victims of tuberculosis were of course isolated in ways when they were ill. Yet I could not recall in any of these writers' memoirs, or in any of their biographies, or in any of these composers' cultural productions even a passing mention of the general healthy public's use of masking — let alone "health" directives that called for the "distancing" of healthy people and that compelled them to stay indoors for months at a time.

Indeed, *The Magic Mountain* is set in a tuberculosis sanatorium; there are many scenes of inhabitants taking strenuous outdoor hikes, devouring healthful meals, and being made to lie bundled up in fur sleeping bags on sleeping porches outdoors, to benefit from fresh air and sunshine. But "masks," "distancing," and being kept forcibly indoors together were not at all part of the regime.[70]

Tubercular people in the past were at times quarantined or sent to sanatoria, but never before in this history of dealing with serious airborne illness had the human race "distanced" the healthy from one another in order to deal with the risk of this kind of pathogen. If "distancing" and "masking" had "worked" with regard to serious airborne respiratory illnesses, why was this presumably tremendously important discovery now news only coincidentally with the onset of a brand-new illness in 2020?

The question naturally arises: how did we deal with similar medical crises in the past?

The answer: for all the devastation these crises wrought, civilization and commerce were not brought to a standstill.

In fact, America has lived through waves of infectious diseases ranging from yellow fever in Boston in 1693,[71] to smallpox from 1775–82,[72] to cholera outbreaks the mid-nineteenth century,[73] to waves of tuberculosis from the late-nineteenth to the mid-twentieth centuries.[74] But we remained America — and free, after 1776, with a constitution and rule of law — in spite of these waves of disease and indeed in spite of two world wars.

Even in the worst instances of waves of serious or fatal diseases, schools sought to reopen as soon and as safely as possible. In *Jane Eyre*, the heroine's boarding school Lowood is closed after an epidemic of typhus fever kills students. But after an investigation into the causes of the spread of the disease, wealthy benefactors improve the building and its location, the diet, clothing, housing conditions and treatment of the children, and "[t]he school, thus improved, became in time a truly useful and noble institution."[75]

The terrible Spanish flu epidemic of 1918–19, with which COVID-19 has been so often compared — but which, in fact, cut a much more harrowing swath through society (not only taking many millions more worldwide, but particularly targeting young adults) — did not bring to a permanent stop commerce, arts, worship or assembly worldwide. Europe likewise had long sustained waves of infectious disease, including cholera and typhus in the nineteenth century that killed tens of thousands.

But none of it dissolved North American or European culture or community. Indeed, the periods of disease in North America and Europe coincided with periods of great human achievement. People suffered in medical terms, of course; people died and were mourned. The tragedies of infectious diseases unfolded on grand scales. But culture and history, innovation and capital markets did not stop.

Western children lived through such difficult times and survived, even thrived, because they had each other. They had parents. They could speak and hug and play. And they had around them the organic local culture. The American Psychological Association notes that kids can survive many crises, even wartime, with mental health intact if they have loving and expressive home situations.[76]

Indeed, people in the West sustained communal achievements during crises and bad times generation after generation. It was during the yellow fever epidemics of the 1790s[77] that Philadelphia saw the creation of some of its most beautiful architectural structures.[78]

During the typhus and cholera epidemics in Britain in the 1830s and 1840s, Charles Dickens produced *The Pickwick Papers, Oliver Twist,* and *Nicholas Nickleby,* Robert Browning wrote *Sordello,* and Elizabeth Barrett Browning published her first book. Charlotte Brontë brought out *Jane Eyre.* The examples of productivity during hellish medical crises past are endless. In each case the writer was surrounded by, and reflected, the dynamism of life in the great capital and regional metropoles; he or she was absorbed by the social and economic life of the community and went freely to church, to baptisms, and to funerals and traveled to transact business and to meet friends.

It's not as if people were indifferent, or that no precautions were taken. In the years before antibiotics and modern treatments, infectious diseases, including airborne respiratory illnesses, were of course greatly-feared and addressed, if imperfectly, by sunlight, nutrition, exercise, fresh air and better sanitation. Everyone who reads Western novels and knows Western history is well-aware of this.

In Crimea, in 1854–56, the British nursing pioneer Florence Nightingale famously lowered rates of airborne illness in wartime hospitals by insisting on bringing into dark, unventilated conditions sunlight, nutrition, and ventilation: "hygiene, sanitation, fresh air . . . a good diet."[79] Her results were measurable, and they changed public health practices. Building on this knowledge base, America's settlement movement in the Progressive Era sought to ease crowded, stuffy, multifamily households, where infectious diseases flourished, by changing building codes so that airshafts and courtyards allowed for air circulation in the home. The Tenement House Law of 1901 ensured flush toilets and airshafts to limit disease and set minimum requirements in building codes for light and ventilation.[80]

This understanding of the health impacts of sunlight and ventilation even led to the building codes that required stepped-back skyscrapers in New York City, to allow sun and air circulation to reach crowded urban streets.[81] Settlement reformers got cod liver oil, with its high levels of Vitamin D, to the children of the poor[82] and lobbied successfully for public parks and playgrounds.[83] The reason? They understood that sunlight, Vitamin D, nutrition, exercise, and fresh air were potent enemies of then-otherwise-untreatable airborne infectious diseases.

Everyone knew this.

Yet now, weirdly, in state after state, policies and media messages were promoting precisely the opposite. The message was not "Go to the park, go to the beach! Exercise! Open the windows! Get sun! Take Vitamin D!" but rather, "Stay Home! Bring the adult children home into crowded multigenerational households! Stay indoors, continually stressed with fear! Put a piece of fabric on your face!"

It was hard to fathom how we had so quickly lost our collective cultural memory.

The ready access of enclosed and depressed people to marijuana and alcohol under the directive not to leave home further degraded the likelihood of healthful outcomes.[84]

The masking, the enclosure, the isolation, the lack of community, fresh air and exercise, the fear, the cabin fever, the generations piled on top of one another, the alienation engendered by computer screens — they all took their toll. People grew pale, fearful, obsessive, phobic, and sad. And unsurprisingly, many got sick and many died.

———————

The everywhere-promoted "masking" quickly became a fetish. In all cultures and at all times, masks have represented de-individuation and dehumanization. Thieves wear masks. Executioners wear black masks so their victims cannot see them. Torturers are masked. On Halloween, masked children assume the avatars of ghosts, monsters, and devils; at Carnival in New Orleans or Rio de Janeiro, masks endow their wearers with a scarier or more powerful persona.

On the other side of the equation, masks allow for people to be more easily punished and victimized. In Pentonville prison, where the poet and playwright Oscar Wilde was incarcerated for "gross indecency," prisoners were masked as a way to reinforce their isolation:

> [T]he guiding principle of this system was to keep prisoners completely apart, as a form of punishment . . . When prisoners left their cells, only for exercise and to attend chapel, they had to wear a "Scottish cap," which was a type of baseball cap with a large peak forming a mask so that they could only see through narrow slits. Even in the chapel the prisoners had to sit in cubicles, rather than in open pews. Wilde would have already experienced this at Pentonville. There were 250 cells in Reading Prison, on three landings — all single occupancy.[85]

So isolation, masking, and "distancing" were part of the regime of punishment and psychological torture in a Victorian prison.

And yet in 2020–21 these were reintroduced to the West as an optimum lifestyle.

Culturally, masks are always what the Viennese founder of psychoanalysis Sigmund Freud called the *"unheimlich"* — the uncanny, a symbol that triggers unconscious feelings of unease, of being "not at home," which provides a sensation that is creepy or weird. How many characters in horror films, from *Ghostface* to Jason in *Friday the 13th*, are masked?

It is not surprising that masks are so destabilizing to see, so unnerving. We see from expressions if we are among friendly people or people who are dangerous to us. Human beings need to see faces in order to feel safe.

I recall around June of 2020 seeing an adult stranger, a woman, approach a five-year-old who was beside her mother. The older lady just wanted to say "Hi" and to chat, as she had with children for decades, as we all used to do before 2020. It was second nature to her, and of course such casual interactions are basic to children's socialization. But this child, unable to tell if the masked stranger approaching her was smiling or not, began to cower in fear, and to cling desperately to his mother.

Early in the "masking" regime, there were victims of sexual assault describing online how triggering it was for them not to be able to see faces and assess expressions. "Everyone in a mask seems like a predator," as one survivor put it.

"Social distancing" — "mask up" — "we stand together by staying apart": these proto-Marxist idioms and Newspeak linguistic aberrations in the culture were like hideous toadstools in what had been a familiar, fresh, green forest of Western languages.

———

For the first time in human history, what was expected, and on a grand scale, was that kids would stay tethered to their screens for hours every day.

But what is school?

It's not just learning facts from a curriculum or in a textbook. School is also a promise to teach children how to grow up to navigate the physical and human world.

School is how small human primates imitate the skills they need to become socialized, educated human adults.

School is not just a curriculum on a page or a screen. School means learning how to put your coat in a cubby; how to take turns on a slide; how to avoid the mean kids and identify kids who seem as if they might like you back. From a facial expression, from body language, by way of a shy smile across a lunchroom or a sneering glance across the homeroom, you figure out how to find friends and avoid enemies. School is field trips, being boisterous and noisy on the bus, or being shown arrowheads while sitting in a circle around a patient museum curator.

School presents to a human child the special role that humans have in engaging with the extraordinary physical world, and it promises to help the child unlock its secrets. School is the promise of the interpretation of what seem to children like miracles, whose interpretation is the human task.

Primates learn from imitation. That is why human beings huddle close together when they learn and why they stand side by side to engage in observation and commentary while learning.

As a child, you stood next to another little human when you first looked into a microscope or when you learned how to solder in shop class. You watched together. You discussed what you were seeing.

As a child, you sat in a circle around your teacher and looked at her face as she read a story, and you felt the magic of human narrative in a collective context. When you grew a bit older, you may have sat side by side with other children around a campfire at camp, listening to a story — that quintessential human initiation into the miracle of narrative unfolding in the context of community. It takes being close, within a couple of feet, to relate to other humans socially. It can't be done otherwise. And it needs to be in person.

School is molding clay and watching the miracle of a little pot being created, to be taken home and displayed proudly; it is growing a bean seedling in an egg carton and watching the miracle of a plant unfold into the pale classroom-window light. It is looking into a microscope to see the miracle of tiny microorganisms in rainwater darting around on a slide. It is playing recorder in your music class and catching the miracle of that moment when thirty-two awkward, furiously focusing kids — kids from different backgrounds, with different interests and physiques, maybe speaking different languages at home — all get caught up as one in the harmony of "Für Elise."

School is socialization: learning how to be human in a human community, learning how not to get beaten up, learning how to make allies in Red Rover or Kiss the Girls, and later learning how to have a girlfriend or boyfriend, learning how to flirt at a locker or over a pipette or while passing a team stretching on a playing field. The folklorists Iona and Peter Opie began to study the schoolyard culture of children in the 1950s and found that games and rhymes such as "Ring Around the Rosie" had been passed down via generations of children for centuries. No one had disrupted that transmission for centuries, in the West.[86] Now the culture of childhood was disrupted, disconnected, like little circuits being detached from one another.

School is about how to be human in groups — learning how to lose at a game and keep going. Learning how to win graciously. Learning how to pass the ball. All of those are preparatory to any great endeavor involving "teamwork," which is a trite word for the miracle of human beings engaged in coordination, collaboration, and competition from which our arts, our civilization, our commerce, and our defense all arise.

School teaches us how to please, care for, argue with, provoke, and conciliate people outside of our immediate families.

School is emotional learning, as recent educators have pointed out. Teachers don't just teach. Fellow students don't just sit next to scholars inertly. The community of school expands the emotional field of the students outside of the family, so they learn to have emotionally successful relationships with people outside their mother, father and siblings. A relationship with a teacher is the first relationship with an adult most modern Western children have outside of their families. The emotional life of school gives a child practice to learn what pleases and what displeases, what fosters connection and approval from others and what closes it down. With every suc-

cessful emotional interaction, kids learn mastery and confidence; they acquire power.

Additionally, not every family is healthy. Kids with narcissistic parents who can't see them often learn from a teacher or peer group what it means to be seen. Kids who are beaten at home learn what it means to be physically safe. Kids whose parents suffer with addiction learn what it means to engage with people who are able to respond.

The reason that people around the world have struggled, and still do, at great cost to themselves, to build schools, or to pass laws to get children into schools, or to go without so their kids can afford a school uniform and be educated, is not just so that a child can have facts in his or her head. If that were all that education was, then free libraries — or, yes, maybe even "distance learning" — would be enough.

The extra-"factual" nature of education, the social nature of education, is why parents and the progressive movement moved heaven and earth to put children in physical schools, with human teachers. Because school is a living daily promise that is kept to draw a child into a holistic community of enrichment, a thought-through institution based on rules and agreements about behavior and deliverables that extend past what is inside of textbooks, a proto-civilization of the educated that surrounds the child with a 360-degree experience of being with the educated and being expected to prioritize and value the tasks and goals that go along with being educated.

But suddenly, it was ok — indeed, it was "necessary" — to provide no school for the kids. To offer no community college or university for the young adults.

Because, because . . . COVID.

Parents all over were praying that kids could go back to school in the fall of 2020. They did not know that decisions were already being made, above their heads.

CHAPTER FIVE

THE "NEW NORMAL"

A t the same time as the living classroom was killed off, so was the living office. "Remote working" or "working remotely" became terms in the new lexicon — as opposed to the more organic "not showing up for work" or "being absent from the office." Suddenly, after two hundred and fifty years of an Industrial Revolution in which many Western people *went* to work, the importance of the office, that workplace outside of the home, simply vanished.

Abruptly, vast messaging surrounded almost every white-collar worker, communicating that one could stay home — stay home! And work "remotely," on a platform such as Zoom or Microsoft Teams.

Indeed Zoom — which was a platform that a tiny minority had navigated before April 2020 — was suddenly everywhere.

As with "remote learning," Zoom rolled out everywhere as a cultural expectation without question or variation. It wasn't as if some businesses met or polled their workers or created a hybrid model — no, the social norm was established almost overnight. Everyone suddenly knew how to navigate it, and a whole Zoom culture appeared at once.

At first it seemed impossible — this staying at home with working parents and kids tethered to screens could never be a widespread or enduring solution. Women have been asking to "work remotely" for decades, and business interests have always had reasons not to allow it.

But suddenly this massive shift in human activity every day, this shift of not going to work, was not just tolerated, it was promoted everywhere. In the blink of an eye it was "the new normal" — another phrase that appeared out of nowhere in the early spring of 2020. (Zoom's stock, by the way, peaked in October 2020).[87]

Lifestyle articles talked about "Zoomers" (cute!). "Coronavirus and Zoom have marked a generation," we read in 2020.[88]

Fashion pages discussed what it meant to wear sweatpants all day down below and a well-put-together look on top. Adorable, slightly sassy features tsk-tsked at how men working at home would hog the good surfaces and wives would have to find a corner in a bedroom. But few really seemed to question this massive shift in the expectation of how human beings should spend their days. And after "mandates" were passed to force us to stay home, resistance was futile anyway.

Still, it seemed extraordinary: kids were expected to be on a computer for multiple hours a day in one room, while a working mom, or a homemaking mom, was also nearby, and a dad might also be in the next room working on a computer. If there were siblings, they were expected to be on computers.

I knew from decades of being on panels about working mothers and "balance" — and also from having been a working mom with small children myself — that this expectation was impossible.

Whoever had issued this bizarre sudden edict seemed not to have dealt with something that had bedeviled feminism and employers for forty years: who would watch the children? No, that question was completely done away with and over the course of some weeks. A new expectation was now prevalent all over America, and indeed the West. Strange and head-spinning as it seemed at first: *no one* was watching the kids.

The time-honored American, Canadian, Australian, and European social outlet of physical shopping also had largely vanished overnight. News articles appeared stating that you could get sick from touching surfaces: "What's the Risk of Catching Coronavirus from a Surface? Touching Contaminated Objects and then Infecting Ourselves with the Germs is Not Typically How the Virus Spreads. But it Can Happen."[89] UC Davis Health would later note that "[t]ests have found traces of COVID-19 on surfaces, but no research has established that the virus is viable in those places."[90] What a gift for e-commerce!

Menus vanished, as they presumably carried fatal diseases (except that they didn't), to be replaced with QR codes that could geolocate you.[91] "Contactless" offerings appeared everywhere: "Curbside Pickup," Grubhub, Seamless.

Almost as suddenly, to solve the problem, at least for the affluent, of being discouraged from physically shopping for groceries whose surfaces could kill you (except that they couldn't), meal kits appeared — they would be delivered to your doorstep! So many, many meal kits were suddenly advertised everywhere: Home Chef, Marley Spoon, Green Chef.

HelloFresh was one such meal kit company. It had not made money for years after its founding. It was supported by the startup studio Rocket Internet; Insight Venture Partners led a $50 million round in 2014.[92] By 2017, HelloFresh was still unprofitable. But Rocket Internet's stake in HelloFresh was worth almost $980 million.[93]

What a benefit, though, the "stay at home" orders were to this formerly money-losing meal-kit company and its internet-industry investors: HelloFresh's revenue more than doubled from 2019 to 2020, then nearly doubled yet again in 2021 (Figure 1).[94]

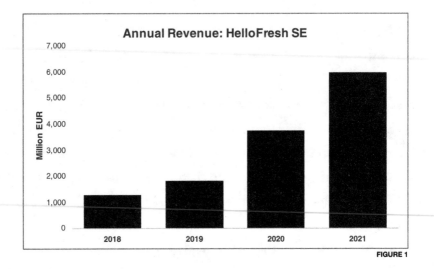

FIGURE 1

The meal kits appeared, like magic, for every taste, at least for the upper-middle class, and pacified them. The working class people who could not afford them or who could not afford to get to Walmart or Costco, or who had no car, were suddenly trying to stay healthy in food deserts even more deserted than the food deserts that had bedeviled their lower-income neighborhoods before March 2020.

———————

In the digital world, almost every major website or platform suddenly had a "COVID-19" warning.

That has been the case now for two years. That is hard to accomplish. Google showed you where testing sites were, when you were just looking for directions to a nearby gas station. Our phones suddenly showed a scary, spiked, mucus-green "COVID virus" emoji when we typed the word "virus."

Other tech moguls funded evidence for "lockdowns." The Blavatnik School of Government at the University of Oxford built a "COVID-19 Government Response Tracker," which purported to show how school closures, "lockdown" policies and other restrictive measures affected health and economic outcomes in 180 countries.[95] In the middle of the "lockdown," the Blavatnik School's "COVID-19 Stringency Index" was widely cited in the US news media alongside case counts to show that "locked-down" states purportedly did better than open states.[96] Subsequent studies did not, however, confirm this claimed difference in outcomes.[97]

The Blavatnik School, which is a public policy institution and not a medical one, was funded by Len Blavatnik, a Ukrainian-born billionaire with both US and UK citizenship. He is a major donor to both US political parties and has ties to Russian oligarchs. Blavatnik's portfolio includes Access Technology Ventures, "a portfolio of foundational companies that touch millions of customers across the consumer and enterprise technology ecosystems."[98] This portfolio shows how mega-elites profit from both the CCP and the West, thus blurring the objectives of traditional nation-state adversaries and reveals how many have a vested interest in a "locked-down," post-humane world.

The group invested more than $2 billion in tech and related companies worldwide.[99] Its holdings? Companies boosted directly by "lockdowns" and a "contactless" world.

Blavatnik's portfolio has included Alibaba Group (a major online retailer, similar to Amazon and one of its chief competitors), Tencent Music, and ANT Financial (all Chinese companies), Zhihu Inc, "an iconic online content community" and one of the top five online content communities in China,[100] Facebook, Snapchat, Spotify, Square (the digital payment processor), Amazon, and Rocket Internet — the HelloFresh investor.[101] All these platforms are boosted by a post-humane world, in which we do not meet, party, make music, or transact in person.

The Blavatnik School also offered the "Pathways for Prosperity Commission on Technology and Inclusive Development." One of the program's three co-chairs? Melinda Gates. The program was "founded and managed by the Blavatnik School of Government and the Bill & Melinda Gates Foundation."[102]

Before anyone really processed what was happening, before we could catch our collective breath, this somber catastrophe, or what was alleged to be a somber catastrophe — one that in times past we might have dealt with in 330 million individual ways, as Americans had always dealt with catastrophe — morphed into a uniform, top-down, almost cozy "lifestyle" that was, as a form of house arrest, well, tolerable.

That is, if you were affluent.

What we did not know was that the "academic" studies, the media messaging, and the tools for the cozy lifestyle all derived from, and then benefited, the same small group.

People were still locked in their homes. People feared going outside, feared touching others. The terror-inducing articles were relentless.

In the spring of 2020, The New York Times *memorably reported that the city had deployed a set of forty-five mobile morgues. The morgues were photographed lined up in a municipal parking lot, terrifyingly ready to absorb the purported excess number of bodies.*

City functionaries now entirely altered the usual method of how bodies were disposed of in Manhattan. Previously, it was standard practice for funeral homes, which are not state or government entities, to retrieve bodies from hospitals to be processed for burial. But in this "emergency," the city had replaced this system with its own, under the aegis of the office of the chief medical examiner.

A spokeswoman for the office told The New York Times *that in addition to the forty-five mobile morgues, eighty-five additional units were due to be delivered by FEMA.*[103]

Yet in fact, according to Mike Lanotte of the New York State Funeral Homes Directors' Association, this "bottleneck" had been created because cemeteries had been forced to reduce their hours of operation, meaning that the number of bodies they could bury in a day had been restricted. In other words, the bodies were stacking up so graphically and alarmingly not solely because their overwhelming number meant there were too many to process, but also because the cemeteries had not been allowed to process them during normal working hours.

The medical examiner's office further declared that "under the final phase of its plan, the medical examiner's office would coordinate with all local cemeteries to bury the dead in the 'temporary mass internment method.'" The horrifying article concluded that under this method, "Ten bodies in caskets are placed lengthwise in a long, narrow section in the ground . . . The foot end of one casket is placed in close proximity to the head end of the next."[104]

It was, needless to say, traumatic reading. Who wanted such an end for a loved one?

But I was puzzled by the accompanying images of dead bodies on gurneys or under bright-vermilion plastic tarps being transported from hospitals to morgues; the bodies appeared to be tightly bound in medieval-looking winding sheets revealing their human shape. Even weirder, they were being rolled outside of the hospital loading docks, down ramps, and out onto the sidewalks on city streets, all but paraded in front of news cameras.

Under normal circumstances, when a funeral home retrieves a body from a hospital morgue, it is put on a gurney, fully covered, and immediately placed into a hearse or a minivan. The funeral director comes at any time of day or night to talk with the family of the deceased and to safely take custody of the deceased's body. This is why you don't typically see dead bodies being transported on the sidewalks of New York. The hearse or the funeral home minivan backs up to the loading dock of the hospital. The transfer, under the care of the funeral director, is typically discreet and private.

So I did not doubt the deaths. But I knew media messaging, and media availability, and I was struck that the discretion and privacy of death as handled by private funeral directors had been replaced by a graphic public display of dead bodies to the cameras from multiple angles, as well as by the fact the city's emergency officials, having taken over the process of handling the bodies, had evidently leaked to the press not just documents sure to terrify readers, but had made the bodies available to the cameras.

Also notably, news stories, accompanied by vivid photos of multiple caskets awaiting burial, described how Hart Island, off the coast of the Bronx, would be the final resting place for the COVID victims whose remains exceeded cemetery capacities in New York City. News features showed aerial photographs of vast trenches being dug deep into the ground on Hart Island and uniformed workers stacking plain pine caskets one on top of the other within the trenches. The images were shot from above, by drones. They were entirely shocking to most people seeing them.

As it happened, though, I knew about Hart Island, as before the pandemic I had been researching it for a book. It is a "Potter's Field," a burial ground for all New York City's five boroughs. I also knew that shocking as the images truly were in 2020 to those unfamiliar with Hart Island, they were in no way unusual for the uses to which Hart Island had been put over its long history. Indeed, for a hundred years the facility had been used to bury the unclaimed indigent in mass graves, the graves dug by prisoners. So, as gruesome as the scene in the photos seemed to those unfamiliar with how business was done on Hart Island, what they showed happening on Hart Island was in no way out of the ordinary. Indigent New Yorkers had been buried in deep trenches in plain pine caskets in mass graves on Hart Island for decades as a matter of course.

"Mass burials on Hart Island began in 1875," explains the website of a volunteer group devoted to documenting its history.[105] Over 70,000 people have been buried on Hart Island in mass graves since 1980.[106]

What I also knew was that no one was allowed onto Hart Island without government permission. It is a government facility. So I was especially struck by the aerial footage of caskets being buried in a mass grave, images reproduced and described in shocked tones by the BBC, The Washington Post, *Sky News, and other outlets worldwide.[107] I knew full well that drones cannot fly over Hart Island without official authorization. So unless someone was violating the law, government officials would either have had to provide the images or given permission for a news outlet to shoot them.*

———————

Over the course of the spring and summer of 2020, Governor Cuomo had rolled out one spectacle of medical terror after another. On April 2, 2020, the Navy hospital ship USNS Comfort, *a massive white hospital ship docked dramatically at Pier 90 and was secured to great fanfare by the governor. The visuals were stunning.*

The ship was an instant iconic symbol of disaster. It had a thousand beds. Yet by April 30, it had quietly departed, having treated fewer than 200 patients, and at times as few as 20, though the hospitals were full. Confusing.[108]

The morgue vehicles ranged before the cameras on Thirtieth Street were succeeded by Governor Cuomo's announcement that Central Park might be used for a field hospital. By April 17, 2020, Samaritan's Purse, a private nonprofit organization aligned with Mt. Sinai hospital, had indeed set up a field hospital in East Meadow in Central Park, made up of fourteen massive white tents. The field hospital made for new highly disturbing images in the news. Samaritan's Purse ran stories about the desperate surge in cases.

But by May 2, 2020 — "Field Hospital that Treated Coronavirus Patients in Central Park to Close," announced CBSnews.com. It had been up for fifteen days and then disassembled.[109] A similar indoor facility in Queens had cost $52 million dollars to assemble and treated a total of 79 people before closing after one month.[110]

Finally, Governor Cuomo also announced that he was moving COVID patients into nursing homes, which seemed bizarre to me. [111] I had never heard of that happening before.

At the same time, I heard from a cousin that my elderly relative was in a nursing home, but, "because of COVID," her family was not allowed to see her. Infected people were being moved in by the governor, but healthy family members were being kept out? I did not understand this. Why couldn't she have visitors while seated safely outside? A sociable woman with many grandchildren who loved her, this isolation seemed like it would be a form of torture for her.

I was already noticing that the media was not citing primary sources for COVID "cases" and deaths. For instance, CBS often cited . . . CBS. On May 2 the network reported "There have been a total of 309,145 cases in New York State since the crisis began, and 18,909 deaths, according to CBS New York."[112] This self-citation was curious journalistically, to say the least. And if you clicked through to the source link, the data looked very different: "In the 24 hours leading into Saturday, the number of "confirmed" COVID-19 cases in New York State was 831, down slightly from the average of 900 a day the state was seeing recently, to a total of 309,145 cases."[113]

So this fine print, which you only saw by clicking through to what presented itself as a "citation," contradicted the scary news story; it explained that there were not in fact 309,145 cases of COVID-19 in New York State on May 2, 2020, even though CBS.com reported on the primary page that everyone read that there "have been" 309,145 cases in New York State "since the crisis began," implying an ongoing emergency of that kind of scale.

That terrifying figure was completely misleading. As if things weren't bad enough, this was needless scaremongering on an epic scale.

In fact, there were 831 "confirmed cases" of COVID-19 in New York State on May 2, 2020, out of roughly 20 million people, down from about 900 on average in the days before.[114] The 300,000-plus figure was reporting totals of all time in New York State, and it was a figure that did not subtract from the total the people who had recovered.

On that typical day at the height of the pandemic in New York, May 2, 2020, 299 more New Yorkers were listed as having died of illnesses "related to" COVID-19, bringing the total to the 18,909. Again, terrifying sounding. Except there are roughly 20 million people in New York State, so what, in fact, that "deaths related to COVID-19" *figure meant was that every New Yorker had a minuscule chance of dying in a death "related to" COVID. Indeed, all this time later, though New York throughout the pandemic had one of the highest mortality rates of any state (at 3,529 per million population)[115] a New Yorker's chances of dying in a death "related to" the virus was 0.3529%. 3,529 is 0.3529% of one million.*

Not much of a scare headline in that.

It would not be possible to get millions of people to stay inside for two years to avoid this kind of risk.

But because we were being systematically lied to, and because CBS and other media were not doing their jobs, and were cynically misrepresenting the data, for far too long, like millions of others, I was terrified, and so were the people I loved.

———————

A commentator on social media posted: "The train today was stopped because someone phoned in a suicide threat and put his head on the tracks, and they were looking for the body while I was on the train."

I stood at the Wassaic train station myself later that day, waiting for the train heading into Manhattan. An announcement came over the loudspeaker, stating that it was now national Amtrak policy that everyone had to wear a mask on the train.

The Amtrak website said: "Amtrak requires Facial Covering for Added Layer of Protection." "Help Us and Others."

A possibly attractive cartoon Amtrak passenger showed her green eyes above the "facial covering."[116]

I understood that this seemed, medically, like a reasonable request given the exposure of staff to respiratory pathogens. But I trembled too, as I understood another boundary was now breached.

I did notice, when I boarded, that Amtrak and Metro-North trains windows had not been altered, and still could not be opened. All the air in the car was unhealthily recirculating.

I remember my heart sinking, as I sat down and positioned my mask on my face. I understood that this demand, this "order," had crossed a line in a free society, and that the power to "mask" represented a new kind of power over citizens in America. It had not arisen via law, and not even via emergency measures that were under regular review and responsive to public pressure or changing conditions. So I understood that I now lived in a world in which citizens could be masked by force — and that they would soon be forced to do other things.

I had read history. I understood that now nothing would prevent new orders to mask all the community, in venue after venue, and that all measures limiting our physical bodies, and the bodies of others were now on the table.

CHAPTER SIX

HOW EMERGENCY POLICY IS MADE

S o it took much longer than it should have for anyone but a handful to understand that the pandemic had created a pretext for 360-degree social control. This is because we're a trusting and good-hearted people, and many citizens had little understanding of how policy is crafted in an emergency/opportunity context.

Most people naturally assume emergency-related policies are made as a direct response to the needs of citizens. But they could not be more mistaken.

Former President Clinton's operative Rahm Emanuel famously told a *Wall Street Journal* forum how some political operatives actually regard horrific situations: "[Y]ou never want a serious crisis to go to waste."[117]

Having been around global decision-makers in media, politics, and tech gives me insight into what can happen in the rooms where responses to crisis are crafted. While at a national or even a state level it is a given that the policy response to a crisis will always be presented to the citizenry as addressing their own needs, in actuality, no matter how awful the emergency may be, one of the first thing insiders need to know about an emergency is also whether it offers an opportunity to promote their interests.

This is why a lot of emergency policy can seem illogical to citizens on the receiving end.

Behind the scenes, in conversations that media do not cover, dozens of lobbyists and assorted billionaires oftentimes have a say in what that "emergency" legislation or health mandates look like.

The hidden special interests can range from Big Pharma executives to real estate investors, to telecom and tech companies to insurers. These days lobbyists can, and do, include foreign nations — even foreign nations that, far from being our immediate allies, are our sworn adversaries.

Of course, when the policy or the health-department directive is announced, those dozens of hands and scores of fingerprints belonging to the lobbyists for the mega-corporations and billionaires that shaped it are invisible. The policy is rolled out as being driven solely by medical necessity and peer-reviewed research.

This is often a lie.

Yet it is received as truth by citizens, and never more so than in the panic of the crisis, not only because they have no way to see "how the sausage is made," but also because they are afraid.

Indeed, the outcomes sought by the elites can't be accomplished nearly as readily in ordinary times, times where lobbyists certainly play a part, but find their roles constrained by the normal legislative process. But in a COVID-closed or COVID-managed society, there is none of the scrutiny that routinely accompanies the making of legislation; normal debate is suspended; reporters can't — or, even more than ordinarily, won't — ask hard questions. Policy to comprehensively control people's behavior and movements at scale is crafted in darkness,

Emergencies create unbelievably lucrative opportunities for the ramping-up of corruption.

———

I am often called a "conspiracy theorist." The reason is simple. Unlike all but a very few other journalists or nonfiction writers, I've been a political consultant to a presidential campaign and advisor to a vice president. And as a result of those experiences, I know how the powerful react in a crisis — especially when their self-interest is involved.

A quick story. It is August 1998 and my then-husband was a White House speechwriter. We'd left Washington on vacation and were journeying through the Atlas Mountains of Morocco with our three-year-old toddler. Over crackling radios, we heard about a breaking scandal; we could barely make out disclosures coming closer and closer to an alleged sex act in the White House.

Our guide, who spoke little English, explained only: "Clinton. Dress. Scandal." Monica Lewinsky was about to testify to a grand jury about her relationship to the President of the United States.

A few nights later, an emergency unfolded in the United States.[118]

"Changing the subject" during a scandal or a run of bad press is political-insider shorthand for "making people forget." It is the goal of every political consultant or chief of staff under duress.

A factory in Sudan had been bombed "on the direct orders" of the president.[119] The factory, alleged to have been involved in the making of threatening substances, was "pulverized," reduced to "broken concrete and iron bars."[120] The "subject was changed." Abruptly, in the news media, the focus turned to the great threat this factory had posed to our safety in the United States, and to our very way of life. The media showed images of the post-bombardment wreckage. Triumphalist coverage attended this show of our force.

Soon enough the dust settled. When it was reported that in actuality the target had been a medicine factory, White House spokes-people countered that it was in fact a "disguised chemical weapons factory" and that soil samples showed a substance connected to the manufacture of nerve gas.

By the time the news cycle had moved on, and Sudan was once again relegated to its usual status as a US foreign policy backwater, a few brief news stories conceded that in reality the bombed building had never been a chemical-weapons factory. It had been a pharmaceuticals factory. It was one of three factories in the Sudan that made medicines, including anti-TB and anti-malarial medications. Jonathan Belke, in *The Boston Globe,* pointed out that the loss of domestically produced medicines would lead to thousands of avoidable deaths in Sudan.[121] It hadn't worked out as President Clinton's staff may have hoped — the press quickly returned to the salacious allegations of the president's infidelity, with news outlets once again getting to say "oral sex" and "blue dress" and eventually even "cigar." The scandal was simply too irresistible a gift to the media to ignore.

But I never forgot that an entirely innocent night watchman died in the attack. [122]

The truly powerful go to enormous lengths to control the narrative, and in general achieve great success.

What the most powerful people always want is certainty. Randomness and risk are their sworn enemies. What they never want is any possibility for chance to affect events and outcomes. Chance might allow the other side to win, and then all the billions will flow to the other side and their cronies. Chance allows that stock on which your friends have bet to tank. Chance allows populist movements to emerge that upend your best-laid plans.

When I am attacked as being a conspiracy theorist, it is when I make predictions based on having witnessed the behavior of those at the center of power and observing how it was directed 24/7 at getting rid of organic historical or market processes, and thus doing away with much-dreaded chance.

Why would powerful men and women *not* want to control all the outcomes in the world? In many cases, it is the fiduciary responsibilities of these men and women to control all possible risk in outcomes. "Conspiracy theorist" is a handy term of abuse, thrown around (and never more than in 2020–22) by bought media and bought social media influencers to deride those who know better how power really operates in private. The smear also serves to deter citizens from recognizing the fundamental but dispiriting truth that powerful people *always* seek to control history and markets and limit their risk in a systematic way — and the corollary that they themselves are often powerless.

Powerful people seek to bring about historical outcomes without leaving written evidence, using nonprofits, cutouts, relatives, lawyers, or friends of friends. They don't issue press releases. Everyone who works at the highest levels of government understands the need for deniability; the job is to get the implied wishes of the principal accomplished, without direct instruction, let alone written memos.

This high-level aversion to risk and this aim at "no fingerprints" and no paper trail is not conspiracy theory, it is reality. It is simply the way that global elites operate, assisted by the highest-compensated lawyers and lobbyists in DC, paid for advancing world-historical outcomes *without* public disclosure, or a messy set of documents vulnerable to exposure in the event of a subpoena.

Indeed, though the bombing prompted perhaps by President Clinton's affair with Monica Lewinsky redirected media attention briefly from a damaging topic, no fingerprints were left behind. Why? Because inside the White House, in 1998, it is close to certain the president never actually said, "We need to bomb an ambiguously-understood factory in Sudan to get the press focus off of me and my young former girlfriend." It is very unlikely that any chief of staff or White House operative ever spoke any words connecting the pressure of the sex scandal to the appeal of making a dramatic strike.

But as I saw relationships unfold in the White House and in the Naval Observatory, everyone would have understood the unspoken need to simply change the subject: *Will no one rid me of this meddlesome priest?*

Was that a "conspiracy"? Maybe not technically. But did large impersonal forces chillingly align to bring about a world-historical outcome, with no fingerprints? We know the answer.

And so an innocent man died, and maybe ultimately thousands more, as collateral damage.

In the same way, but on a vastly larger scale, crimes were committed in 2020–22. They were committed against the entire human race, by small powerful groups of people to bring about outcomes which they saw as well worth of the sacrifice — that is to say, the sacrifice of us.

———————

We stayed in the woods, inside. Our neighbors stayed inside.

We all heard about the fact that a field hospital was being set up in Central Park, and this news chilled us mightily. But we did not hear that it had been packed up a mere fifteen days later.

We also heard loud and clear that there were 309,145 "cases" in New York State. We did not hear that that figure was cumulative, and that on May 2, 2020, there were in fact fewer than 900 "cases" in the whole of our populous state.

My neighbor up the road was told his elderly father had COVID, and the neighbor was distraught at the prospect that his dad would be moved into a field hospital in Central Park — a certain death sentence, he reasonably feared. That must have been one of the worst times of his life.

But my neighbor was not informed that the field hospital had been expensively packed away. He was allowed to suffer with now-baseless dread.

Governor Cuomo's nightly television briefings were both riveting and absolutely nightmare-inducing.

He named and named and named the deceased.

No one told us on the major news platforms that studies were showing that young adults were not at great risk from the virus, even then. No one explained that, even then, studies were showing that children were at almost no risk of being killed by the virus. (Though I religiously read the major news outlets, I did not learn these facts until I interviewed Dr Jay Bhattacharya, a signatory of the Great Barrington Declaration, months later.)

In August of 2020, I hugged a twentysomething who had visited us, and wept; I begged him not to go into the city. I wept and it upset him. I did this emotional damage — on a day that the young man had zero point zero plus chance of being seriously harmed if infected. If the news outlets I read had reported on how little risk there was to healthy young adults, I would not have caused, or myself suffered, this traumatizing distress.

Though it was now summer, playgrounds remained closed off. Children were restless and pale, hoping to go back to school in the fall. But no one was firm about whether they could resume in-person learning. This uncertainty rattled children, and it wore down parents.

A relative became very ill with COVID. He was given no therapeutics. His lungs were scarred.

A dear friend was very ill with COVID. She had to sleep sitting up. She was sick for months. Her doctors, the best that could be found, gave her no therapeutics — they said to go home to let the illness "play itself out."

In general, there were no therapeutics given to people suffering.

Any discussion of possible therapeutics was attributed to the obtuseness of President Trump and his racist, science-hating supporters.

The medical regimes that did exist in our educated liberal circles, though, seemed pre-Victorian to me. These sufferers were told to come back to the ER if their oxygen levels dropped dangerously.

The New York Times ran story after story, in ghastly detail, on the grisly deaths suffered by COVID victims placed on ventilators.[123]

The New York Times discussed "white-glass lesions" on lungs as an aftereffect of COVID. Their reporting graphically depicted lung transplants and permanent lung damage.[124]

The press was full of appallingly intrusive images of dying people on ventilators.

I felt at times that there was an unusually theatrical, horror-show quality to the reporting, and even to the political drama produced by Governor Cuomo.

People were suffering, as they do in waves of illness.

But they had not yet collectively lost their minds.

On news channels there were suddenly weird features about business moguls saying things such as "the handshake is dead forever" and showing how they were fist-bumping, or even more awkwardly, bumping elbows in greeting — an unnatural dance demonstrating how to avoid exchanging deadly viruses. When I first saw the "elbow-bump" promoted as a COVID trend, I thought: "no socially literate human being would have come up with that." The cultural logic and imagery suddenly in play had a strange, Asperger's-like quality.

In August 2020, The Guardian *reported that the city of Preston, England "bans households from mixing as infection among under-30s rises at 'an alarming rate.'"*[125]

You could not have friends over, and children who lived in different homes could no longer play together. Many friendships were suspended nationwide in Britain.

In Britain, you were not allowed to gather with more than two people in your own garden. "Bubble" became a term in both the United States and Britain — in Britain you could not visit households outside "your bubble." There was a ban on group meetings of more than six people. As if out of a CCP fairy tale, this was called "The Rule of Six."[126]

Indeed, if anything, things in Britain were worse than at home. By the end of 2020, some colleagues in Britain had not seen anyone outside their household members for months. There were "rules" at times on how often one could go outside during the day. These became more and more narrow. Soon people were allowed a single walk a day "for exercise." And then only with members "of their households." You had grief-stricken mothers posting on social media about children gazing longingly at other children outside, with whom they were forbidden to play.

Prime Minister Boris Johnson announced new "rules" in November 2020:

We are going to go back instead to a regional, tiered approach, applying the toughest measures where COVID is most prevalent. While the previous local tiers cut the R number, they were not quite enough to reduce it below 1, so the scientific advice, I am afraid, is that, as we come out, our tiers need to be made tougher.

In particular, in tier 1 people should work from home wherever possible. In tier 2, alcohol may only be served in hospitality settings as part of a substantial meal. In tier 3, indoor entertainment, hotels and other accommodation will have to close, along with all forms of hospitality, except for delivery and takeaways. I am very sorry, obviously, for the unavoidable hardship that this will cause for business owners who have already endured so much disruption this year.

Unlike the previous arrangements, tiers will now be a uniform set of rules.[127]

This dramatic declaration turned out to be based on utter falsehoods. "The scientific advice" that correlated COVID-19 spread with "our tiers need[ing] to be made tougher" turned out to be imaginary or plain wrong and came from conflicted scientists modeling baseless computer projections.

The citizens of the United Kingdom did not, however, know this, for the most part. And much moralizing went along with this edict: those who followed "the rules" were lauded in the press; those who asked questions were derided as "COVID deniers" who wanted to "kill Grandma."

Our country was not much better or saner.

The "restrictions" were dizzyingly confusing and erratic.

I did not understand how any of this made any kind of sense, rational, epidemiological, or otherwise. But I saw the psychologi-

cal damage, and how nations held hostage to relentless propaganda were losing all sense of any alternative and quietly, unprotestingly giving up long-cherished inalienable rights.

The media was full of images that I thought were unpleasantly insistent about how we must handle our predicament. I recognized influence campaigns from my own training as a PR person and as a campaign advisor.

There was a campaign to get people to accept that distance was good. Distance was how you showed love.

A commercial sentimentalized scenes of a little girl holding up her hand to the glass of a window, on the other side of which an elderly woman also held up her hand to the glass. The slogan was: "Apart together." Or variations: "We Stand Together by Staying Apart." Our pop culture, I thought, had always sentimentalized connection; why were so many corporates, indeed an obvious, expensive influence campaign, now sentimentalizing distance and isolation?[128]

I also knew how long influence campaigns took to plan out, shoot, edit, and distribute. Why such an investment of time and money in a health crisis that could subside next week?

Media and social media echoed the idea that if you really loved someone, you did not go near them. Media and social media were full of the discourse that you could "kill your grandmother" if you saw her by being an "asymptomatic carrier." "'Don't Kill Granny with Coronavirus,' Warns Matt Hancock" headlined London's The Times. *Matt Hancock, the UK Health Minister, used a soundbite that was repeated in hundreds of other countries and news stories.[129] The soundbites were so global that eventually* The

Times of India *would protest, 'Who Killed Granny? Shameless Emotional Manipulation has Shaped too much of Global COVID Policy, Disastrously.'"[130]*

Young adults and children were told "Don't Kill Granny" in a massive, highly funded UK government propaganda campaign documented in Laura Dodsworth's A State of Fear: How the UK Government Weaponized Fear During the COVID-19 Pandemic.[131]

The discourse posited the notion that you love your elders best by not going to see them, by not touching them, by not visiting them — ever. Love was turned on its head.

We were bombarded by images of loving families connecting with their elders not by physical hugs and visits, but through the safe, sanitary digital screen. That was real love.

Children, especially, were traumatized by the message that a hug of theirs "could kill grandma." I saw the emotional conflict that this message created in the minds of the very young. I met a little neighbor up the street, a very bright, talkative five-year-old, with her mother; and we chatted at a distance of twelve or so feet. After I had made conversation with the little one directly, about subjects that interested her, I saw her impulsively start to run toward me to be closer and to talk more; her mother drew her back. I saw the look of confusion, self-doubt, and fear that supplanted the child's natural interest to move in the direction of curiosity — and toward warmth, conversation and connection.

The "Zoom class" was working online in this strange new way. We quickly got used to it. How not? It was strangely cozy, even as it

*slowly strangled your social capital, slowly cut you off from your col-
leagues, your larger acquaintanceship, and new ideas and alliances.
You could hold a meeting while still wearing PJs and slippers below
the desk level.*

We were learning the culture of Zoom meetings.

We were learning the culture of "Quarantinis."

We saw our friends on screens.

*The "essential workers" — truck drivers, delivery people, nurses,
laborers — were on the "front lines," another new (or in this case,
repurposed) phrase, and were all day, every day, exposed to the virus.*

*People in the South Bronx, my former neighborhood, along with
Queens, had the highest death rates from COVID in the entire city.
Most working people in Mott Haven were "front-line" workers, and
did not have the luxury of staying home to "Zoom."*

*Our superintendent's mother had died from the virus. I remem-
bered the devastatingly poorly supported South Bronx hospitals.*

*When I saw him briefly, to retrieve some items from our former
apartment, he was stricken with grief, but had to work in spite of
his mourning.*

*Manhattan, the wealthiest borough, in contrast to the Bronx, had
the lowest rates of infection.[132]*

*No matter how "right on" the upper-middle class was, no matter
the social-justice proclamations of my former liberal, affluent urban
"tribe," no one really expressed any objection to this unequal distri-
bution of risk and harm.*

CHAPTER SEVEN

THE UNVERIFIABLE PANDEMIC

The global onslaught against human assembly, commerce, and community, managed and driven largely by tech companies, was undergirded by a new digital product: the suddenly-ubiquitous "COVID-19 maps," also known as "COVID-19 dashboards." X/Y axis graphs, they showed the incredibly alarming numbers of deaths and infections in sensationally-depicted detail.

The dashboards employed colors with particular creative flair. In *The New York Times*'s dashboard, the often nearly vertical right hand slope recording "Weekly Cases" was in lurid magenta-red — the vermilion color that seemed to be the "brand" color of the disease-related fear campaign; in contrast, the welcome rising vaccination rates would be tracked in a cool and soothing medicinal green.[133]

We quickly became familiar with the dashboards, believing as we did that the data they revealed was behind official statements, politics and policies. We watched the graph peaks and valleys with horror or (rare) relief, certain they represented "the science" and "the numbers" in purest form. When Dr. Anthony Fauci pronounced, in his trademark

Brooklyn accent, his favorite phrase, "When you look at the data —" the media reacted by referencing these X/Y charts.[134]

But I began to notice that while Dr. Fauci of the NIAID and Dr. Rochelle Walensky of the CDC continually invoked the phrases "follow the data" or "follow the science," they almost never provided the raw data or peer-reviewed publications. Instead we were left to rely on these ubiquitous non-government, third-party-produced COVID dashboards and on press release-type news stories describing studies exactly as officials had summarized the studies' findings, but without actually linking to them.

Thus, the conclusions drawn by the media, citing these platforms especially, were impossible to confirm. Why? Because many of the most-referenced dashboards were based on flawed methodologies and unverifiable datasets. They were phantoms.

———————

As it happens, I was familiar with dashboard technology because my tech company, DailyClout.io, builds dashboards based on exactly the same process and using exactly the same technology as do the COVID maps. We also, purportedly like the COVID maps, use government data. It is in some ways a simple and, in the world of digital data, fully understood process. In other words, there is no magic to the process of creating a dashboard out of government data. Building these kinds of maps and databases is a standard feat of coding.

So I knew that the third-party dashboards that were showing the world "COVID cases" or "COVID deaths" must be based on an API. In order to be real and verifiable, the dashboards there would have to be based upon state health department data derived from real death certificates and real, working clinical tests being fed continually into an API.

What is an API?

An API, or Application Programming Interface, is like a firehose of data. It allows one software application to talk to another to send or receive information. If the data retrieved through an API are messy (usually the case), programmers have to make sense of the data, and develop ways to deal with any unexpected results they could receive from an API "call."

To make the data useful for a dashboard, programmers also have to clean, combine and format the data into workable datasets. These datasets can then be fed "into the backend" of the dashboard — that is, the part that developers and webmasters can see, but users themselves cannot.

Developers can then take the nicely formatted data and create ways to show that data visually to users, building code to turn the data into what users see "on the front end" or the "UX" (for user experience). The way readers navigate the website "on the front end" is called the "UI" or "user interface."

This "front end" is what readers of the digital *New York Times* saw when they looked at the COVID map that was featured every single day on the paper's digital front page, or what those who went to the Johns Hopkins University Medicine Coronavirus Resource Center site (a dashboard that has had various names throughout the pandemic) saw when they went there in search of updates on COVID cases and deaths.[135]

The story of "cases" and "deaths" was told by multiple media outlets using the various third-party dashboards as their terrifying illustration, their "proof."

Yet few reporters clicked through to try to locate the raw datasets to verify for readers that what the dashboards showed them "on the front end" was really the full story. And few checked to see if there were really indeed verifiable state health department data being aggregated, or some other nonsense altogether.

For the first month, perhaps, this ignorance could be excused as part of a learning curve around digital data. But when a year passed and two years passed, and reporters were still citing digital dashboards uncritically, without understanding or, it seems, showing even any curiosity about what they were looking at, the excuse vanished. As noted, an API is a simple technology that can be explained in ten minutes to any lay person.

What reporters would not understand is: a digital dashboard is not in fact a medical product.

It is not a scientific product.

A digital dashboard is not necessarily even generated from anything at all that corresponds to physical or biological reality.

"Cases" tabulated on a digital dashboard are not necessarily generated from actual tests that are generated from real human biological samples. "Deaths" tabulated on a digital dashboard do not necessarily derive from any actual dead bodies recorded by real coroners in real hospital morgues or from funeral directors retrieving bodies from homes.

A digital dashboard is simply a product of code that counts data inputs in a certain way. It counts what the developer told it to count.

This data on a COVID dashboard that calls itself "cases" can be based on a real positive nasal swab, from a real human nose, translated into an accurate positive real test done at the correct cycle threshold, which result is then translated accurately into a snippet of code.

Or the data calling itself "cases" can be just — a snippet of code.

The data on a digital dashboard that calls itself "deaths," implying deaths "from COVID," are only as good as the forms filled out to claim a cause of death or the way the deaths are counted "as COVID."

Anything at all can be counted as a "case." And any death can be mis-identified as a "death."

———————

If the reports of "cases" were from flawed tests, such as the now-infamous PCR tests that counted both real and not-real nasal swab material as "positive" depending on the PCR test cycle thresholds, then the dashboard would count all that data as "cases."[136] As data scientists like to say: "garbage in, garbage out".

Whatever the backend was told by the developer to count as a "case" was counted by the dashboard as a "case"; the "front end" — the part that you saw as a reader, the part that was the graphic display reproduced in a million news outlets and newspaper front pages — represented this aggregation to readers in a jagged line on an X and Y axis. A jagged line that day after day, scared people to death.

When it came to COVID fatalities, the counting was likewise subjective and dependent on whatever the developer told the operative code to count. If "deaths" were defined as "PIC" deaths — "pneumonia, influenza and COVID-19," a category that the CDC came up with months into the pandemic — then that was the number that the "front end" of the dashboard presented to the world as "COVID deaths." The correct definition was lost somewhere in the fine print.

If "deaths" were counted by the developer as "deaths *with* COVID-19" — and if the data retrieved by the API included anyone who'd died 28 days after a positive PCR test, even if, as documented cases have shown, that person actually died of a car crash or cancer —

then the code likewise counted those deaths as "COVID deaths," and showed them on the front end as "deaths" in a graph that usually had a clever way of not saying directly "DEATHS FROM COVID-19."

Often the graph would say "Total Deaths" under the headline "COVID-19 DEATHS" or "Deaths to Date," but it would have a legalistic wording to *not* claim that all those deaths were "from COVID-19."

So again: accessing the *raw* data is what all those supposedly most invested in the facts behind the most monumental story of the era should have done on a regular basis.

News reporters should have, and scientists should have, and epidemiologists should have, and politicians should have. And citizens who considered themselves informed should have done so as well.

By linking the raw datasets, any honest, conscientious reporter would have been able to see and verify real deaths, in real contexts, or else ask hard questions about datasets that were anomalously compiled, or about missing information. But there were no raw datasets linked.

Mainstream media reporting took the "conclusions" of the dashboards at face value. So credulous and ignorant was the reporting, so lacking in basic skepticism, that to so much as raise questions about their veracity was seen as attacking science itself. For reporters the dashboards' mere existence represented irrefutable fact.

———

There were other problems in addition to the absence of complete linked raw datasets.

A serious one involved methodology: *how* the data were counted and *what was* actually being counted. As noted, a COVID "death" might have been based on a real dead body; or the "deaths" data might have been amplified artificially by setting the API to count death certificates that had already been changed to heighten the likelihood that document would record a "COVID death." This happened at scale, as Dr. Henry Ealy of Portland, Oregon and his team reported, when the CDC moved the reporting of "COVID" as a comorbidity to Part I of the death certificate. As Dr. Ealy explained, since this section was the one counted by the health departments, this meant that if someone with a positive COVID test died of cancer or suicide, the death would still be counted as a "COVID death."[137] Dr. Ealy, along with two Oregon state senators, Sen. Kim Thatcher and Sen. Dennis Linthicum, went so far as to call for a grand jury investigation charging the CDC with "willful misconduct" in this form and other forms of mishandling and misrepresenting COVID-19 data.[138] (Their filing was docketed by a federal court on March 4, 2022.)[139]

A dashboard can thus count a "bad" category, such as deaths "with COVID." If the dashboard reports "deaths," as many do, but without adding the words "from COVID," then the final tally displayed is not necessarily one of "deaths from COVID" at all.

Another problem had to do with chain of custody of the data, as Dr. Ealy's research team points out.

A verifiable dashboard is one that does not have an intermediary handling the data after the time it leaves the state health departments or, in the UK, the NHS.

But there is growing evidence that third parties were invited into the handling of the data related to the pandemic, in ways that degraded its integrity and that, intentionally or not, inflated numbers in various ways.

Indeed, the basis for the grand jury investigation filing presented by Dr. Ealy and his colleagues was that government data must be handled according to certain regulations, and it is a violation of these regulations for data management and access to be outsourced to third parties.[140]

But according to a grand jury petition filing in which Dr. Rochelle Walensky is a defendant, that is exactly what the CDC did. Dr. Ealy and his colleagues detail these alleged violations of regulations in a paper titled "COVID-19 Data Collection, Comorbidity & Federal Law: A Historical Retrospective," featured in *Science, Public Health Policy and the Law*.[141] They argue:

> On April 14th, the CDC adopted a position paper authored by the Council of State and Territorial Epidemiologists (CSTE), a 501c (6) non-profit organization, with the assistance of 4 CDC-employed subject matter experts (Dr. Susan Gerber, Dr. Aron J. Hall, Sandra Roush, & Dr. Tom Shimabukuro). This document was sanctioned by Dr. Robert R. Redfield, Director of the CDC.
>
> Not only does this appear to be a potential conflict of interest, it also bypasses the OMB oversight for the IQA & PRA, as directed by Congress and is rife with *ex parte* communications. *Ex parte* communications in general violate ethical standards.
>
> By employing a non-governmental organization (CSTE), free from the oversight of the OMB and the laws detailed by Congress via the IQA & PRA, the CDC bypassed the oversight of the OMB Director's Information Resources Management policies, plans, rules, regulations, procedures, and guidelines for public comment. We allege this is a violation of 44 US Code 3517(a), which requires an

agency to provide interested persons an "early and meaning-ful opportunity to comment."

This violation has inevitably resulted in COVID-19 data for cases, hospitalizations, and fatalities being artificially elevated, and definitively compromises prudent decision making at federal and state executive levels. This includes policy enforcement for a public health crisis that may not have existed had the CDC abided by the laws that ensure the accuracy of data collection.

For example: The CSTE position paper in Section VII established rules for COVID-19 data classification and col-lection that allowed for probable diagnoses unconfirmed by lab testing, a test-based strategy for lab testing, and set the stage for people with no medical licensure to contact trace and illegally diagnose American citizens they have never seen.

In short, according to Dr. Ealy and his colleagues, the CDC partnered with a third-party nonprofit to allow "probable" cases to replace lab testing in terms of data collected.

It is interesting to note that shortly after the grand jury investi-gation petition was filed by Dr. Ealy, Oregon State Senator Dennis Linthicum and Oregon State Senator Kim Thatcher, the CDC made a statement to Reuters that its algorithm was "accidentally counting deaths that were not COVID-19-related." [142] 72,277 COVID deaths were removed from its website. And *The Guardian* also reported that the CDC correction in children's deaths came after that newspaper had reported on that issue: "The agency briefly noted the change in a footnote, although the note did not explain how the error occurred or how long it was in effect."[143] Dr. Ealy and his colleagues had raised concerns about overcounting a year and a half previously — the CDC now blamed it on a bug via the machines.

The CDC's statement that the overcount resulted from a "coding logic error" seemed to be counting on ignorance from the American public about the fact that it is the job of the CDC leadership to *tell* the developers to design the code to count what should be counted, and that it is their responsibility to review the website for accuracy. The CDC's claim that a coding bug had lasted for months seems to rely on the public not to realize that bugs are supposed to be worked out in "QA" in advance of a launch — if they aren't, they are to be fixed within 24 hours.

But follow-up questions by the press about this major overstatement of both the general public's, and of children's, alleged COVID deaths went largely unasked.[144]

———————

By the fall of 2020 and into 2021, my disappointment in my fellow journalists had become acute. To their shame, reporters had become acute. Reporters continued to take it on faith that the dashboards were transparent mirrors of solid, verifiable government data, updated in real time by the magic of what they presumed to be accountable engineers.

In the United States, most of the news about COVID in 2020–21 was being drawn from two sources: Johns Hopkins University's COVID chart and *The New York Times*'s COVID chart.

But when I checked on the datasets, what I found was head-splitting. The Johns Hopkins University COVID database, The COVID Tracking Project, Worldometers.info, *The New York Times*, and in

Britain, the NHS and UK.gov and ONS dashboards — all seemed deeply flawed.[145]

A contractor who had been hired by Johns Hopkins to create visualizations sent me the actual datasets in a Github account. A Github account is where developers often keep raw datasets or computer codes.

I was surprised to receive these, but they were not sent to me off the record.

Looking at the Github of what were described as being leaked datasets, I saw at the time only six US states were reporting actual COVID cases and deaths to the Johns Hopkins database. If there were other datasets, they weren't in that Github.

The COVID Tracking Project was another of the most frequently cited platforms for the first six months of the pandemic. It was identified as being "At *The Atlantic*," whatever that meant. But, for 2020 and 2021, it was staffed by "volunteers." Consequently, the data uploaded at that crucial period was presumably uploaded by these "volunteers." Who could be anyone.[146]

When I looked on that platform at COVID data for the Bronx — where I had recently been living — the source data for The COVID Tracking Project showed five "cases" uploaded for the Bronx in one week. But by whom? No way to know. Were these duplicates? No way to know. How was a "case" defined? No way to know. Who was uploading the "cases"? Could be public health experts. But . . . it could equally well be political operatives. Or bored housewives. Or an unemployed video gamer in his mom's basement. Or it could be The COVID Tracking Project's staff themselves. No way to know. The data were thus meaningless because there *was* no verifiable methodology.

Had there been honest, independent journalists reporting on those five deaths, they would have made sure they had been uploaded to the platform in real contexts, with identifying codes (not names).

Then they would have called the hospitals in the South Bronx and gotten confirmation that each was a real death. But no one anywhere was doing any such reporting.

An example of the human cost of this bad set of methodologies was dramatized in my visit to my mother in Corvallis, Oregon, in November of 2020.

New York, with all of its controlling policies, had been relaxed compared to Oregon. I arrived to a state in a condition of hysteria. Terror of a virus "surge" saturated the local press.

The Oregonian called November 2020 "Officially Oregon's Deadliest Month."[147] Governor Kate Brown "ordered" a two week "freeze," restricting businesses and worship, and limiting social get-togethers to no more than six people.

"In terms of individuals, I am not asking you" she declared. "I am ordering you."

News reports warned that violating her "orders" was a Class C Misdemeanor.[148]

What was causing this statewide freak-out?

In November 2020, there had been 224 "fatalities" in Oregon.[149] The press would shriek that "cases" or "deaths" were "up 30 percent," but when you looked at the actual numbers, in both absolute terms and relative to the state's population, they didn't support the panic.

There were over 4.2 million people in Oregon in 2020.[150] So my mom's chance of being a "fatality" related to COVID in November 2020 was one in 18,916.[151] For comparison, the average American has a 1 in 9,094 chance of dying in a car crash over the course of a year.[152]

The Oregon press, as news outlets everywhere did, avoided stating "fatalities from COVID-19" but gave the impression that COVID-19 was the direct cause of these deaths.

In my mother's county, Benton County, heading into the third year after the start of the pandemic, there have now been sixty-four cumulative deaths since the start of the pandemic. So, thirty-two a year on average.[153] In contrast there were 131 deaths from heart disease in 2020 alone — over double the two-year tally of Benton County's COVID-related deaths.[154]

For over two horrible years, my mom was terrified every single day of something that was just one quarter as likely, in her county, to happen to her, as her dying from heart disease.

Due to the ceaseless fear drumbeat in the Oregon press, and from Governor Brown's office, my mom could barely summon the courage to hug me even after I had stayed for five days in a hotel room for the germs from the plane ride to wear off, and after I had received the negative results of a PCR test.

She endured this terror in her daily life, and this breach in human contact and comfort, at a time when deaths from COVID-19 in Oregon came in at number seven on the cause of deaths scale, below the rates of deaths from strokes and Alzheimer's disease, numbers four and five. Below cancer, heart disease and unintended injuries.[155]

A whole state's worth of elderly people, instead of enjoying their mature years, socializing, and seeing family, were instructed by misreported numbers to cower indoors alone, and they did so.

———

The Atlantic, where The COVID Tracking Project was "at," was a grantee of the Bill & Melinda Gates Foundation — receiving $500,222 in 2019 alone.[156] For what? The unidentifiable topic, "Postsecondary Education, Public Awareness and Analysis." Duration of the grant? 24 months. So: into 2020 and 2021.

Who owns a majority stake in *The Atlantic*? Laurene Powell Jobs, the widow of Apple founder Steve Jobs.[157] Her group "The Emerson Collective" is an activist investment entity that seeks social outcomes, including education reform.[158] A scary, unverifiable pandemic chart leads, among other outcomes, to a rationale for school closures, which presents booming "EdTech" opportunities for the parent company's owner and her investing friends.

Ms. Jobs was hardly alone. Before the pandemic, other tech heirs and heiresses and moguls were buying up other legacy media outlets that would play so key a role in "informing" the public. "Most auspiciously, in 2013 the Amazon founder Jeff Bezos bought the ailing *Washington Post*, quickly investing, with significant success, in its journalism and in its digital reach."[159]

The Washington Post, too, would play a leading role in fanning COVID hysteria.

In short, those managing the dashboards' data and promoting the results were often the very same tech companies that stood to most benefit from skewing the numbers upward. Microsoft co-founder Steve Ballmer founded USAFacts.org.[160] Bloomberg Philanthropies funded the JHS dashboard.[161]

Johns Hopkins's Center for Health Security "in partnership with the World Economic Forum and the Bill & Melinda Gates Foundation" was also the site of "Event 201," which I thought until I looked at it was surely apocryphal. It was a real "high-level" pandemic exercise simulation, held on October 18, 2019. Per the scenario description, "Event 201 simulates an outbreak of a novel zoonotic coronavirus transmitted from bats to pigs to people that eventually becomes efficiently transmissible from person to person leading to a severe pandemic."[162] This simulated outbreak would require "reliable cooperation among several industries, national governments, and key international institutions."[163]

Other tech moguls created the COVID toolkit. Microsoft, along with Salesforce (whose co-founder Marc Benioff sits on the World Economic Forum's Board of Trustees),[164] built a digital vaccine passport prototype, anticipating that "governments, airlines and other firms will soon start asking people for proof that they have been inoculated."[165] Imagine the data these Big Tech giants could collect — and where it could end up.

Google, well-versed in the business of consumer data, was directly involved in COVID testing. Google owns Project Baseline[166] ("Together, we can invent the future of data-powered healthcare"), a key partner of Rite Aid in their administration of COVID tests.[167] As part of the pre-test authorizations individuals had to sign, Google and Project Baseline collected data from thousands of people who got tested for COVID at Rite Aid.[168]

Of course, "testing" now became compulsory in many contexts, as when you were forced to test just to work or fly or see family. In 2019, Google's revenue was $160.40 billion.[169] Two years later, with PCR testing everywhere compulsory, its revenue was $257.64 billion.[170]

The fact remains jaw-droppingly incredible, but it bears repeating over and over again: the same Big Tech companies profiting by the billions from the "lockdown" and oppressive pandemic policies were tasked with presenting the data that drove and justified and sustained the "lockdown" and oppressive pandemic policies in the first place!

By November of 2020, we'd been locked in with one another in the woods for five months. I love my husband and no doubt he loves me, but you must talk to more than one other live human; it was all starting to feel vertiginous. No worship, no dinners, no events. No other people except onscreen.

People were lonely.

My husband put trail cameras in the woods on our property. We got to know, by sight via the trail-camera footage, a mother bear and her two curious bear cubs. There was an arrogant badger that traversed our porch at night, that drove our elderly dog into a furor of outraged barking. Via the footage, we watched the deer languorously saunter down to the stream to drink.

We talked a lot about our dog, and about Twitter.

My habit of leaving the caps off toothpaste tubes started driving him crazy, and his habit of leaving socks on the floor started to make me irate. Like very elderly people, who live mostly indoors, our world was shrinking.

Before my other loved ones came to visit, I had to quarantine for ten days, as everyone at that time still believed you could infect everyone else "asymptomatically."

I was on social media a lot. So was everyone. My attention was increasingly drawn to a few outspoken doctors. They were not on board with these "lockdown" policies. I had begun to think of these perfectly normal public health experts as "dissidents," because it was clear that a consensus had formed and was being policed in a strangely un-American way, and they were contradicting some of the edicts I heard repeated endlessly on social media and on NPR and in The New York Times.

Dr. Peter McCullough. Dr. Robert Malone. Dr. Kulvinda Kaur. Dr. Patrick Phillips. Dr. Paul Alexander. Dr. Andrew Bostom. Dr. Harvey Tenenbaum. Dr. Sunetra Gupta. Dr. Martin Kulldorff. Dr. Sunetra Gupta. Dr Simon Goddek. Dr. Jay Bhattacharya, whom I've mentioned. Highly credentialled people. Harvard, Oxford, Stanford; experienced epidemiologists, public health experts and statisticians — they were raising alarms in various ways. The lockdowns were harmful; the data methodologies were wrong; the PCR tests were misleading. I watched them be attacked, smeared and censored.

The New York Times *never engaged constructively, it seemed, with such critics.*

But The Times's *COVID reporter, Apoorva Mandavilli, had started to refer to "variants" with the Bela Lugosi-type language of "mutants."[171]* The BBC referred to "double mutants."[172]

Dr. Paul Alexander explained, as did many of the "dissident doctors" and researchers, that every virus ordinarily creates multiple variants. This epidemiological fact was not reflected in legacy media reporting, which treated every "variant" with a hysterical unveiling of a brand -new name, like that final scene in "Fatal Attraction," when the seemingly dead villainess astonishingly rises up again to murderous life.

I guess that "double mutants" had eventually been a bridge too far editorially. "Variants" were back in editorial fashion.

I noticed that Ms. Mandavilli, who replied to me on Twitter, did not tell me how the COVID dashboard on which she was basing her reporting had been created, nor did she refer me to the creators of the dashboards. She called the creators of the front-page dashboards, "the guys."

I warned her on Twitter that the data on the other dashboards were incomplete. I asked her where The New York Times's COVID data map — front of the front page every single day — got its data. Was it sent in on a unified form in all fifty states?

She almost always replied to me, but I could not get real answers. I asked her to let me interview the developers so I could check the raw datasets. She did not direct me to any sourcing for The New York Times datasets — datasets on which she was basing her reporting every day. This amazed me as a journalist. Wouldn't you want to check if someone raises alarms about the integrity of the data on which you are basing your daily reporting?

Eventually she blocked me.

———

By late fall of 2020, the world was still "locked down." Roads were still empty. Restaurants were shut. Day after day, my husband and I watched animals emerge from their hiding places, away from human noises and crowds — because there were almost no human noises, certainly no crowds. People posted on social media scenes of turkeys, foxes, and coyotes curiously and confidently exploring dead, ghostly suburban streets and abandoned downtowns.

The New York Times *did not let up on its terrifying coverage.*

The pandemic's "restrictions" rolled out worldwide in lockstep. Businesses were still forcibly shut, as were schools. In California, playgrounds were still closed, hiking trails were closed, beaches were closed.

By now it was clear to me that we were not going to be "let out." Videos were my only way of experiencing community, and on them I started saying that the pandemic would never be declared to be "over."

They are never going to let us out, I started telling disbelieving friends and loved ones — and when we did emerge, I explained, we should not expect to have our rights back.

I went back to Manhattan, for a visit, in November of 2020.

The landscape was completely changed. It seemed as if at least half — maybe most — of what had been the quirky small businesses were gone. The hole-in-the-wall restaurants; the tiny cafés with eccentric themes; the small boutiques with niche clientele; the boutique for trans women looking for high heeled shoes; the boutique for leather fetishists; the boutique for expensive monogrammed sheets; the tattoo artists; the corner bodegas everywhere, with variations on the breakfast egg and bacon sandwich and coffee for working men and women; the tiny florist with room for one refrigerator and a six-foot-long counter on which to assemble four dozen roses a day; the shoemakers with a single last; the pet-care store with an orange cat skulking about — indeed, the endless texture, the dizzying human innovation that Jane Jacobs had described in looking at New York City streets in her classic The Death and Life of Great American Cities — *most of those I recalled, it seemed, were dead: a graveyard of commerce; a junk heap of mom and pop dreams. All closed.*

What was in that same real estate — literally in a matter of eight months?

A new Starbucks was where the Spanish tapas place had been. A TD Bank was in place of the Shanghai noodle shop with hand-pulled noodles, which had employed fifteen immigrants. A Chase Bank was where the low-cost boutique with good-looking fashion knockoffs for aspiring working women had been. The little café whose owner lovingly hand-selected the coffee beans from Brazilian importers, and who had placed graceful hanging plants in arcade containers at every corner, and where NYU students could afford to sit in the trendy warmth and do their homework when it was cold outside and the windows were steamy: gone, gone. In its place was a FedEx outlet, and a struggling young woman in a mask.

I looked across the river at my beloved South Bronx neighborhood. The once-lively streets were deserted. They were ghostly. The small-business collective that I had joined before March 2020 — with its snazzy hip-hop murals that paid tribute to the culture and history of the area, its chic white café-to-be with the green plants waiting in readiness and its vibrant multiracial community — had closed its doors. All the little businesses that were being incubated there were scattered.

The great residential buildings that were to be built along a newly developed waterfront park were incomplete. The construction had been forcibly stopped, "because of COVID." Never mind that construction workers work out of doors.

So, after all, there was to be no riverside park any time soon for the children of the South Bronx — no fresh air walkway to help strengthen their lungs against the high risks of asthma. Children no longer thronged the streets, talking and laughing in groups as they flowed home from school or hung out in the local playground. They were locked indoors. On screens.

Bodegas were shuttered. The little West African restaurant on the corner where the cab drivers used to gather at all hours to watch Senegalese soap operas and news broadcasts had shuttered.

The juice bar had died.

The death rate from COVID-19 in the South Bronx had been atrocious, among the worst in the city. The governor's psychotic "pause" policies meant that the elite class stayed in, maskless and on social media, relatively safe, ordering food and products that my former neighbors in the Bronx, on "the front lines," delivered.

There had been people here from every part of the world; smiles and conversation could be had on every corner, with faces from everywhere telling stories from everywhere. Now you could not see people's faces at all above their masks. Where were they from? What did they think? Differences weren't "melted" into a rich melting pot, they were simply erased. The whole mass of humanity was anonymized.

It had been a neighborhood of a million languages. Now? No one was talking.

CHAPTER EIGHT

"LOCKDOWN" IS NOT "QUARANTINE": WHAT "RESTRICTIONS" REALLY ACHIEVE

The invitation was to fear, and to fear endlessly. This fear was followed by escalating "restrictions." Restrictions in movement, assembly, and commerce. That rollout in turn permitted the massive transfer of wealth from the many to the few — the brazen mass theft of 2020–22.

Nominally directed at public health, the behavioral checks on citizens of the formerly free West, its restrictions multiplying dizzyingly, left people flailing, tossed about by strange unknowable currents. Like the afflictions streaming from Pandora's box, they bore great ill and endless new harms.

Each time there came a new "restriction," we, the reasonable people of the West, engaged with it at face value, at least at first. Must I stand six feet away from others? OK. Must I leave my loved one alone in the hospital, in spite of decades of hospital policies' allowing loved ones to be with one another? OK. Must I accept that my unvaccinated nine-year-old can't enter a building in Manhattan? OK. Now must I accept that my unvaccinated five-year-old cannot enter a building in Manhattan? Well . . . I guess . . . OK . . .

So what were these "restrictions" really for? Why were they proliferating and shape shifting day by day and week by week?

Gradually, it became clear. The true reason had nothing to do with medicine.

The true reason is that, in the elites' war against Western humanism, "restrictions" had become the weapon of choice. Why? Because historically "restrictions" disempower the restricted and leave them open to the theft of their lands and assets.

"Restrictions" endow the ruling class with unlimited power and reduce ordinary peoples' power to that of medieval vassals.

Presented as "public health necessity," the menu of "restrictions" was deployed largely without resistance, at least initially. But their imposition succeeded also because the peoples of hitherto free nations — in North America and Europe, Australia and New Zealand — for a long time did not recognize what they were losing, or why. Born and raised in free nations to presume the best of others, propagandized into panic and fear, they confronted a situation as unfamiliar as it was deeply disorienting.

Why unfamiliar?

We in the West grew up in a very unusual and blessed time. We came of age, as did our parents, in the sacred space and dimension of liberty. It is not a coincidence that such affluence and cultural growth accompanied this post-war period of liberty in the West. Material and cultural wealth are a constant byproduct of freedom.

In fact, 1945–2020 was a beautiful and aberrant pause in the often horrific timeline of human history. Yet those of us born in that period came to take it as much for granted as the air we breathe. In this time of seemingly endless promise, widespread prosperity, relative harmony, and the establishment and growth of equal rights for all, we became complacent. It became easy to forget that in the great timeline of human history, all of it had to have been won, and at great cost.

Easy, especially, for Americans. The peoples of Europe have a longer history, and more to forget.

In France, for instance, from the bloody Revolution of 1789, through Paris Commune of 1871, from the depth of bigotry exposed by the Dreyfus Affair through to the Vichy government's unapologetic collaboration with Nazism fifty years later, it was codified in the national DNA, or it should have been, that rights were precious things, and always subject to loss.[173]

Indeed, in much of Europe the rule of law as a universal principle, and the modern Western liberal idea of universal human rights, blossomed only after the Second World War with the unprecedented expansion of civil society liberties — understandably, the world having just concluded a bloody war against a totalitarian regime of unprecedented evil.

The developing world, too, made historic advances during this period in seeking and often adopting human-rights-based law.

On December 10, 1948, the United Nations adopted the Universal Declaration of Human Rights, encapsulating the idealism in which, in that Cold War era, even totalitarian regimes had to profess to believe.

Translated into more than five hundred languages, the UDHR paved the way for the adoption of more than seventy human-rights treaties, affirming, among other things, the right of everyone everywhere to be free of discrimination; to be treated equally; to enjoy freedom of movement inside their own countries; to leave their countries; to not be arbitrarily deprived of their property; to be secure in their persons; to not endure "arbitrary interference with his privacy, family, home or correspondence, nor to attacks upon his honour and reputation."[174]

From March 2020 to 2022 and even afterward, these rights, so laboriously won through so much blood and treasure — these rights that formed the matrix of what it meant to be Western — were suspended, dissolved, ignored, trampled.

And most people — including the French, who had staged a bloody revolution that terrified the crowned heads of Europe, and the British, who within living memory had shown the definition of courage under fascist bombardment during the Second World War — accepted, or rather meekly submitted.

In less than two years, the rights enumerated in the UN Declaration of Human Rights were suspended in the West, as the American Constitution was effectively suspended in many states. By February of 2021, I was astonished to hear State Rep. Melissa Blasek of New Hampshire tell me something that should have been one of the biggest news stories of the century: forty-seven states were under emergency law.

It happened without any conventional army rolling into any European or North American street, and without a shot being fired.

It was accomplished by stealth.

I became more and more horrified that the global imprisonment in which we found ourselves was being mislabeled a "quarantine."

In fact, the emergency orders imposed restricting assembly and commerce bore no relationship to quarantines in the past, which were limited geographically and in time, and separated only the sick or newly arrived travelers from the rest of society.

What was happening now was completely different.

Yes, of course, versions of this "lockdown" — mislabeled "quarantine" — had happened before on this planet. Totalitarian and fascist societies have long used mass restrictions of movement, curfews, and other ways of restricting free association and free movement to keep their citizens in check. North Korea and China have cordoned off entire regions and put them under no-movement rules. Long before the COVID pandemic, China under the CCP was among the few modern societies to restrict citizens' physical movements nationally and regionally.[175] As dissident escapees from North Korea report, North Korean nationals have also long been unable to move freely around the country without proper documentation, even for family visits.[176]

Nor was Europe immune to "lockdowns" in the past — but that was in countries that suffered from fascist leadership. In 1935–36, the passports of Jews in Germany were restricted, and thereafter laws imposing increasingly severe restrictions on the movements of Jews put members of the Jewish community into effective "lockdown" as citizens within the larger German society.[177] Tragically, restrictions on leaving the country would finally keep Jewish Germans from escaping altogether.[178]

But medical quarantine, as the term is properly understood, has a different history. Webster's has defined "quarantine" as:

> Specifically, the term, originally of forty days, during which a ship arriving in port, and suspected of being infected a malignant contagious disease, is obliged to forbear all intercourse with the shore; hence, such restraint or inhibition of intercourse; also, the place where infected or prohibited

vessels are stationed. *Quarantine* is now applied also to any forced stoppage of travel or communication on account of malignant contagious disease, on land as well as by sea.[179]

This isolation of the infected members of a community is of ancient origin. Throughout the Hebrew Bible and the New Testament, ill people are isolated. It was understood that within the camp of the Israelites, people infected with contagious diseases could "defile" the rest of the community. Leviticus prescribes how to handle the dreaded fear of contagion of leprosy from a member of the community: "His clothes shall be rent, his head shall be left bare, and he shall cover over his upper lip; and he shall call out, "Unclean, Unclean!"[180] P. J. Grisar, writing in *The Forward*, adds the example of Moses telling the Israelites to place outside the camp, "anyone with an eruption or a discharge."[181] Some analysts of ancient Jewish practices such as these, with their emphases on cleanliness and strict attention to what is "fit" and "unfit" to touch or eat, argue that some rules may have had to do with upholding sanitary practices in a time when infections swept through communities with devastating impunity.

Some historians of science refer to quarantine as a primitive "technology": A. A. Conti, in "Quarantine Through History," notes that quarantine "is overall one of the oldest and most disseminated and, despite its limits, most effective health measures elaborated by mankind."[182] And in the centuries before germ theory was understood, and before vaccines, quarantine — physical isolation of the infected — was indeed among the few methodologies societies had to manage terrifying outbreaks of suffering and of death.

So, yes, in the absence of modern medical interventions, such measures were long used, and often proved at least somewhat effective.

But "quarantine" has virtually always meant the restriction of movement for those who are ill or possibly infected.

With COVID, and a society-wide shutdown, including the closing down of all economic activity, all that changed. Illness was messaged from the top down as a public health matter, with the state assuming a central role, and limitless authority, in managing our own bodies and the bodies of others. From our temperatures being taken in front of strangers, to announcements of the infections of public figures on social media, COVID's lethality was used to explain away any expectation of individual privacy or autonomy.

With COVID, we in the modern West were all re-positioned as being hypothetically ill. As PPE specialist Megan Mansell would later explain, we were all re-identified as if we were all immunocompromised.

Political leaders rolled out messaging around restrictions of movement, as labeling this form of citizen immobilization a "quarantine" to lend it the legitimacy of precedent. In fact, for Western democracies it was a new social experiment on this scale.

What can "restrictions" of this kind ultimately do? They prepare the way for wholesale theft or transfer of assets.

———————

What prepared the groundwork for such an easy victory against Western liberties was the quiescence born of seductive comfort — that, and a growing ignorance on the part of the citizenry of the structures of democracy that were being systematically dismantled.

Westerners had come to believe things would always be as they were. They would always have access to museums and cultural events, lovely train trips that went seamlessly across borders like a knife's edge drawn smoothly across the surface of a bowl of cream, lovely human-rights guarantees, lovely assembly, lovely property rights, lovely mobility.

For seventy-five years, Westerners had become accustomed to this unprecedented level of freedom and acceptance of human rights. They had become accustomed to protesting *en masse* when a policy upset them; indeed, for two generations, nothing less had been their readily exercised right. They gathered in public in great crowds — for festivals, for outdoor rock concerts, for religious processions. They traveled freely and joyfully throughout their own countries, exploring landscapes and heritages. The delights of free movement were very democratic; it did not cost much to explore one's beautiful country. It was affordable, usually, to buy a bus pass, and it cost little to bike or hike.

Westerners went camping, they explored antique shows and motor-cycle rallies, they went to tennis matches, they gathered for wine tours, they walked to Compostela on religious pilgrimages. Europeans of all backgrounds and economic levels took long-distance trains in August to the coasts in France or to little hostels in the Alps for fresh air and relaxation. They crossed borders to visit relatives and friends; they went to conferences. In cities, they wandered and drifted and assembled, freely as birds flying solo, or as flocks of birds. They convened in bars and cafés and at popups and film festivals, and in dance halls and bistros, and at dinner parties and pot lucks, at conventions and stamp-collector meetings, and on walkways by rivers where local politicians screened films on summer nights. They wandered past the booksellers on the Seine, at their own pace. They drifted into museums to see the latest Corot exhibition at the Louvre or to revisit their favorite stele in the Assyrian collection at the British Museum. They tried the latest res-taurant tucked into little alleyways. They caught up with their friends with a café crème at the corner *tabac* in Paris, or started the day with an ouzo in the little local café in Mykonos or in Athens.

Certainly there were quarrels — about nationalism, or immigration, or environmentalism. But on the great scale of free versus unfree human conditions, these quarrels were at the margins.

Masses in open parks listened to music. Masses explored ancient cities in privacy. People enjoyed private consultations with physicians. Parents made private medical decisions about their children. No one demanded papers.

We thought this was it, and this would last forever.

When others clamored to immigrate into our countries it was understood that it was not just the economic opportunities that beckoned, but the freedom.

People basked in those freedoms and certainly appreciated them. But did we understand them? Did we grasp how easily the substructures of our rights could be dismantled, what a fragile edifice they were?

Not really, at least none but the most aware.

In Europe, especially, under the European Union, people seemed blissfully unaware of what was at risk. Because of the horrors they'd endured during the cataclysmic wars of the twentieth century, the European Union seemed a political Godsend; a modern idealistic invention to knit European countries so closely together there could never again be large-scale war on the Continent.

And at least on its public face, the European Union did deliver widely popular policies on matters ranging from workers' and tenants' laws to education and the environment. Barriers to travel were erased, a common currency established. The peoples of Europe, for so many centuries at daggers drawn, went happily into the new and now easily accessible sociopolitical landscape. Croatian businessmen had lunch meetings in Munich. Swedish arts festivals invited Spanish dance troupes to visit. Students amassed languages and friends and trips and documented it all on Instagram, ebulliently.

It was so humane, so civilized.

Yet it came at a huge cost: the surrender of individual nations' sovereignty to Brussels.

Indeed, behind European Union's public messaging, buried in legal briefs and incomprehensible documents not readily available to the public, the people's hands were being removed quietly from the actual machinery of both national and EU-level governance. And governance itself receded from actual transparency.

This dismantling of access to the structures of national democracy in Europe was cloaked in jargon. When I started reporting on this issue in 2016–18, in the wake of Brexit, I was shocked to realize that very few continental Europeans, *including journalists*, actually understood how EU governance worked. Most Europeans believed that the European Union was like a federal system, similar to that in the United States, uniting disparate entities but leaving each with a significant degree of independence. Many educated, influential Europeans and Britons with whom I spoke believed, mistakenly, that even if they could not describe it in detail, the European Union was an accountable, if complex, meta-democracy.

This was not surprising, given the degree that the European Union's true governance was cloaked in obfuscation. Its webpages provided only incomprehensible graphics with seating charts and arrows that contradicted each other and could not be followed. Even as someone who ran a website devoted to explaining the founding documents and democratic governance to American audiences, I was consistently baffled; I kept poking around on EU websites and tweeting, annoyingly no doubt, to the EU press office: Where are the EU's complete set of founding documents? I asked. What laws undergirded the European Union's powers of governance? How could citizens lobby? We could organize as citizens to change our Constitution. By what method could

European citizens organize to change the existing EU foundational agreements?

Where was the upcoming proposed legislation?

I then had the unnerving experience of EU spokespeople pointing me in this or that direction, but never to the foundational laws demonstrating the governance of the European Union and showing how citizens could affect or alter it. They pointed me to a "legislative feed." But that showed only bills after the European Parliament had voted them into law.

It was during this process of trying to find these answers that I was invited to Madeira, Portugal, to speak about my book *The End of America*. Madeira is a beautiful archipelago, an autonomous region of Portugal, in the North Atlantic Ocean.

Madeira is lush with small green forests, mists clinging to the sides of valleys, heaped with curvaceous little mountains covered with grass that slope down to the curling waves of the Atlantic, and with a rich history as a contact point between traders and sailors. It has winding main streets with nineteenth century cottages trimmed with carpenter's gingerbread from its time as a destination for foreign invalids who sought out the gentle climate.[183]

I was on a panel with a Portuguese civil servant who spent much of his time dealing with the EU. Since I had been speaking about civic action, people were asking us about how to engage politically. One issue that came up repeatedly was that there was poor flight service to Europe from Madeira — generally you had to fly one and a half hours to Lisbon. Business owner after business owner made the case that the local economy could not grow without a decent airport able to handle more direct flights.

It seemed simple enough. "Can't you lobby your elected officials?" I naively asked.

Impossible, explained the civil servant unhappily; aviation was managed from Brussels.

That astounded me. But surely they could lobby their own Portuguese representative in the EU?

No. It did not matter. If the European Union did not want a better airport in Madeira, the merchants of Madeira were powerless, he said. Portugal herself was powerless.

Later, we convened for a meal. The setting was a beautiful teahouse halfway up one of these dreamy green mountains.

The civil servant and my host explained the European Union to me in terms I could not mistake. Their tone was directive, as if they were handing me a task. They could not do anything about it. But they wanted people to know.

My host explained: the European Union is not a governance entity. It is an economic alliance, and Germany is by far the major influence.

The civil servant explained: "People don't understand the structure of lawmaking in the EU. The unelected diplomats usually propose new laws. And," he added, "Brussels has the second highest number of lobbyists after Washington, DC."

I was astonished—this was legerdemain on a high scale. Western Europeans thought of the European Union as a state above states, a democracy above democracies. But it simply wasn't. It was something else. It was not just "a bureaucracy" that was "complex" — too complex for ordinary citizens to understand, though this was the common messaging point in the news.

Rather, it was "too complex," for a reason. It was democracy theater. The real power was in unaccountable hands.

Having read the history of totalitarianism, I knew what that meant. And that was why this Portuguese politician, who loved his country, took the time to disclose this insider view to me.

I knew that no matter how great things looked in Europe on the surface — the beautiful mobility, the thrilling cultural events, the busy commerce, the admirable language of human rights, and the semblance of freedoms — the powers of the European nation-state had been drained.

European nation-states had been made vulnerable, and people would be left unable to defend themselves in any real way if, heaven forbid, the now-benign, now-smiling, now-well-messaged European Union turned hostile or abusive or — tyrannical.

What I saw all around me that looked so lovely was no longer built on a structure belonging to or owned by the people.

As they would learn in 2020–22, the puppeteer's hand could sweep the entire action away in a moment. The edifice of the beautiful drama of "European democracy" and human rights could come crashing down at any time.

In fact, having for so long lived under EU governance left continental Europeans especially easy prey for the COVID tyrants. Many of these formerly free peoples, most of whom had been born too late to experience totalitarianism firsthand, were quick to follow governmental directives, as in their lifetimes most governmental directives had been benign or at least not malevolent. And even when disoriented by these "restrictions," most of these people failed to recognize them early for what they were, let alone mount effective resistance.

We were vulnerable, too, in the United States, and largely for the same reasons.

Our legacy of freedom was still more accessible to us than was that of continental Europeans. But day after day, "in the midst of the pandemic," our grasp of democracy grew fainter.

We also had too readily forgotten our history, part of which, had we been paying attention, is understanding that restrictions drain human capital and blunt human civilization.

Indeed, we had seen that understanding play out in practice in our own past, for we have seen groups in America subjected to precisely such restrictions.

———————

"Restrictions" irrevocably changed the destiny of Native Americans, for example. Formerly freely traveling and transacting Native Americans tribes were the victims of a massive appropriation of lands and wealth almost unprecedented in Western history. How was it accomplished? By the United States government "locking them down" in reservations, forbidding them to move freely, subjecting them to state "restrictions" on language, dress, currency, and culture. The book *Prairie Fires: The American Dreams of Laura Ingalls Wilder* shows how laws such as the 1830 "Indian Removal Act" restricted Choctaws, Creeks, Cherokees, Osages, and more to certain narrow strips of land.[184] Endless restrictive legislation followed. Separated from the rest of society by compulsion, tracked and monitored by the state, these once formidable and often wealthy nations were forced into defeat and compliance, their destinies constricted to this day.

By way of contrast, even the poorest European-descended settlers of the time in the United States enjoyed freedom of movement and speech and could engage freely with towns, cities, and educational institutions. In her extraordinary books, Ingalls Wilder vividly describes moving from place to place as a child, making new friends, and learning from teachers in humble one-room schoolhouses, all part of growing into the curious, well-read young woman who'd become a world-famous author. She did not have wealth as her inheritance. What she had rather, in contrast to the "restricted" Native American children whom she and her family were displacing, was freedom.

Indeed, the story of America is the story of capital generated by poor people who used their ability to save up a little money to buy a boat ticket to a more promising venue: to peddle a pushcart with a handful of inventory down a grimy street that they were free to traverse, to go door to door selling brushes or offering to repair tin pans.

The story of America is the story of people fleeing countries with "lockdowns" and "restrictions" that made them poor, illiterate, and miserable, so they could become educated and prosperous, thereby contributing to the cultural wealth of their new home. An America that gave them freedom of movement also gave them freedom of worship, speech, and thought, and that in turn facilitated their accumulation of assets, notably land and housing.

In *Financial Exclusion*, in a chapter called "The Jim Crow Experience," economist Robert E. Wright demonstrates that Jim Crow laws and discriminatory "redlining," which restricted movement and assembly, correlated directly to economic harms for African-Americans in the United States. Housing segregation and restrictions on movement and commerce imposed on African-Americans created a "self-fulfilling prophecy that limited their ability to profit from the ownership of real estate."[185] Wright describes how the Great Migration northwards to a less "restricted" cultural context allowed for immediate improvements to those African-Americans' economic success.

The Pity of it All and *A Bookstore in Berlin* both detail how restrictions on the mobility and assembly of Jews in Germany, and in Vichy France, respectively, led to the curtailment of their economic strength, and prepared the way for the eventual transfer or draining of their assets.

Freedom and the securing of wealth are correlated.

Freedom of movement equals cultural achievement, economic achievement, and political influence. "Restrictions" kill all those forms of civil power.

The goal of the "restrictions" that technology companies, via governments in their pockets, imposed on humans in 2020–22 was the same goal restrictions have always had everywhere: to weaken those restricted, to steal or transfer their assets, and to blunt them as a potential source of opposition.

This war was one waged by the lords and ladies of technology; they used technology — and leveraged the culture and civilization of technology — to wage asymmetrical combat against the whole of humanity itself and to strike out against human movement, speech, touch, ingenuity, bodies, religion, families, schooling, and especially culture.

Restrictions in human history always preceded theft: theft of the lands, assets, and opportunities of the restricted. It was so this time too.

For the first time in our species' history, those restricted were not one or even several distinct subgroups, but *humans as a whole.*

Those who restricted them had human form, but they were traitors to humanity.

Headlines in the mainstream news media were almost like how-to manuals for generating mental illnesses: **November 16, 2020** *brought "Holiday Stress: How to Cope During the Coronavirus Pandemic."[186]*

The New York Times *reported on how "stressful" Thanksgiving shopping was. By doing so it ensured that Thanksgiving shopping would be stressful: "How Do I Make Thanksgiving Grocery Shopping Safer?" the headline read. The news and lifestyle stories praised readers for not seeing their families, not hosting a holiday gathering or traveling.*

"So you've canceled your Thanksgiving travel plans, quarantined the college student and created a scaled-back, family-only holiday menu. Good job."[187] November 19, 2020, showed us "When Holiday and Pandemic Stress Collide." [188] November 24, 2020, brought, "Everything's Different This Year — So Why Not Holiday Stress?"[189]

Even if you were fine, you were instructed not to be fine.

The messaging began to feel very wrong to me. I had been a civilian during one war as a child and around a war as a young adult. I had been taken to our apartment building's bomb shelter in Jerusalem during rocket attacks as a twelve-year-old, and later, I had embedded with the IDF as a young reporter; I had seen the rubble of apartment buildings after bomb attacks on Southern Lebanon. I'd traveled decades later as a reporter with field workers for the International Rescue Committee through Sierra Leone, which had been ravaged by civil war.

What anyone who fights in or reports on or survives a war or a humanitarian crisis knows is, in a real crisis, there is unlikely to be nonstop messaging that there is a crisis. Events speak for themselves.

Why were we being told and told and told how bad this was?

Why were we not being allowed to figure that out for ourselves?

———————

By November 2020, I had noticed the news coverage of the Great Barrington Declaration, an open letter drafted by three highly credible epidemiologists arguing that time-tested public health practice suggested that while the elderly and otherwise vulnerable should be supported and protected, everyone else should be left alone to live their lives. It was convened by Jeffrey Tucker of the American Institute for Economic Research.

Its lead signatories — Professor Jay Bhattacharya of Stanford, Dr. Martin Kulldorff, then of Harvard, and Dr. Sunetra Gupta of Oxford University, all mentioned above — warned of the looming damage to humanity that, to them, "lockdowns" clearly portended. They predicted that the harms would be most severe among the poor, the elderly, children. Their "Declaration" was signed by tens of thousands of physicians and scientists.

While the objections of this group of brave public health experts were primarily economic — they talked about how the most impoverished would starve by the millions — they also talked about physical and emotional "collateral damage."

The brave epidemiologists were right.

In spite of endless news stories claiming the contrary, these experts warned that "locked down" states and nations would do no better in reaching the stated public health goal that ushered them in than did states and nations that never "locked down."[190] Restrictions did nothing except harm populations in countless ways, they explained, including in terms of public health.

Initially the response to this bracingly direct and reasonable-sounding open letter, which argued that "Covid-19 policy should focus on protecting the elderly and vulnerable, and largely re-open society and school for others," was neutral to positive.[191]

People were tired, and the strangeness of what was happening to us, was becoming more apparent.

Dr. Martin Kulldorf voiced several concerns over "lockdowns" to The Lancet Respiratory Medicine in November 2020: "We are seeing plummeting vaccination rates, people are not getting diabetes treatment, they are not attending for cancer screening, cardiovascular disease outcomes are worsening, and the restrictions are putting a huge strain on mental health . . . These are not short-term problems — closing schools, for example, can have serious consequences that last a lifetime."[192] He claimed a significant portion of the nearly 100,000 excess deaths in 2020 from conditions other than the virus stemmed from effects of the "lockdowns": "If you are not in a vulnerable group, the collateral damage of lockdown is far more destructive than the virus."[193]

But even at that time, these public health experts and their message questioning the "lockdown" narrative had powerful enemies.

As the Great Barrington Declaration was garnering some initial respectful attention, Dr. Anthony Fauci, the director of the National Institute of Allergy and Infectious Diseases, was communicating with NIH director Francis Collins. The emails were obtained in December of 2021 via a FOIA request by the American Institute for Economic Research scholar Phil Magness.

Behind the scenes, Dr. Collins was calling for "a quick and devastating published take down" of the premises of these scientists, whom he called "fringe" epidemiologists.[194]

In the months to follow, Dr. Collins would get what he had commissioned; "mud would be slung" at the scientists in abundance.[195]

I saw, without knowing about these internal communications, how these admirably credentialled experts making a reasoned case, were immediately smeared.

In spite of these brave and credible voices, what was becoming recognizable as "the narrative" unrolled apace.

I began to ask questions.

———

I was starting to recognize what I called "the totalitarian third-person plural." In individualistic America, news outlets and influencers kept phrasing directives in an unprecedented way: "We must," as in, "To defeat this virus we must all stay home." "We must sacrifice in-person holidays in order to do our part in defeating the virus." Headlines read, "Everyone is," as if we were no longer all different people with different choices and lives. It was a communitarian phrasing culturally alien to the United States, and to the West for that matter. "We must"?

We Americans could not in the past agree even on the ideal color for an SUV, for Lord's sake.

Now, news outlets and health policy spokespeople were describing what "we must" do — not only with our own bodies, but with the bodies of others, and used the language of closed societies to do so.

The language echoed the 2006 film by Florian Henckel von Donnersmarck about agents of the Stasi in East Germany tasked with surveilling the private, intimate moments of citizens, The Lives of Others *— an intrusiveness that was depicted in East Berlin in 1984 as being ostensibly for the common good.*

Americans now seemed also not to understand what their own country was made up of or how it worked.

We were following orders — that were not even orders.

CDC "guidance" was being followed and cited by schools, universities, and businesses as if it were law. But it was just "guidance." Dr. Fauci appeared on scores of news outlets saying what you "could" and "could not" do. But Dr. Fauci's agency had no enforcement authority. His job was just to advise the president about science.

We were free people. None of these officials actually were supposed to control us. But few seemed to realize that.

CHAPTER NINE

FROZEN WITH FEAR: A CULT TAKES SHAPE

The virus was now being spoken of the way a villain in horror movie might be — with its own theme music and looming, Satanic personality. It wasn't described any longer the way we had described smallpox, or typhus, or tuberculosis. It was being positioned as the awe-inspiring antihero in what we were invited to join as a collective cult.

It was Milton's Satan.

By November 2020, I'd started reading a range of sources, including independent commentators on social media, libertarians and conservatives, *The Epoch Times* and Children's Health Defense. I was reading the peer-reviewed studies. I often saw that the studies themselves bore little relationship to the way they were being reported.

I read *The New York Times* article which suggested that you could get sick from passing someone on an outdoor path: "An open-air café may seem safe, until people start walking by on the sidewalk without masks."[196] But in papers studying aerosol transmission, for instance, the conclusions were much more nuanced than *The Times* article led readers to believe. Many aerosol studies of COVID-19 transmission were primarily theoretical, basing their findings on mathematical models.[197]

Nonetheless, the image of a toxic cloud heading toward a hapless victim on a path had scared my mom, and many of my friends and loved ones, to death.

I spoke with John Beaudoin, a researcher, who showed me Massachusetts Department of Public Health statistics on who was dying from COVID in that state. The average age was seventy-nine — in line with America's average life span.[198]

I was invited in January 2021 to become a Fellow at the American Institute of Economic Research by Jeffrey Tucker. I had long admired his work — he was a well-known and brilliant libertarian essayist and under his oversight, AIER was producing the best and most fearless and thorough reporting on the pandemic.

In this beautiful stone house at the top of a mountain in Massachusetts, I spent every day with a thoughtful community of liberty-minded economists, AI theorists and historians.

I remember the first day I walked in: Mr. Tucker ran the Institute with the kind of respect for personal choice that had been simply "America" before 2020. I entered into a tastefully appointed living room in which a group of twenty or so Fellows and staffers, all beautifully dressed, were chatting and having cocktails.

Like normal.

I was shocked that they were maskless, standing near one another, and socializing like human beings. At AIER, there was hand sanitizer in abundance and there were baskets of masks everywhere, and everyone could choose his or her own comfort level and level of risk. That was how we used to live.

Some people were working from home. Others "distanced." Still others just hung out together comfortably. I was enchanted and delighted, and I made the choices that were comfortable for me.

Every day I had lunch with twenty or thirty Fellows around a dining table and every evening we had cocktails or tea and coffee and conversation about the issues of the day in the salon, sitting with one another as normal people did.

There was good ventilation; no one coerced anyone; people kept to the distance or closeness that suited them. And to my knowledge, no one got seriously ill and no one died of COVID. But life continued excitingly apace.

So with this community around me, I had a tiny foothold in the realm of expectation of respect for other people's bodies and choices that used to be the world we took for granted.

I was able to think about the great fear gripping the rest of the nation, with a firsthand experience of events in the community of which I was now a part being fairly safe and fairly easily manageable. And I had a direct experience of my own day-to-day life not stopping.

I didn't get sick. Brian didn't get sick. It was an intellectually rich time, filled with new friendships and stimulating conversations.

But most of the rest of my friends and family were still in a state of locked-in, suspended animation. They worried about me terribly when I said I went into an office every day.

I thought about the AIER community not getting very seriously sick *en masse*, and I thought about the Amish community, which had not "locked down," also not getting very seriously sick *en masse*, and I thought about the Orthodox Jewish community to which my relatives belonged not getting very seriously sick *en masse*.

And I wondered why there were no studies of communities that did not "lock down" — communities in which people chose their own levels of risk while providing support to those who wished to "isolate" or who wanted to protect their own, more vulnerable immune systems while others made different choices.

I wondered why no one wanted to know what was becoming of them.

————————

At about this time, the Great Barrington-based synagogue we had joined told the community not to expect to gather again in person for the foreseeable future. It had already been a year that the synagogue was physically closed.

The rabbis said proudly that there were "epidemiologists" advising the board about staying closed.

But I felt spiritually drained by Zoom meetings to discuss Jewish short stories, instead of actual worship in front of the sacred Torah scrolls. I wanted to worship. I craved worship in a community. That form of gathering had sustained our people for four millennia.

The rabbis explained to me that no one was going to open the sanctuary. They used holidays to make their points, as other spokespeople had done, as if this were a script.

Not by Purim, they said. Not by Hanukah — ten months into the future.

How could they possibly know what the status of this disease would be that far into the future?

I suggested to a synagogue committee I had joined that any people who did in fact want to get together in person were welcome to come join me in my living room to follow the Zoom Shabbat services.

A hail of hostile emails to me from members of that committee followed what I had thought was a modest suggestion. The rabbi was on the email chain too — and did not comment.

I asked the rabbis again later when we could expect that the sanctuary would ever reopen. They said that reopening simply could not be expected.

It had been a year, I pointed out, and we had moved to a new area, but we had yet to meet a single member of the congregation in person, or worship even once in the sanctuary. I had never set foot in the synagogue.

The synagogue across the Hudson had been closed for just as long as our synagogue had been closed.

In Jewish tradition, a "minyan" — the gathering of ten or more people — is considered sacred.

There was no minyan, indoors or out.

There was nowhere to worship. There were no plans to reopen. There were no alternatives being proposed.

Jewish life, which had survived for more than four thousand years worldwide under the most hostile of conditions, was dying. Spiritually, I too was dying.

At my Jewish summer camps, outdoor worship on Sabbath evenings had been magical and moving. It did not matter where we were as long as we were together with God.

I asked the rabbis if we could just put folding chairs at a distance from one another outside the temple, in the parking lot perhaps, for those who did wish to worship in community. Others who preferred to isolate could still Zoom in, couldn't they?

No, said the rabbis, firmly; we could not consider worshipping in the parking lot, or anywhere, or at a distance, or in any in-person context. They did not give a reason.

I said tensely to the rabbis on that call, "If I were a rabbi and someone wanted to pray with me, I would meet with them in a *bus shelter*."

Soon thereafter the rabbis let me know I that was not a "good fit" for the congregation.

My congregation essentially broke up with me, and returned to me my membership dues.

———————

My synagogue was by no means alone. I noted all the closed churches in my area. Methodist. Catholic. Episcopalian. Baptist.

No in-person worship anywhere in New York State. Epidemiologists and public health officials were now somehow on many institutions' Boards.

My friend's mom had enjoyed her local Texas church as the mainstay of her life. She said that her friendships were now withering away because the church was not congregating. A widow, she was now entirely alone.

I thought of my childhood synagogue; how a congregant whom I will call Emmie, an older adult with Down Syndrome, had come every Friday night, without fail, to Shabbat services. She too lived alone.

Emmie had few teeth, and as I recall, she always wore the same well-worn dark blue dress with a pinafore front, and the same white collared shirt beneath it, when she came to services. She often had crumbs on her clothing, and she wore eccentric hats. She did not have much, materially.

But every Friday night she had a beautiful, brightly lit, dignified place to be, and she was treated with great respect and given a cordial welcome by our truly honorable rabbi, Rabbi Saul White. She was greeted by her fellow worshippers; she had friends.

That is what a synagogue — or church or mosque — is *supposed* to do.

Emmie ate the kiddush treats after services, and she took some cookies and cakes home every week in a napkin placed gently in her purse.

Every week, whether we wanted the hugs or not, she warmly hugged me and my brother. They may have been the only hugs she had all week.

She gave us, and our family, every Friday night, her immense smiles.

She was entirely alone in this world. But she wasn't.

Temple Beth Shalom was her home.

Now people like Emmie — people like me; like all of us — were existentially alone in the world again.

What is religion? Properly understood, it is a community. It is a home — that's where God actually lives.

By January 2021, in the Hudson Valley, there was no Jewish or Episcopal or Catholic community anymore. There was no home.

Whoever had hated our belief, and the strength it gave us — whoever had wanted our faith communities to die out — had won.

———————

As a result of this primary research and of seeing human beings living normally at the libertarian think tank where I now worked, and as a result of being in touch with such scientists as Dr. Bhattacharya, Dr. Goddek and Dr. Vatsal Thakkar, who researched how Vitamin D boosted immunity, I realized that I had to follow the *actual* science.

I had to stay healthy and boost my immune system and be in ventilated spaces. I should not sit face-to-face with someone who might be ill in a closed room for fifteen minutes. Indeed, I should avoid crowded, unventilated spaces. I had to get sunshine and Vitamin D. I had to exercise to avoid hypertension, a major risk factor for COVID-19, and obesity, the second top risk factor. These were not terrifying messages — they were reasonable goals. While the disease was scary, indeed, and serious for many, these messages based on the science cited by the "dissident" doctors and researchers, were not messages that made one feel helpless. People could take action to make good decisions to promote their chances of protecting their health.

But many of my friends and family were not reading these sources, and the primary messages they were getting were about staying inside alone in terror of a holistically threatening world. So they were frozen with fear.

Many news outlets continued to miscommunicate studies, or to feature flawed studies, all of which tended to heighten the level of their readers' fear and sense of helplessness.

The New York Times was reporting on COVID "droplets" and communicating the message, essentially, that you could get infected from any air in any context. "As the CDC now advises, 'Avoid large and small gatherings in private places and public spaces, such as a friend's house, parks, restaurants, shops, or any other place.'" *The New York Times* showed a diagram of a single study from Guangzhou, China, that purported to show how "families A, B and C" became sick from a single unnamed family that had purportedly traveled 520 miles from Wuhan, China the day before Wuhan and its surrounding province locked down and then had lunch in an unfortunate restaurant.[199] The article was a death knell for the restaurant industry, as it concluded that air conditioning must have spread the disease and that even spacing tables was no panacea. *The Times* cited the CDC in relaying this message.

Was this Chinese study, however, in a separate peer-reviewed publication?

No: "Chinese researchers described the incident in a paper that is to be published in the July issue of the *Emerging Infectious Diseases*, a journal published by the Centers for Disease Control and Prevention."

So the study was not published in a separate peer-reviewed journal: the CDC was actually citing . . . the CDC.[200] *Emerging Infectious Diseases* is a CDC publication.

Another flaw: "The field study has limitations. The researchers, for example, did not perform experiments to simulate the airborne transmission."

Still another flaw in how this study was reported was replicated in many studies cited by legacy media: correlation is not causation. The Chinese researchers saw that someone in "Family A" got sick; they saw that within two weeks, nine others who had also been in the restaurant "tested positive." Four of these could have gotten sick elsewhere, they surmised: "But for the other five," *The New York Times* wrote, "the restaurant appears to have been the source of the virus."

But why could the other five not also been infected elsewhere? A COVID infection does not have a timestamp.

Indeed, even the scientists who'd done the study — scientists living under the CCP regime, with a watchful eye over scientists and research — had not made the certain claims *The New York Times* implied that they had. Even these scientists acknowledged that the sick patients could have been infected elsewhere.

Which is to say, even under CCP oversight, the Chinese scientists were far more hesitant in their conclusions than was *The New York Times*.

But once again, what my mom and my relatives and my friends saw was a memorable schematic in a newspaper they all trusted, showing round tables with diners infecting one another, right there, circled in lurid red.

Cautioned *The Times*: "The social nature of dining out could increase the risk. The longer people linger in a contaminated area, the more virus particles they would likely inhale."

So there was the takeaway from the vaunted *New York Times*: Breathing, talking, certainly dining socially, could all horribly sicken or kill you. And, by the way: "Simply spacing tables six feet apart . . . may not be sufficient to safeguard restaurant patrons."[201] All of this was meant to illustrate "some of the challenges that restaurants will face when they try to reopen."

This article mattered immensely. Throughout New York, people who'd regularly dined out their entire lives, providing the backbone of the city's restaurant industry, were now sure that dining out could be a death sentence. This article and others provided the grist for governors such as Cuomo and Massachusetts' Governor Baker to "restrict" seating in bars and restaurants, or to close them altogether. Once these measures were in place, they would not soon let up.

Indeed, a full year into the pandemic, *The New York Times* was still claiming that bars and restaurants were a key source of COVID infections. They showcased another study that purported to correlate open restaurants with increased infections. Who was *The Times* now citing? The CDC's Dr. Walensky. And what was she now citing? A CDC study.

Nonetheless, even then, anyone who bothered to actually read the CDC's study could not have failed to grasp its limitations. Among them, as the CDC itself confessed, "the analysis did not differentiate between indoor and outdoor dining, adequacy of ventilation, and adherence to physical distancing and occupancy requirements."[202]

Restaurant owners, horribly hard hit already, were driven to take issue with the "science" that the CDC was presenting as justification to keep their entire industry closed or restricted:

> On Friday night, the National Restaurant Association, which represents one million restaurants and food service outlets, criticized the CDC study as "an ill-informed attack on the industry hardest-hit by the pandemic."
>
> It pointed out that researchers had not controlled for factors other than restaurant dining — such as business closures and other policies — that might have contributed to coronavirus infections and deaths: "If a positive correlation between ice cream sales and shark attacks is found, that would not mean that ice cream causes shark attacks," the association said in a statement.[203]

The restaurant owners were correct about the CDC and its methods. They were absolutely right, both logically and morally.

These articles and proclamations had not come close to proving with replicable experiments or controlled studies published in peer-reviewed journals that open restaurants, with proper ventilation, sanitation, and seating, directly caused dramatically higher rates of COVID than did other venues.

Stubbornly, published studies showed that households were environments ripe for transmission — the same places we were corralled into to "stop the spread."[204]

After tens of thousands of restaurants had closed, a study showed that restaurants accounted for only 1.4% of infections.[205]

But for all those businesses, for all those independent, hardworking business owners, many of them immigrants and members of communities of color, the facts could not help them anymore. It was already too late.

———————————

January 2021: *I called a colleague at a university in Northern England. He had been prevented for months from going outside except for an hour a day to exercise.*

In the middle of our conversation about ordinary professional stresses, he began to cry.

I'd hired a remote technologist through a platform that connects women techies in the developing world to companies that need them in the global north. It is a great idea and had been empowering many women, from Saudi Arabia to Jordan to Central Europe and Latin America and the Philippines. The WordPress webmaster we'd hired had been a bright young woman; her profile picture showed her in a crisp blue blouse and neat skirt, hair shiny and expression hopeful and determined. She had been organized, professional, and productive when the "lockdown" began. By January 2021 her work was suffering. In our Zoom calls, she explained that the population in the Philippines, where she was located, was only allowed out on alternating days and then only for groceries or medicine. Children were not allowed out at all, she said.

The technologist had a boyfriend — they had been dating for years — but when they walked in public now, a stick was placed between the two young people, by a public health officer, making sure they were six feet apart. They could not touch or hold hands.

By February 2021, her punctuation and grammar were erratic. When she made mistakes, she seemed unable to care.

On calls the formerly hyper-professional young woman was unkempt and pale; her eyes had grown dull. She seemed no longer to have the energy to brush her once-smooth black hair. She was always in one room.

She was so depressed as to be almost immobile.

With sorrow we had to let her go.

But the dissident doctors, such as the Canadian ER physician Dr. Patrick Phillips, were increasingly speaking up on social media: "Elders are coming in dying of starvation," reported Dr. Phillips. "People are dying of depression. People are dying from missed cancer screenings."

Dr. Simon Goddek, a German biologist based in Brazil, was warning that there was something wrong with the PCR tests. Curious, I did an interview with Dr. Goddek — one of my first.

He told me he had faced backlash from his university for breaking the important story that the journal Eurosurveillance, which published the signature study claiming the PCR test could identify COVID-19 — had passed peer review for the article in a little over a day, when the average timeline, as Dr. Goddek proved, was dozens of months. Dr. Goddek was shaken but insistent that the truth come out. His outrage was the pure outrage of a scientist. Something was wrong.[206]

I started to interview more of the dissident voices that I saw on social media, and their persuasiveness and general aura of personal integrity impressed me and shook me.

Dr. Vatsal Thakkar was trying to sound the alarm that keeping people indoors would kill them. Vitamin D saved lives, he explained. He showed me, as had Dr. Goddek, dozens of peer-reviewed studies showing that Vitamin D raised resistance to severe harms from COVID-19.[207]

Kevin McKernan, who runs a PCR test lab in Beverly, Massachusetts, was starting to warn as well, from his own knowledge base, that there was something wrong with the PCR tests.

Snapping out of the fear-based torpor that had made the world go into a standstill, and that dragged at me as well, I forced myself to act like a reporter. Having reached out to him, I actually went into the world to speak to him face-to-face — the world that was represented as killing us at every turn.

It was kind of nice to be out in Beverly, Massachusetts, by the water, in the evening, and nice to enter an office building, which I had not done for seven months.

Mr. McKernan let me tour his PCR test lab, with my husband Brian recording our discussion. The lab was clean and bright. I was struck that the scientists here were going to work every day and acting the way people would have without the "mandates" of "distancing." They'd found their own comfort level regarding where they sat and stood and walked, and it seemed to be working out fine. Male and female, casually dressed, or in white lab coats, the scientists intently discussed their work. Masks were provided, but no one was wearing one. The employees sat an organic ten or twelve feet from one another. The ventilation was exceptional and refreshing. Lush green plants flourished at the broad windows.

No one had yet been ill, Mr. McKernan said.

He showed me that the PCR tests in use for COVID could pick up evidence of weeks-old cold or flu in the nasal passages and mis-identify it as "COVID-19." He explained that all many colds are "coronaviruses," so I realized that a news outlet saying that 70,000 people had died of "coronavirus," without further identification, could imply more than just deaths from COVID-19. He showed me the missing data line that should have been present, if human COVID-19 was really being measured by the PCR tests now in use. He explained that if you run the PCR tests at high cycle thresholds, you often get false positives. Mr. McKernan's colleague Bobby Malhotra, a data designer, dialing in from Vienna, confirmed what Mr. McKernan was saying.[208]

The information was stunning.

Every day for months, the COVID-19 dashboards had reported the results of PCR tests as if they were golden, bulletproof evidence of rampaging COVID-19 infections. But both Dr. Goddek and Kevin McKernan had independently confirmed, and both were openly and persuasively demonstrating, that what people were being told was not correct. There were glaring flaws in the tests' method of collecting the data, to add to the flaws about which I already knew of in the method of digitally interpreting and displaying the data.[209]

At about the same time, early 2021, Dr. Jay Bhattacharya and Dr. Martin Kulldorff and Dr. Sunetra Gupta were trying to warn that children should not be kept out of school, as they were not at serious risk for COVID.

I interviewed Dr. Bhattacharya; a pleasant, upbeat, genial professor at Stanford who radiated reasonableness; his tone was measured and judicious. Yet he too was now being painted as a wild-eyed science-denier or conspiracy theorist.

Dr. Bhattacharya said that while older and vulnerable people should be supported in "sheltered protection," young adults should go about their lives. I thought of college students whom I loved, and who were suffering, and I was chilled.[210]

Were we suppressing the young people for no good reason?

Dr. Patrick Phillips of Canada described the horrors of cancers, and other illnesses, that had worsened due to "lockdowns."[211]

I watched as more and more of these scientists and doctors were being trolled and hounded digitally for their messages.

And when I posted my solidly sourced interviews with these highly credentialed people, based on primary source reporting, including a visit to a PCR-test lab, I watched in amazement as I myself was trolled, and then hounded, and finally frozen out digitally.

———————

Restaurants were still completely closed in Massachusetts. I interviewed Paul Massimino, of the beloved restaurant Massimino's in

Boston. His father had founded the restaurant. He was distraught. He had twenty families' breadwinners depending on him to reopen and yet the Board of Health kept changing the rules: 25 people — 50 people — 25 people. I had never before seen the face of a decent man who was at his wits' end, in an ever-changing, illogical environment, trying to find a way to keep food on the table for twenty families dependent on a breadwinner's honest work — when that breadwinner was being prevented from working. It was a troubling sight.

On March 15, 2021, Governor Cuomo made the truly weird declaration that while weddings and catered events could now resume, wedding guests had to dance apart, be masked, and could only remove their masks while seated and eating or drinking:

"Venues were restricted to 50% capacity, with no more than 150 attendees per event.

All attendees must have proof of recent negative test result or proof of immunization prior to the event.

Sign-in with contact information was required to assist with potential contact tracing.

Venues had to notify local health departments of large events, above the social gathering limit, in advance.

Ceremonial and socially-distanced dancing would be allowed only in designated areas."[212]

By the start of 2021, millions were getting vaccinated with mRNA vaccines, rolled out under Emergency Use Authorization. In March 2021, I began to see women on social media with appalling accounts of menstrual dysregulation after vaccination. Young healthy women were reporting two periods a month, or a period that lasted fifteen days at a time. A number of women who had been postmenopausal for years began to menstruate again, a truly bizarre symptom if you know about women's health and the fertility-related reason for menses in the first place. One mom said her twelve-year-old daughter had gotten a fourteen-day period — her first — immediately on having been vaccinated. Many women described horror stories related to their post-vaccination menses: agonizing cramps and the hemorrhaging of large clots of bloody tissue. A nurse described recently menstruating women in the hospital passing large clots of bloody tissue.

I am a writer on women's health, and feminism teaches us, "first, listen to women." It was by listening to women's early anecdotal reports about their own bodies, or about their babies, that we learned about the dangers of thalidomide and vaginal mesh, silicone breast implants and Mirena.

All that bleeding, about which I was hearing online and from women I knew, was just not normal. And you didn't have to be a rocket scientist to understand that a dysregulated menstrual cycle was going to negatively affect fertility.

I talked about this set of symptoms on Fox News and on the political podcast War Room.

The reaction?

My Twitter account was suspended; the reason given was that I had committed "medical misinformation."

Reporter Matt Gertz of CNN and MediaMatters, in a detailed, carefully illustrated takedown, cited my reporting on menstrual dysregulation and labeled me a "conspiracy theorist."

A few months earlier, CNN had received $3.6 million from the Bill & Melinda Gates Foundation directly to fund its reporting. The grant was to extend for more than three years.[213]

CHAPTER TEN

"THE SOFTWARE OF LIFE"

B y April 2021, even more people, at least in my former circles, were getting mRNA vaccines. Soon people were "double-vaxxed." They boasted online about being "Team Pfizer" or "Team Moderna." All over social media, you would see smiling influencers rolling up their sleeves and proudly showing off their Band-Aids. Legacy media wasn't much better.

How organic was all this cheerleading? TheBlaze uncovered a money trail straight to the legacy media:

> TheBlaze.com FOIA'd the Department of Health and Human Services, and found that HHS had bought advertising from major news platforms such as *ABC, CBS* and *NBC*. Via HHS, millions flowed to *Fox News, CNN* and *NBC; The Washington Post, The New York Times, The Los Angeles Times* and *Buzzfeed.com*. The money derived from Congress' having appropriated one billion dollars in 2021

for HHS, using CDC as its distributor, to "strengthen vaccine confidence in the United States."[214]

The ad dollars went to print and TV and digital advertising, and to influencers on social media, and to influencers from hard-hit communities. The mission was clearly spelled out as being the kind of management of messaging that we saw ramping up 2021: the CDC and other agencies were allowed to award contracts to both private and public organizations to "carry out a national, evidence-based campaign to increase awareness and knowledge of the safety and effectiveness of vaccines for the prevention and control of diseases, combat misinformation about vaccines, and disseminate scientific and evidence-based vaccine-related information, with the goal of increasing rates of vaccination across all ages [...]"[215]

Some states, using funding from the CARES Act, led their own messaging campaigns. Colorado alone paid over 120 influencers on platforms such as TikTok "up to $1000 a month" to tell people to get vaccinated.[216]

This presented a whole new model of funding that in just a few months completely corrupted American civil society and affected many legacy media outlets' messaging. US taxpayer dollars were being used to pay individuals and groups to push a product made by donors to the administration,[217] with a crossover business alignment with Big Tech.[218] Big Tech, in turn, via social media platforms, was supporting the propaganda push.[219] It was a circular current of influence on a scale never before seen.

By May 2021, the influencers were sharing stories of having vaccinated their teenaged kids.

I did not get vaccinated.

I have nothing against other safety-proven vaccines, but I had been absolutely petrified simply from reading the Moderna website. Its competitive advantage, as it pitched to shareholders, was that its mRNA vaccines, in a novel lipid nanoparticle delivery system, would enter bodily cells and produce a spike protein. The Moderna website claimed that the new technology was, in the metaphor they chose, "the software of life."[220] Running a tech company, I knew well that "software" requires "updates" as time passes and technology evolves. Was Moderna really *that* transparent about its vaccination "business plan," even in its use of a metaphor?

Based on this pitch to investors, before anyone had heard of "boosters," I predicted on social media that there would be repeat injections in the future. I also looked at peer-reviewed studies of lipid nanoparticles. This scared me even more, because the biotech world was so excited about this new technology. The massive investment in and excitement about lipid nanoparticle research was not coming from medicine alone, but, I was alarmed to see, from biotech companies: "Solid Lipid Nanoparticles for Drug Delivery: Pharmacological and Biopharmaceutical Aspects": "Pharmaceutical applications of lipid nanocarriers are a burgeoning field for the transport and delivery of a diversity of therapeutic agents, from biotechnological products to small drug molecules."[221] These articles were euphoric about the potential that lipid nanoparticles had for biotech engagement with bodily processes, as well as for drug delivery.

In that breathless tech-media coverage of lipid nanoparticles, I recognized the "gold-rush" excitement of venture capitalists running rampant. Indeed, "[t]he field sometimes resembles the early stage of a gold rush," as Wired.com reported.[222] Silicon Valley sees the oceans and earth and sky, and the human body itself, as the last frontiers, the only remaining Wild West left to conquer via digital colonization. I did not want my body to be part of their "gold rush."

Tech moguls resent being limited to computers. They want to get into the commons of the environment all around us, and they want to get inside the human body — that gold mine of data.

Because of the intense market-forces excitement about lipid nanoparticle technology from the biotech community, I simply did not trust the quickly produced vaccine. I was wary that there had been so much development money poured into the lipid nanoparticle technology even prior to any COVID-19 emergency. The delivery technology had not been developed for this emergency specifically but in hopes of its serving other purposes.

I was also startled that doctors I knew seemed so ignorant about the mRNA technology let alone the lipid nanoparticle casings. I was badgered by a relative who is an MD, who seemed to be reading from a script on the CDC website on how to prod stubborn unvaccinated family members to "do the right thing." I asked him if he knew what happened to the spike protein. He could not answer the question.

In another context, a doctor asked me if I had been vaccinated yet, a question I always found intrusive. (I actually have a serious neurological condition, which also was a factor in my reluctance to experiment with an already impaired nervous system. This factor too was no one's business but my own, of course.)

I did not answer, but asked him if he knew what happened to the spike protein: where it went. He replied with the answer that public health spokespeople were providing: that it stayed in the muscle where it had been injected.

Lastly, there was a paper that reputable physicians and epidemiologists, including Dr. Sucharit Bhakdi, sent to the European Medicines Agency. They described the mRNA vaccine's likely damaging effect on the walls of the blood vessels, including the tiniest ones; and they foresaw strokes and thrombotic events simply from the way the vaccine's mechanism was constructed:

> It must be expected that endothelial damage with subsequent triggering of blood coagulation via platelet activation will ensue at countless sites throughout the body. We request evidence that this probability was excluded in pre-clinical animal models with all three vaccines prior to their approval for use in humans by the EMA . . . If such evidence is not available, it must be expected that this will lead to a drop in platelet counts, appearance of D-dimers in the blood, and to myriad ischaemic lesions throughout the body including in the brain, spinal cord and heart. Bleeding disorders might occur in the wake of this novel type of DIC-syndrome including, amongst other possibilities, profuse bleedings and haemorrhagic stroke. We request evidence that all these possibilities were excluded in pre-clinical animal models with all three vaccines prior to their approval for use in humans by the EMA.[223]

Their letter seemed well evidenced about the risk to the vascular system, and seemed to ask important questions. They asked the agency to allay or respond to their concerns.

Everything about which they warned came to pass.

I sent the letter to my loved ones and friends.

Beginning to be completely devoted to a gathering narrative in which mRNA vaccination was "our way out of this" and the unvaccinated were stubborn disease factories to be ostracized, many friends and loved ones asked me not to send them anything of that nature again. These were judges, journalists, editors — critically thinking people.

By now the frenzy of people wanting to escape from "lockdown" via "the only way out," the vaccine, was in full force, like the tulip mania of seventeenth-century Holland. By now, the media was relentlessly casting the unvaccinated as Trump-obsessed infectious racists and depicting getting mRNA-vaccinated as the only way to be a decent human being and to serve the community.

My friends and loved ones in the blue cities were falling into a group consciousness that I could not fathom.

It seemed to me that they did not want to see anything that went against what was becoming a solidifying mass delusion.

———————

During the summer of 2021, Brian and I drove across country, to the fear and amazement of many of our friends and loved ones. It was absolutely fine. In red states, people were respectful of each other's personal space and used hand sanitizer and seemed otherwise to go about their business. They were lovely.

The national news had been full of stories of people dying en masse in South Dakota, whose governor, Kristi Noem, had refused to "lock down." When we asked about all the video footage playing on CNN and NBC showing people lying on gurneys in the hallways of the local hospital, allegedly ill and dying of COVID-19, the orderly actually laughed. He said that that footage was from 2019, when a lot of young people had come into the ER seriously hung over from a huge party.

We stopped in Sturgis, South Dakota. We asked a young woman at the curio shop where we stopped about the local biker rally that had been reported as a "superspreader event," and about COVID's impact on her town.

She showed exasperation.

There were a few sad deaths of elderly people, she said, at the start of the pandemic, as in every other little town. Some other people had gotten very sick at the beginning of the pandemic.

But the consensus in town and among attendees to the biker rally was that it had not been the site of the spreading of any unusual level of illness.

Of course, this was the opposite of the message that had been conveyed about Sturgis to viewers of CNN and NBC and to readers of The New York Times, *and by extension, to all the consumers of the mainstream media that follow* The Times's *lead. A* Times *story published after the rally was headlined "A Motorcycle Rally in a Pandemic? 'We Kind of Knew What Was Going to Happen'" and made it sound as if hundreds of people had been infected at the Sturgis rally. "In the rally's aftermath," it read, pointing out the South Dakota's governor was a Republican, "hundreds of people have gotten sick and Sturgis has become a rumbling symbol of America's bitter divisions over the coronavirus, even now, as cases continue to surge, surpassing more than 121,000 daily infections on Thursday, and the nation's death toll crosses 235,000."*[224]

It took a close reading to figure out that many of those reported to have gotten sick with COVID actually fell ill a month later, when they were back home in New Hampshire, Wyoming, Nebraska and elsewhere. Indeed, The Times *did not link to any evidence showing that the cases had "spread" from attendees at the biker rally to colleagues or family members in distant states. Those who fell ill, as tens of thousands were during that period, could indeed have gotten sick at the politically incorrect red-state rally. Or they could have gotten sick entirely unrelatedly, back at home.*

But to those seeking reassurance for their own obsessive masking and sheltering-in-place and obedience in general to the ever-shifting regime of mandates, it did not matter. "The Biker Rally" in Sturgis, SD, became shorthand for stupid, self-destructive Trump-voting "liberty" fetishists, whose fault the whole pandemic's spread would be. As The New York Times *reported, these selfish, feckless jerks had had their fun in a crowd, then gone home to kill off their families. Worse, those beer-swilling, hard-partying superspreaders had put in jeopardy the "careful," solitary, indoors-dwelling, mask-wearing upper-class progressive urbanites, the "good people" who "followed the science," and thus readily accepted one limitation after another on their freedom and well-being.*

And now, finding ourselves in Sturgis almost a year later, it was clear that things were mostly fine. Few people were now ill, and no one seriously.

And our acquaintance at the curio shop was saying she resented how the pretty little town and the people who came from across the country to be present with one another had been so misrepresented in the media.

I was struck at how completely back to normal things were in Sturgis, in a state where the governor, had declared "I don't have the right to close anyone's business." South Dakota struck me as one of those few places left in America where people still moved, talked, and smiled like Americans, a state that had not been traumatized: a state that had never been "locked down."

The nice young woman in the curio shop told us everyone was looking forward to the next biker rally.

———

Obviously, none of this is to suggest there were not actual dangers. As noted, peer-reviewed studies indeed showed that you should not sit at close range speaking directly to people face-to-face for fifteen minutes or more in an unventilated room. Nor did it seem wise, based on those studies, to gather in tight dense crowds when there was a serious respiratory disease circulating.

But all risk is relative and all risk is personal, as we used to know.

What I am saying is that "the science," as it was presented by the CDC and The New York Times, and repeated in talking points in news outlets around the country, failed to give Americans solid, honest data or an accurate explanation of real risk. It grossly inflated the certainty of cause and effect and levels of risk to the otherwise healthy population as a whole.

As a result, readers of The New York Times — like my mom, my friends, my loved ones — endured emotional suffering. Here was mental dysregulation throughout the country, on a very broad scale.

———————

I kept trying to explain to those in my circle what was wrong with the articles that kept coming out in The Times, but it did not matter. I tried to explain that serious scientists were challenging the methods and statements of the FDA and Dr. Fauci and the CDC, but it did not matter.

My beloved elderly relatives were isolated in their homes, refusing to go out or even to chat with a neighbor even at a distance.

The articles they read in The Times helped to establish a "virtue" in popular culture (which soon became a popular religion or cult).

That is to say, it helped to establish the notion of "better" and "more valuable" and "cleaner" educated New York Times *readers who were willing to embrace being alone indoors, ordering from Amazon, observing CDC guidance, masking and double-masking, and worshipping Dr. Fauci's pronouncements. These virtuous souls were pitted against another group, who most certainly did not read* The Times *and in any case tended to do things very differently.*

This other group, so looked down upon by the elites, kept gathering and worshipping, taking responsibility for their own health decisions and using their best common sense. This group continued to live pretty normally, witness events in real life dimensions, and stay in human contact. It is true that many in both groups got sick; many died. But the two different belief systems and lifestyles did not determine the different people's fates.

All the while, the other group stayed inside, some for almost two years, alone, or with a few loved ones. As in Plato's allegory of the cave, all that was left for them was to read the world via projections of the fire on the cave wall.

This group, sheltered and isolated, grew more and more vulnerable, impressionable, gaslit, subjective; in the end, some became severely mentally ill. Many got COVID anyway, sadly; as mentioned, many tragically died.

Yet The Times-*reading group went on in their submission and isolation, increasingly believing themselves to be the "clean" ones, the virtuous ones, the redeemed.*

CHAPTER ELEVEN

HOW MASKS SUPPRESS THE HUMAN ADVANTAGE

Knowing what we now know about how Big Tech resents the human advantage, and seeks to kill it off, the fetish that came to surround masks takes on new meaning.

It was increasingly clear masking was a threat in some ways to physical health.[225]

But, if anything, its effects on emotional health were even more harrowing.

Online I saw a commentator named Megan Mansell enumerating the ways "masking" was counterproductive, even potentially damaging, and reached out to interview her.

For me, that interview was pivotal. It confirmed with telling specificity my sense that the "mask mandates" already in place in state after state were a disaster — not just potentially dangerous, especially to children, but illegally dangerous.

Mrs. Mansell has served as a Florida-based district-education director managing "special-populations integration." Her program serves students who are profoundly disabled, immunocompromised, or autistic, and includes "other challenging placements." As she explained, she is experienced in writing and monitoring protocol implementation under full ADA and OSHA compliance. She also has a background in hazardous environments and PPE applications, which includes knowing how and why which masks and respirators work.

By now I was distraught about a nine-year-old child I loved, who was being forced to wear a mask all day at school.

"Mrs. Mansell," I began, "tell me what you feel about the science behind masks. Are they useful?" I asked.

Mrs. Mansell: What I believe we have more than anything is a large number of people who newly feel they identify as immunocompromised and feel unrepresented by the public sector. And then we've had a PPE misapplication.

Here is what I mean: COVID particles are the size of 0.06 to 0.14 microns when there's a pressurized exhale. Behind that mask, you're taking any droplet and you can force-filter and aerosolize that droplet; added to that, there are already aerosols being generated within that respiratory outburst — whether it's a plosive-force-generating event like a cough, a sneeze or a scream, or if it's just general respiration.

But the droplet can then be forced-filtered through a mask or respirator, depending on the fit and on the amount of pressure being released.

But then you're taking what would have otherwise fallen in a predictable six foot arc [if you were not wearing a mask], and you're sending it now, with a mask aerosolizing it, into an eighteen- to twenty-foot trajectory, where it remains aloft within respiratory range for hours.

At the beginning, the CDC and the World Health Organization came out and said, "We believe this is solely a droplet based pathogen." So all of our mitigation measures were based solely on droplet based pathogens. But when we introduced airborne into the mix, there was never a pivot at any of our nation's test sites or testing facilities.

In the outside world you don't have restricted airflow, and so I don't think outside we need to be taking anywhere near the precautions that we are. And: are you outside huddled under a pergola with sixty people who are transmissively positive? Or are you across the basketball court huddled in a mask, mad that somebody across the basketball court is not also in a mask or passing them on the sidewalk and mad that they are not wearing a mask?

Naomi: You are confirming what I as a non-scientist understood. I changed how I lived my life after having read the aerosol studies. I don't want to be huddled face-to-face with someone who's symptomatic for 10 to 30 minutes, even outside. However, if there's a walkway which is completely desolate, along a river front or waterfront, but my governor says I have to wear a mask walking along there, is that nonsensical?

Mrs. Mansell: That is nonsensical. Also, the person who is trying to protect themselves, their immune function has a lot to do with it. How healthy are you? At the beginning of this, somebody should have come out and said: Some of you are going to die. Some of you are going to take added risk that you shouldn't have; you will designate yourself incorrectly and some of you will be wrong just as some of you are wrong every time you get behind the wheel of a car — just as some of you were wrong every time you engage in high risk sports activities and things of that nature.

But we've taken free will and personal risk mitigation out of the conversation, and especially educated personal risk mitigation; and we're telling people use this mask — we're handing it out at health departments — but it's something that expressly and by design does not protect people from the pathogen at hand. That would be analogous. According to the Americans with Disabilities Act, you cannot discriminate against people who can't wear masks or won't wear masks.

Naomi: Our Governor Cuomo proposed a vaccine passport. Those are discriminatory under the Americans with Disabilities Act?

Mrs. Mansell: Those are. Under ADA, you don't get to know what's wrong with somebody else. Also, under IDEA, all children within the American school districts have a right to the least restrictive educational environment. There are children required to wear helmets with preexisting biting conditions who were 350 pounds; and they want you to try to keep a mask on them all day. It would be horrifying for the nonverbal child, who's not understanding what you're doing to them and why.

And medical consent is required in the use of any kind of mitigating apparatus, in addition to medical clearance within workplaces, under OSHA. By law, you can't force someone to wear a mask.

Cloth masks are expressly non-mitigating, expressly "non-PPE" under OSHA, so they should not be required for airborne pathogens in any workplace.

And certainly masks are expressly non-mitigating for airborne pathogens; they are porous by design and are for catching splatter or large droplets in close proximity settings for blood borne pathogens, like dental practices and surgery settings.

Naomi: So it's actually against the Americans with Disabilities Act to discriminate in any way between mask wearing people and not-mask wearing people? And you pointed out that it's against the law in terms of medical consent to ask anyone if they've been vaccinated or allow them in or out of settings based on their status?

Mrs. Mansell: Yes, it is illegal.

Naomi: I've also been hearing from parents of kids who have hearing disabilities, kids with autism, kids who are on the spectrum; they are worried that kids with any kind of learning challenges, or hearing challenges, can't learn; their social-emotional learning is impaired, and their brain development is impaired, by not being able to see people's faces.

Mrs. Mansell: That's so important. I was going to take it back to infant development and young childhood development too, because so much of what you garner for social and emotional and language development involves teeth, tongue and lip placement for language development.

So much of our expressions and our social understanding is from mimicking caregiver expressions. And so, you're going to have a lot of children identify as on the spectrum who otherwise wouldn't have just because they don't have the ability to see faces to mimic those expressions, and those therapies are extensive that will be required.

I've been observing children losing expression on their lower faces and losing appropriate eye contact because there's nothing to see, and losing the ability to pick up social cues, and losing communication skills. I don't think that anybody should have to wear a mask if they don't want to. I think that human touch and personal interaction and presence and proximity are important, no matter how immunocompromised you are. And I've seen the really depressing side of children who spent years in isolation, and I don't wish for that on anybody.

There exist zero efficacy standards for a child-size mask, because if you see a mask on a child it is untested; it probably was some homemade unsterile thing that likely does nothing for anything close to the COVID size particulates. However, it anonymizes the child and makes them unable to even communicate.

Naomi: It sounds as if a lot of how this has rolled out is illegal.

Mrs. Mansell: It is a violation of IDEA.[226] That's the federal education integration law. That's what people should be using to push back against their school systems.

Naomi: You said masks aerosolize what would otherwise be droplets. If we don't wear masks, if God forbid we're infected, the droplets will fall within six feet. But when we wear a mask, we aerosolize that contagious material and it can go further and hang out longer in the air — is that what you're saying?

Mrs. Mansell: Yes, and I have excellent citations on that. Hospitals are giving N95 masks to COVID-positive patients upon release, and those masks produce this complete jet stream of focused particulates and are ineffective exhale filtration for aerosols. Those do not filter particles under 4 microns and so certainly not COVID particles at 0.06 to 0.14 microns. So the COVID particulate is just sent out in a pressurized stream. It is so bad.

People are providing their own masks, and the situation is dangerous. I visited the same girl working in a grocery store, over a two-week period. She wore the same filthy surgical mask, while she was handling leaky chicken packages and counting money. And she was adjusting the mask constantly — the same mask for two weeks.

And she's lucky that she's alive. I mean, Legionnaires' Disease and a whole host of other disgusting things are in there: microbial challenges, as well as deoxygenating and hypercapnia-inducing effects, are there.

Naomi: What are some things that can happen to you from wearing a mask for two weeks?

Mrs. Mansell: The fibers can come loose and your body cannot shake them free. Fibrosis is a very real concern there. Deoxygenation is when you have a lower access to respiratory inhaled oxygen for an extended period of time and with hypoxia you have increased inhaled CO2 levels.

You also have the microbial challenges of not only what you wipe on a mask or if you are wearing a mask in a public restroom and you pick up particulate from that disgusting flush plume. But then also your body is constantly trying to get rid of things, whether it's a pathogen, whether it's if you cough or you sneeze. Your expiration — that is, what you are breathing out — is what your body is *rejecting*. What you are breathing out is what your body is trying to get rid of. And so when you wear a mask you're constantly cycling that back into your body.

We need to be really conscious about the effects of masks and deoxygenation on human development, both for children and for the unborn. We have stillbirth rates up fourfold in developed countries, and in the mask-happy countries, we have an estimated 300,000 fewer births this year. Three hundred thousand fewer human beings are coming into the world. These babies are being lost and never had a chance, because their mothers needed to keep their jobs and are being required to wear these masks for eight, ten hours a day. I've had three children; I know what a sensitive process pregnancy is.

And to require something that never would have passed an ethics review before, it's a real tragedy. It's something that the working class has no recourse in relation to right now. And they're the ones that this will affect more than anybody else.

Naomi: Do you have evidence that there is a correlation between stillbirth or miscarriages and hypoxia from wearing masks?

Mrs. Mansell: We know that there are many birth conditions that can be from deoxygenation during birth, and during late pregnancy. Cerebral palsy is the big one that everybody is familiar with. But we are not saying, "Hey, a lot of kids got cerebral palsy from an umbilical cord being twisted or wrapped around their necks during birth, and they have lifelong effects from this deprivation of oxygen." So why aren't we considering the impacts on the unborn of create the same effect throughout that entire child's gestation period?

We don't yet have studies on what deoxygenation from mothers' masks does to fetuses and babies because it's such a new thing. It's a huge experiment on humanity. But I am confirming that there's a higher rate of stillbirth and miscarriage in moms who wore masks.

When you're giving birth, so much of what happens in the American obstetrical system is to keep your baby from losing oxygen as it passes down the birth canal. We know that even a minute with low oxygen can cause lifetime irreparable damage to newborn babies or to fetuses. So many C-sections come about from the baby losing oxygen and the heart rate slowing. When oxygen levels drop for the baby, that mom has to be rushed into a C-section because that baby cannot be without oxygen for more than a very short time or else there's permanent brain damage.

Now, we're seeing that baby inside that pregnant mom has to have decreased oxygen for hours a day for nine months. And mothers-to-be are masked now while they are giving birth — while the baby needs oxygen the most.

Naomi: Walk us through why humans need oxygen and why babies in utero need oxygen.

Mrs. Mansell: Oxygen fuels your cells. It's what keeps every cell in your body alive. And it's also what keeps cells dividing in utero. The supply of blood-based oxygen from the umbilical cord — from the mother to the baby — is a process that you wouldn't want to try to stem. To stem oxygen from the umbilical cord means that fewer nutrients are getting to the child.

Some women have jobs during pregnancy where they are exerting themselves. So exerting yourself while wearing a mask means you're breathing more CO_2 and more CO_2.

Naomi: I can't help remembering the warnings we were given when we were little, when you were told, "Do not breathe into a paper bag." If you breathed into a paper bag, our parents warned us, then you were breathing your exhaled breath, and you could pass out.

Mrs. Mansell: There's a reason you pass out. You pass out because your brain needs oxygen all the time and not CO_2. So by replacing oxygen with CO_2, you're starving your brain of something it needs to keep you alert, to keep your blood flowing.

———

I struggled to wear masks. Within moments I felt weak and dizzy. Like many people with mobility issues, I have something called "oxygen deficit." Many people who struggle to walk, whether from a health issue, a mobility issue, age or obesity, have an "oxygen deficit."

But by now masks were fetishes. If you adjusted your mask in public or pulled it away from your face to breathe, someone — including government officials in government buildings such as the town hall or the DMV — would gesture officiously, with that suddenly-everywhere gesture demanding that you pull your mask up over your nose.

I met an Iranian woman who said that this gesture — "Cover your nose! Cover your nose!" — was exactly the kind of gesture as the one that the morals police would use in demanding that women tug their head coverings down over their hair so as to conceal any stray strand that may have escaped.

"I left Iran and came to America to be free of that kind of thing," she said furiously.

It didn't matter now if you had trouble walking or breathing. Mask up!

We used to be so nice, because free people are nice. But now we were becoming authoritarian and casually cruel. We were now a one-size-fits-all country, without "exemptions," and so without systemic kindness.

There is a fable called "Stone Soup" in which a traveler claims to be able to create a delicious soup magically by putting a stone in water. But he also calls for a little meat and a few vegetables. Suddenly there is a delicious "stone soup."

I kept thinking of that fable but recast in a negative context. The virus wasn't the endgame. The vaccines were not the endgame. The endgame was to transform our countries.

We had been people who respected privacy; now we had become people who monitored the bodies of others. We had been kind, generous people with public morals that were truly decent; now we had become people who tolerated and supported cruelty. We had been people who accepted individual needs and requirements; now we had become people who could not accept or tolerate individual need, individual variation, indeed people who rolled right over it without compassion.

We were internalizing the monstrous. Stone soup.

As 2021 unfolded, I began to see children losing expression in their faces, as Mrs. Mansell had warned. A now-ten-year-old child I love became harder and harder to understand when he spoke. As with kids with learning disabilities, it became an effort to understand many children without learning disabilities.

Children looked lethargic. In early 2021 I had written online: "Today it is one or two layers. What if tomorrow they 'mandate' more layers? What if they 'mandate' enough layers that you pass out?" I thought I was being rhetorical but some months later, my stepson's school sent parents a notice that if children could not remember to "wear their masks properly" or "distance," they would receive "physical reminders" including a punishment of "double masking."

This seemed like straight-up child abuse to me.

My reaction was not only instinctive, but also the result of exposure to research establishing that reading facial expressions, touching and imitating one another at close range are essential to learning to be human.

Neurologists have learned the extraordinary communicative gifts of the human face. We have forty-three muscles in our faces, and our faces communicate even before we are consciously aware of our communication. This is due to our nearly magical ability to "mirror" other humans' emotions even below the level of our own awareness. It is automatic. As notes Chris Frith, in "Role of Facial Expressions in Social Interactions," "spoken language plays such an important role that we often forget about the importance of non-

verbal signals. Among these non-verbal signals, facial expressions have a major part in social interactions."[227]

No one at that point had looked into the effects of schools across the country forcing children into masks, of denying them access to the expressions of others, of restricting free breathing, of eight hours a day struggling to breathe, laboring for enough oxygen.

"One cannot think well, love well, sleep well, if one has not dined well," said Virginia Woolf. She understood the relationship of the satiation of the body to free thought and daring expression.

And surely: you cannot write a symphony while struggling for breath. You cannot write a novel if you cannot freely breathe. You cannot even think clearly and freely, let alone at a complex level, if you are struggling for oxygen. Your thinking is reduced to animal survival.

This coercion of people into masks, and the madness that resulted in 2020–22 is in fact analogous to the political role of anorexia — of forcing people to struggle against their impulses, their appetites; forcing them always to be focused on maintaining a level of unnatural deprivation. As I pointed out in The Beauty Myth, *you cannot write well, argue well, if you are faint or hungry. A mask is like a corset. You can't be brave or fight or debate or follow a delicate thought, as Woolf puts it in another context, if you can't easily, freely inhale. You can't dream if you can't exhale. You create a world of humans struggling for oxygen.*

It was bizarre to see the expectation that mothers-to-be must be "masked" as they were in labor. Everyone in the birthing community teaches the critical importance of breathing correctly, for safe births. That well-documented central belief was dropped by the right-on obstetric and doula community overnight.

It was bizarre to see masked yoga practitioners, and to witness the yoga industry not resisting this imposition in any way. The millennia-old understanding of "prana" — the Sanskrit word for "breath" or "life force" — as the key to healing and emotional equilibrium was abandoned overnight.

In forcing people, especially children, to restrict their breath, there was also created a world better suited for the domination of humans by machines, tech platforms, and ultimately by the Chinese Communist Party and totalitarianism generally. Because once you've lost the human advantage of the human face and human freely breathing imagination, you have created a world without empathy.

But masking, above all, makes "IRL" — "in real life" — intolerable; and it makes people race indoors where they can breathe freely, alone with a screen.

CHAPTER TWELVE

THE TECH BUBBLE: VAST WEALTH VIA KILLING HUMAN COMPETITION

E ven as the near-universal "masking" continued to sow division, it further served Big Tech, and the leadership in China, by training the population in obedience and accustoming people to surrender both their human capital and their assets. In short, the world of tech used governments as their handmaidens to wage a war of "restrictions" against — the human race. The result of this was both profits — and damage — nearly beyond human imagining.

Now, via "mask mandates," brilliantly and at a stroke Big Tech had created a world that neutered the power and appeal, the complexity and communicativeness, of the miraculous human face. It had achieved a world that blunted the advantage of the lively, curious human face against those less subtle or responsive. In substituting the "emotions" generated by machines for those of humans, Big Tech had built a cruder world lacking in the deeper understanding that depends on expression and nuance, speech and breathing.

Intentionally or not, the "lockdown" policies had worked to blunt the human advantage, not just in the short term, but also deeply into the future. By limiting children's opportunities to play and by restricting their capacity to see faces and interact socially, by keeping them from school and teaching them to shy away from touch, the 2049 generation had paid a disastrous price in form of the loss of both human and Western legacies.

Indeed, by the end of 2021, after nearly two "masked" years, a study conducted by researchers at Brown University and Rhode Island Hospital reported that the mean IQ score for children born during the pandemic was over twenty-points lower than the averages of prior generations. Reduced interaction, missed educational opportunities and lost opportunities for "creative play," all served to "impact child neurodevelopment."[228] As the study's authors concluded:

> We find that children born during the pandemic have significantly reduced verbal, motor, and overall cognitive performance compared to children born pre-pandemic. Moreover, we find that males and children in lower socio-economic families have been most affected. Results highlight that even in the absence of direct SARS-CoV-2 infection and COVID-19 illness, the environmental changes associated COVID-19 pandemic is significantly and negatively affecting infant and child development.[229]

I spent almost a decade in the "tech space," and seven years as the CEO of a tech company, building digital products. I saw firsthand how, for tech companies, human society is the competitor against which it is vital to strategize.

From Facebook to Twitter to Salesforce to Microsoft Teams to Zoom, most digital platforms seek to persuade people to stop doing something "IRL" (in real life) and instead to do it on that digital platform. It is their business model. They are in the business of targeting private, community-based, human time and space.

While this has always been so, pre-2020 humans still did most things together. When we worshipped in church, when our children were in a classroom, when we attended a town hall meeting, *no data was being generated.* Tech companies saw themselves as losing money every time humans gather in "humane/analog" spaces. This is the reason why a favorite buzzword in tech CEO circles is "disruptive." The primary thing every digital company wants to "disrupt" is a human society from which they are not profiting.

The more that tech platforms and policies are able to shut down human community, and restrict the freedom of humans, the wealthier the Big Tech corporations become.

The goal of almost all tech companies is to gather either "eyeballs," allowing the tech company to sell advertising, or data, whereby they harvest every keystroke you generate on the site and sell that information to advertisers, insurance agencies, marketers, hospital chains, and so on. This unseen market of data purchasing and data warehousing is vast almost beyond imagining. The business model for Zoom (which has servers based in China) is your data and your attention. (The lack of security of Zoom[230] and other similar platforms was the reason that the renowned cybersecurity expert Steven Waterhouse referred to the "lockdown" of 2020 as a "hack" of the intellectual property and data of the West.[231])

The business model for Nintendo is your attention (eyeballs). The business model for Microsoft is your data, subscriptions to its software, and your attention (eyeballs). The business model for Microsoft Teams is a subscription. The business model for Microsoft's educational offerings is data and license sales of the software to school districts.

All these business models gained massive advantages via the suppression of human community and free assembly during the "pandemic."

While the pandemic edicts had no science behind them, from the tech-CEO perspective they ensured that humans — with virtually no "analog/humane" space or culture left, no way to feel comfortable simply gathering in a room, touching one another as friends or allies, or joining together — were almost wholly reliant on digital technology.

Driving all human interaction onto Zoom and other not-always secure platforms was not only a way to harvest all our data, it was a way to ensure (as face-to-face human connection withered and died) that what passes for intimacy and connection in the future will increasingly be online.

It was as if the world had been redesigned by Klaus Schwab in promotion of "The Great Reset". Culture is the great source of strength and fortitude of the human species. But after a year of no worship, no Passover, no Christmas, no school, no Boy Scouts or Girls Scouts, no prom, no Neapolitan chitchat with pizza vendors, no New York chitchat with hot dog vendors, no new openings on Broadway, no galas, no jazz groups improvising, no humans actually meeting unexpectedly, there was nothing to write or sing about, nothing to remember, no history to tell our kids; and the kids hardly even knew there was a world outside their rooms. Culture requires human contact to replicate and develop, and when you isolate humans and don't educate or socialize kids, then culture dies, to be readily replaced by online or CDC (or CCP) directives.

Meanwhile, forbidding assembly kept us from forming human alliances against these monstrous interests. "In a world marked by great uncertainty and volatility," Schwab remarked in 2017 in introducing the brutal Xi Jinping, whom he regularly features as a model leader, "the international community is looking to China to continue its responsive and responsible leadership."[232] Little wonder that such Schwab allies and confederates as New Zealand's Prime Minister Jacinda Ardern (a WEF Young Global Leaders alumna) and Canada's Prime Minister Justin Trudeau (half of whose cabinet, Schwab once boasted, were WEF alumni[233]) would align with tech companies to crack down on free thought and human assembly.[234]

Forbidding human assembly has the effect, and the intent, of preventing new cultures and new business models from arising. By early 2022, we were all still basically stuck with the connections and ideas we had in March of 2019.

Forcing kids to distance at school and wear masks further ensured a generation of Americans who don't know *how* to form human alliances, indeed don't trust their own human instincts, while driving all learning onto distance learning platforms ensured that kids would not know how to behave in human spaces, which are not mediated by technology.

Those are counterrevolutionary training techniques.

In the pre-masking, pre-2020 past, human connection was the norm. People had new and surprising experiences as a matter of course, enriching their own base of understanding and knowledge. Train travel and plane travel mixed up left and right, African-American and Caucasian, rich and poor, techies and journalists, farmers and teachers. The beauty of public spaces where people can breathe and talk unhindered is that they break up encapsulated social and demographic networks. Ideas and knowledge brush up against each other, cultures merge, and new businesses, new ideas, new alliances, and organic new histories are created.

But when that human technology of public space, with breath and speech intact, is broken — as masks and distancing broke and disabled it entirely — people are reduced to machine algorithms for understanding their worlds. Progressives were fed only progressive ideas by the algorithm on their social media; they never bumped into a conservative with whom they could speak easily on a train, at church, or on a plane. Conservatives were fed only conservative ideas; they could never sit for five hours next to someone they liked and with whom they enjoyed speaking, but who would also challenge their ideas. We became even more divided and managed culturally by digital ghosts, by shadows, and by codes. Anything could be said about "the other side" and we were at risk of believing it, because "masking" ensured that those chance, stray conversations that continually educate and surprise free humans, and which constantly undermine tendentious propaganda and ideologies, could not happen.

Indeed, what could be more dangerous to a democratic nation's health than forcing upon its children an extended tutorial on the need for absolute and unquestioning compliance to authority, even when the commands make no logical or ethical sense?

Why develop policies that punish, encumber and restrict human contact in humane/analog (unsurveilled, unmediated) spaces? Because human contact is the great revolutionary force underlying human freedom.

———————

We are relentlessly encouraged by tech companies to think of their technology as enabling human processes, making human actions more efficient. Do your bookkeeping better! Find a restaurant more easily! Talk to a loved one far away!

In fact, the business models of most tech giants, and especially social media giants, most thrive when they have *replaced* human experience and human actions.

And now they have moved on to *suppressing* human experience and human actions.

Amazon wants to persuade you that it is not fun or worthwhile for you to go to your local supermarket or to window-shop in the mom and pop shops on Main Street. Amazon is competing with the pleasure you get from chatting with a checkout clerk, or the unexpected treat of bumping into a neighbor in the supermarket aisle, and even with the small mood boost you get from dreamily gazing at a pile of scarlet mangoes or green avocados and the sensory inputs you receive from picking up the fragrant mango to inhale the scent or running a finger along the rough-smooth avocado to check its ripeness.

In 2019, Amazon's revenues were $280.52 billion. By the end of the first "lockdown" year, *Amazon's revenue was up $105.54 billion* (Figure 2).[235]

Indeed, from 2020 to 2022, the massive realignment in wealth and investment that took place left the five biggest companies in the world, save one Saudi energy company, as tech companies; all are worth more than $1 trillion.[236]

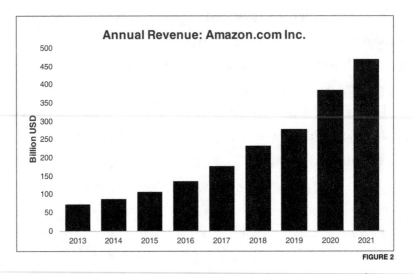

Annual Revenue: Amazon.com Inc.

FIGURE 2

Etsy and Craigslist are competing with the excitement of country drives to real garage sales and auctions, and with the pleasure you get from touching old wood or admiring the shading of paint in real paintings. They compete with the pleasure of attending physical auctions and the excitement you might get from outbidding other humans in a room.

Etsy's business press speaks openly about the boom in profits it sustained as a result of "Lockdown": "'People had to turn to Etsy over the past year . . . The company guided revenue growth of about 10% year-over-year for the fourth quarter, or between $660 million and $690 million . . . people flocked to the site to buy pandemic essentials, like face masks." "The whole conversation since then has been, 'once the world reopens, how much of that will you lose, how much of that will you give up?' and that was a fair thing to ask," the CEO, Josh Silverman said.[237] The business press is open about how "lockdown" policies drove certain sectors' profits.

Etsy's revenue in 2019 was $818.79 million. By the end of the first "lockdown" year, it was up to $1.725 billion: Etsy was in the billion-dollar Silicon Valley club. Its revenues had *more than doubled in a year* (Figure 3).[238] Etsy's initial business model was to offer cute, original handmade, or eclectic goods that small businessowners and craftspeople traditionally offer in little shops. But when you kill off all the little shops, those small craftspeople and one-woman boutique owners have nowhere else to transact than Etsy. A "lockdown" in which small boutiques must close makes a $906 million win for you and your shareholders. In one year.

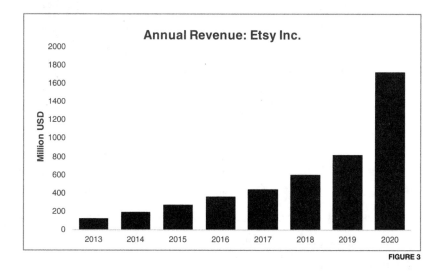

FIGURE 3

Nintendo competes with real bowling leagues, real baseball games, real hiking clubs, real poker tournaments, real billiards halls. Nintendo's sales were $9.96 billion in 2018, $10.91 billion in 2019, $12.12 billion in locked-down 2020; and $15.99 billion in masked, distanced 2021 — a high that the company had not been able to attain since 2010. The "lockdown" years brought Nintendo, quite literally, billions of dollars in new revenue.[239]

Look what happened to Nintendo during the two years your child was prevented from being maskless on a sports team, hanging out with friends unmasked at school, or in any way playing normally with peers: forbidden to play with cards, puzzles, hockey sticks, basketballs, pool tables, ice skates, soccer balls, or footballs — to play or any other sport or game with friends, unmasked (Figure 4).[240]

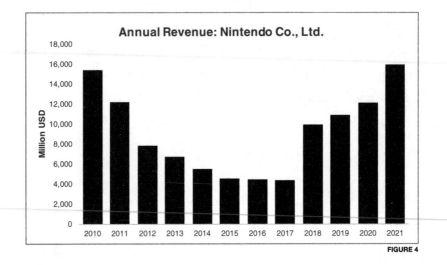

FIGURE 4

"Lockdown" in which children were especially targeted and forcibly masked, saved Nintendo as a moneymaker for its sharehold-ers. The end of the second "lockdown" year, a year in which kids, desperate to breathe, left the blanked-out, muffled faces of their peers, with whom they could have no fun whatsoever, to flee for relief to their rooms so they could breathe freely, and numb their loneliness with a video game — what happened to Nintendo's sales then? The company was up another third of its former total and was racing profitably away from a mid-2010s slump.

What about Apple?

When your kids couldn't talk to their friends in person — when no one could easily talk to anyone in person, we all took out our phones. And for hundreds of millions of us, it was an iPhone. Look at Apple. A vast spike showed in the first quarter of "lockdown," with all of 2021 nearly *double Q3 of 2019 and Q1 of 2022 more than triple Q3 of 2019* (Figure 5).[241]

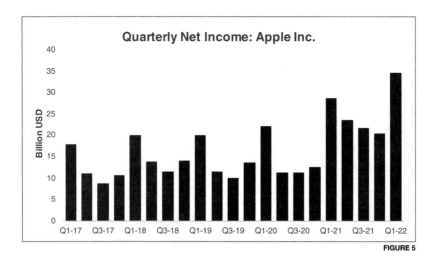

FIGURE 5

I remember standing masked in a hotel, waiting for an elevator, next to another masked woman. Under ordinary conditions we would have smiled, chatted and shared some small talk in the elevator about what shows to see at what museums, or about a great restaurant nearby.

She "smiled with her eyes." I "smiled with my eyes," And of course, since it was going to be awkward in the elevator now, we both took out our phones.

That moment, reproduced around the world, for two years, led to the doubling and in some cases the tripling of income for some tech companies.

So "lockdowns" and "masking" made the whole world and all of human interaction an awkward moment, in which you reach for your phone.

As CNBC reported: "Over the past year, Apple and Microsoft got within arm's reach of a $3 trillion market cap, while . . . Facebook parent company Meta both reached the $1 trillion milestone for the first time."[242]

This is what happened to Microsoft's net income during the two years that everyone was forced indoors and children were kept home from school. Just before the pandemic, its net income was $39.24 billion. What was it after two years of "lockdown," after local and federal governments around the world were forced onto Microsoft Teams to deliberate, when almost no one could visit a human physical office and "Microsoft Education" offered webinars for helpless teachers forced to communicate with each other online,[243] Microsoft's net income went from $39.24 billion to $61.27 billion in two years. Shutting your child inside and closing down human society reaped an increase in annual net income of over twenty-two billion dollars (Figure 6).[244]

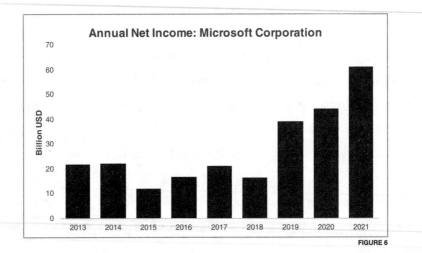

FIGURE 6

And Google? When people are forced indoors and can't ask for directions from other humans, or for restaurant or car-wash recommendations, and can't go to town halls to find out what is happening in their communities and can't ask humans for recipes or hear new jokes from them, and when people across the nation have to sign into Google[245] to get their results from a COVID test they took at Rite Aid, you can see what happens (Figure 7).[246]

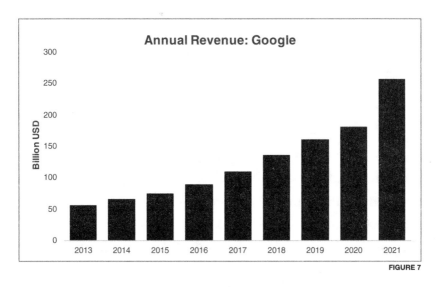

Annual Revenue: Google

FIGURE 7

Educational software? I had known the "space" of distance learning since I analyzed it on behalf of Barnard College's Athena Center for Women and Leadership in 2015. I had also researched creating virtual classes for my own tech company, DailyClout.io. Indeed, a truism of the virtual-university field before the pandemic was that it was difficult to earn substantial money from educational platforms since human students so preferred being in human classrooms with human peers and teachers.

My report in 2015 concluded that Barnard College should not bother with existing distance-learning options as they were unpopular with students and faculty and they did not yield revenues. Coursera, the model distance-learning company, was my object lesson. Coursera was not profitable then. The company stayed massively unprofitable, but the pandemic boosted growth.

Revenue in 2020 increased fifty-nine percent over the prior year. Because the Coursera management were geniuses? No — because millions of students around the world could no longer go to university or college.[247]

The "lockdown" made this multi-million-dollar loser ripe for a staggering valuation and IPO.

"[A]ccording to its SEC filings, its 2020 revenue was $294 million. Its workforce more than doubled. And it kept expanding overseas. Its 77 million learners come from 190 countries," reported Forbes.com.[248]

The company, which benefited from the fact that people were forced to stay indoors and universities were forced to close, went public in March 2021. Its final pre-IPO valuation stood at *$3.6 billion.*[249] "It's now worth nearly $7 billion," reports *Forbes*.[250]

How is "distance learning" growing so fast? A better question: Why did so many schools and universities send their students home, when children are at almost no risk of serious outcomes from COVID-19 and young adults also are at little risk?

Many parents rightfully, and desperately, wondered exactly this.

The reason, in many cases, that schools and universities promoted "distance learning," is that they were paid to do so. Coursera paid $281 million to its 200 university and industry "partners," close to its $294 million in revenue. Usually, it is the customers that pay for the software, but not in this model.[251] The universities create content, and they get paid by Coursera per student, which incentivizes colleges and universities to create "hybrid" learning programs and not just let young adults be humanly present, with no extra royalties coming in, in school or on campus.

Given a choice, most students of course would have preferred in-person learning to being forced to learn online. But they were not given a choice. Given those kinds of numbers, and the deals being done between distance-learning platforms and universities, the phrase "hybrid learning" is going to hound us into the future, pandemic or not. It is unlikely that schools and universities will ever escape the much-promoted "hybrid" model, unless there is a citizen and student revolt.

So much money is low-hanging fruit for Big Tech, if only your child can continue to be kept away from the school lab and sports field and drama club, her friends and her teachers, and shut away safely in her room.

Apple, Microsoft, Alphabet, Amazon, Tesla, and Facebook added a combined *$2.9 trillion* to their collective market capitalizations in 2021, according to data from FactSet. At the end of 2020:

Apple was up 30 percent.

Microsoft was up 50 percent.

Alphabet (Google's parent company) was up 65 percent.

Amazon was up 6 percent.

Meta (Facebook) was up 20 percent.[252]

This dizzying boom, indeed, began to slow only in Q1 of 2022, when people in many American states began in earnest to return to normal life and a movement finally pushed back against restrictions. Policies issued by governors, policed by social media sites with conflicts of interest and enforced by bought-off universities had overnight killed off much of the competition of human-to-human learning, and left devastatingly maimed the beautiful classroom of the "old order."

On July 7, 2021, *I posted a video of Brian reading aloud Dr. Ralph Baric's CV. A University of North Carolina researcher, Dr. Baric had received millions of dollars in gain-of-function research funding from the NIH. I pinned the résumé itself as well.*

Within twenty-four hours, the video had 70,000 views.

A day later, in another hotel room, I read a video of a press release by State Senator Kim Thatcher of Oregon, who would call for an investigation into the misrepresentation of data by the CDC.

As I sought to post the press release, Twitter showed me that my account had been suspended.

We were now in the midst of a great swath of censorship and "cancellations" by Big Tech. President Trump had been kicked off of Twitter. Ben Shapiro warned that CNN was censoring conservatives.[253] LinkedIn censored the Harvard epidemiologist/hero Dr. Martin Kulldorff.[254] And on and on.

Big Tech was deplatforming anyone who raised questions about the mRNA vaccines. And Big Tech was deplatforming conservatives apace.

I had been suspended by Twitter temporarily twice before, so I assumed they would relent eventually, and I went to bed.

In the morning, I saw that news outlets across the English-speaking world had been attacking me with bizarre distortions of my Twitter feed. It was notably interesting that tweets I had deleted immediately for having been poorly phrased — tweets that literally did not exist — had been provided to journalists. In addition, tweets that were quotes from websites, or obvious metaphors, were presented out of context to make me sound deranged. I had quoted, for instance, the Moderna website's metaphor about "the software of life" in a tweet and responded with a metaphor — and yet I was accused in the wave of attacks of believing that the vaccines were literally "software."

I had pinned an FDA white paper that examined the possible effect of spike protein in wastewater and I satirized what was fast becoming vaccine-based segregation by joking about separating vaccinated and unvaccinated people's wastewater; this was presented as my advocating to separate the waste of these two groups.

I had posted a tweet with an image of a teddy bear which had been aimed at luring parents to vaccinate their kids, and reporters claimed that I believed teddy bears should be vaccinated.

These news outlets, many of which over the course of decades had commissioned me to write for them, did not contact me to check for accuracy, for a quote, or for my point of view.

The New Republic, *which was still even at that moment syndicating my work, ran a headline,* "The Madness of Naomi Wolf."

I was interviewed by The Sunday Times *of London, for whom I had written for years. Indeed, I had been a columnist. The young reporter, with her talking points in hand, asked me about my purported belief in "QAnon."*

It was stunning to watch a full-on digitally enhanced smear campaign unfold in real time. Journalism had changed. It was impossible to get corrections. Editors seemed cowed and helpless.

It was not surprising that journalism had so dramatically changed. Tim Schwab, writing in the Columbia Journalism Review, scrutinized the Bill & Melinda Gates Foundation and found $250 million going to media outlets, including BBC, The Atlantic, NBC, *and* The Guardian. [255]

Around the world, headlines declared that I had been deplatformed from Twitter for spreading "medical misinformation" or "vaccine myths."

Soon after, Facebook suspended my account, with its 134,000 followers. YouTube suspended my account, with its 440,000 video views. These suspensions were crippling blows to my digital reach-based company. Some investors in my company asked for their money back.

Now I was shifted rudely over to a whole new life status. I had been a secure member of influential chattering-class circles in New York and Washington. Now, like the dissident doctors, dissident scientists, and the very few dissident journalists, I was stripped of income and reputation, friend groups, and status.

I had in some ways to start over.

I couldn't complain to my senator.

Facebook had donated fifty thousand dollars to his campaign.[256]

Arriving at the train station in Washington, DC, in 2021, I got into a masked-driver taxi. Having just spent five hours on the Acela from New York City in a train filled with the elite — high-level business people and political employees, all thoroughly masked and attached to their screens rather than reading or chatting or talking on the phone, I was eager for human connection. I told the driver I didn't care if he wore a mask — he indicated miserably that he must. He spoke about how he and other cab drivers were barely surviving with so many federal employees working from home. Usually I would chat with the driver about what is happening in his home country — Ethiopia, in this case — and thus get valuable secondhand access to eyewitness accounts of events in other parts of the world. And when asked, I'd in turn offer information that I had. I was usually asked about access to affordable universities for kids.

But now that wasn't possible. After a few muffled efforts, we gave up, and each concentrated on breathing.

So I still don't know what was happening in Ethiopia, from his perspective, that day. And my driver didn't find out if I might have helped get his kids into an affordable college.

By the time I went back to New York City in January 2021, there were far fewer yellow cabs than I remembered. That industry, a cabbie told me, had been killed by "lockdown." In its place were Ubers and Lyfts, which don't give the drivers the valuable equity or chance for independence that a medallion system does. These app-based companies, not incidentally, track both drivers and passengers, creating a social credit system based on how you treat each other.

A goal of the tech elites is to create "Smart Cities," which almost no one but they wish to have. In these "reimagined" cities, your every action is mapped in a digital matrix.

By the time I went back to New York City, the human information clerks had been cleared out of all the subways, and the paper maps had been removed. You had to consult your phone — and generate data and geolocation — just to find out where you were supposed to go.

Now there were QR codes in every restaurant, so that no one would touch the germy paper menus. Customers did not realize, or perhaps no longer cared, that each time they did so they could have been geolocated and potentially connected to the others at the table swiping the code.

I sat at a restaurant with a loved one. "Can I have a paper menu?" I asked the waitress. Why? my loved one inquired, happily scanning his phone to the QR code.

"Because the QR code can scan your data and geolocate you" I replied.

"Oh my God, Naomi, does everything have to be a conspiracy?" said my loved one.

CHAPTER THIRTEEN

"VACCINE PASSPORTS" AND THE END OF HUMAN LIBERTY

B y the end of 2021, "vaccine passports" in many states and nations effectively became the passports to human life. Imposed worldwide, along with vaccine "mandates," they gave tech companies an all-encompassing historic advantage over human beings. In essence, all human experience, fellowship and joy was put behind a paywall.

Do you want to worship? See family at Thanksgiving? Have a job and feed your family? Go to the theater? Get on a long-distance train?

Not without your vaccination subscription. And your "booster" every five to eight months, probably forever, is the renewal of the subscription.

Your body is the credit card. It's what you pay with. Vaccine passports are at the heart of the transition to a world where humans are at the mercy of Big Tech and a few oligarchs.

In 2021, when they were first being floated in the United States, Canada, and the United Kingdom as "trial balloons," I had started warning publicly about the implications of "vaccine passports."

They rolled out early in Israel; Israel submitted to the "Green Pass." Within four months, the "Green Pass" had created a two-tier society.[257]

New York State and California were targeted next, then Canada.

The messaging worldwide was the same: "The vaccine passport is the key to ending the pandemic and regaining 'normal life.'"

Of course, proof of vaccination could be confirmed on a piece of paper. Were digital "passports" really needed?

As CEO of a tech company, I knew exactly why a digital version was "necessary" and the ill that fact boded. I did all I could to warn people that it signaled the potential end of human liberty. In a video that went viral, I explained that digital as opposed to paper "vaccine passports" could require endless "updates" to stay valid. How did I know this? Because a digital product can be made to shut off.

Vaccine passports were truly the last step . . . the last fight that we had to fight. Because once the vaccine passports are accepted, there is no more resistance.

When you sign up on a website or on an app, you sign your name and you choose a password. And then there's a list of terms and conditions. And you agree to them.

This seems insignificant, but it's important because what it means is you have choice. You can read the terms and conditions and you can think: "This is too tyrannical; they're going to sell my private details. I'm not willing to agree to these terms and conditions."

And the password and username mean that you get to decide when you log on to TD Bank, or when you log on to PayPal. You're not walking around your daily life logged into PayPal. You're not walking around your daily life logged into a credit score. You're in control.

With the vaccine passports, in contrast, none of that will be the case. Everyone must be participating all the time.

If you don't participate, you eventually don't get let into the supermarket to buy food. You don't get let into the pub to meet your friends. You can't get into the restaurant. You can't travel on an airplane. You can't travel on a bus. You can't travel on a train. And it's not just that you're forced to participate.

The vaccine passport platform is the first step toward a social credit system, like the one in China that enslaves a billion people.

In China, the CCP can find any dissident in five minutes because of the 360-degree surveillance of the social credit system. It means that when you act like a "good" citizen, you get a boost to your score. And when you act like a "bad" citizen, opportunities get closed to you. Maybe your child doesn't get into college or get into a prep school. Maybe you don't get that job. You don't get that promotion.

The vaccine passports being rolled out in the West could enable the same platform. Once rolled out, I warned, any other functionality could be linked to these passports within half an hour of coding.

It means that with a tweak of the backend, bank account access could be switched off and on, depending on how the underlying AI assesses what you've been saying on social media. So if you've been too conservative or too liberal, or you've used the words "President Trump" too often, or the words "pro-choice" or "Sierra Club" too often, a machine reading it could let your bank know; and your bank could switch off your access to your account, or dial up your interest on a credit card.

Microsoft and Salesforce, as I noted, proposed early versions of a vaccine passport.[258] Development of a digital passport required nationwide would be an incredibly lucrative and immensely powerful contract. The people who housed and managed this data would essentially run the world. They would be more powerful than nations.

This mechanism can also directly manage dissent. With a tweak of the backend, those who control the mechanism can be sure never to grant you a "rejoin-society" or "I don't have COVID" checkmark. You would be at the mercy of what the "passport" says about your status.

So if you're a dissident, you can always be positive for COVID without much recourse to challenge it. And you'd be in a second-class category in society for the rest of your life. Your family would too.

Let's consider a scenario. When you agree to the vaccine passports, when you go to a pub or a play or a restaurant, you will swipe that QR code.

Where does that information go? It goes to a central database, and the information of all the people who are with you, who are also swiping the code, is also going to a central database. This means that the "vaccine passport," which is really a social credit system, knows everyone who's at that table.

And if you're talking online about resistance to the system, if you're talking about staging a protest or writing an op-ed or mobilizing support for a representative to pass a bill to roll back this system, the platform can know. There's a functionality that creates maps of networks of people.

As you all swipe in your vaccine passport to that café or to that restaurant, or even in your living room, the software is geolocating you. It can also tabulate the searches you have done historically. And it can read what happened on your collective social media as a group. And you, as a group, can be blackballed. Your social credit score can dial down.

Or else you are simply all "red," not "green." Or your "shots are out of date."

It can make it impossible for you to get on a subway or a Metro or the Tube in London. It can make it impossible for you to get on a bus. It can make it impossible for you to book an Uber or to book a Lyft.

And this is not "maybe ten years down the line" or "maybe in a more dystopian society."

There is now also a global a push toward government-managed digital currencies.[259] With a digital currency, if you're not a "good citizen," if you pay to see a movie you shouldn't see, if you go to a play you shouldn't go to, which the vaccine passport will know because you have to scan it everywhere you go, then your revenue stream can be shut off or your taxes can be boosted or your bank account won't function.

There is no coming back from this.

I was asked by a reporter, "What if Americans don't adopt this?"

And I said, "You're already talking from a world that's gone if this succeeds in being rolled out." Because if we don't reject the vaccine passports, there won't be any choice. There will be no such thing as refusing to adopt it. There won't be capitalism. There won't be free assembly. There won't be privacy. There won't be choice in anything that you want to do in your life.

And there will be no escape.

In short, this was something from which there was no returning. If indeed there was a "hill to die on," this was it.

But of course my warning was to little avail; the rollout, long planned, continued apace.

By April 2021, two US states were using "vaccine passports,"[260] and the European Commission had proposed a "Digital Green Certificate to facilitate safe free movement inside the EU during the COVID-19 pandemic."[261] By July 2021, people in France could no longer travel by train or eat in restaurants without a vaccine pass.[262] By the late 2021, just as I had warned, citizens of Israel were onto their fourth booster, as the definition of "fully vaccinated" continued to evolve.[263]

———

I was invited to New Hampshire by the Republican State Representative Melissa Blasek. She warned me that forty-seven states were under emergency law. To my astonishment, the statehouse in Concord was closed. The legislators met in the unsecure convention center.

I was invited to Maine by State Representative Heidi Sampson and spoke to a group of legislators about the dangers of vaccine passports.

I was equally amazed that the statehouse in Maine was closed. A state representative sneaked me into the empty building. I looked at the august, deserted auditorium, with its empty balcony where the citizens had once watched the debates of their representatives, and participated in them.

We were hounded out of the desolate statehouse by someone from the governor's staff, who shouted at me, "You don't belong here!"

I could never have expected to experience anything like that in my lifetime.

Was this America?

I found out that the statehouse in Oregon too was closed.

I interviewed Baroness Claire Fox, a member of the House of Lords in the British Parliament. For her part, she could not believe that she and fellow legislators were expected to deliberate on not-secure Zoom and Microsoft platforms.

I thought of Steve Waterhouse, the Canadian cybersecurity expert who had said early on that the pandemic was a "hack" by China of the West.

I started a campaign called the Five Freedoms campaign, to ban vaccine passports, restore free assembly, end mask mandates, open schools, and end emergency law.

I was amazed that such a monumental story — the closing of state-houses across the country — was hardly reported at all.

CHAPTER FOURTEEN

SWITCHING YOU OFF

Before the pandemic, people did not need a subscription to enter human civilization and community. People went to church. No data were harvested. Their kids went to school. No data are harvested when a teacher reads to the class from a book or writes an equation on a blackboard. Nor were data generated when kids played together at recess, or on sports teams, or when they performed a class play, or when they stood side by side to dissect a frog or heat up a solution in a Bunsen burner in science class. That was how we spent time in "The Before Times."

When people get to decide what they want to do with their own lives, there are natural limits to the generation of data. There are only so many software programs or cool e-commerce sites or digital menstrual calendars humans will want to use, if instead they have the option to bowl with friends, dance at a wedding, pray to God in a lovely church or synagogue, go for a stroll hand in hand with a lover and breathe the sea air, watch a movie eating popcorn in a theater, or attend an orchestra.

So the goal — the taking away of the joy of human life, all the power, all the love, all the spontaneity of living in a free Western democracy, and putting it behind a paywall — was not new. Indeed, the paywall has long been the goal of many platforms in the tech world. For as important as it is to lure people onto your site, to have experiences they theoretically want or need to have, a paywall means people have to keep paying for access to those experiences.

I remember being astonished the first time I looked at Google Analytics. We had built DailyClout with the sincere mission of protecting our users' digital privacy. But logging into Google Analytics, I saw it automatically tracked data from any URL or website that Google indexes; so while I could not see the names of our users, I could see in minute breakdowns what their hobbies were; what kinds of publications they read; if they were men or women; what devices they were using to access our content; and more — all laid out in pie charts, in bar charts, in graphs.

Still, all that voracious data harvesting by Google we hoped did only nominal harm to the consumer. Yes, it was intrusive and invasive. But with your "PID" or "personal identifying details" (the tech term for your unique identification details), your name, your location, even what you searched for can all be cross-analyzed and used for any purpose the owner of that data may desire. The IP address was a substantive fig leaf that protected your privacy and veiled your online activity from stroke-by-stroke surveillance. We assumed neither Google, nor the federal government, nor any of the people who bought the data generated by your internet use were able to peek behind that last veil. I could look at the backend and see all the users on our website as an aggregate, but I was not allowed to map the names in the credit card payment-processing platform *against* the activity on our website.

The other protection you have online is the "terms of service" or "terms and conditions" — the clunky, impenetrable legal language everyone scrolls past, which, in fact, is a contract between the user and the digital platform, spelling out the limits of the platform's use of the user's data. Usually the terms of service spell out how the site will protect or not protect — that is, monetize — your data. But the need for the consumer to click the "Agree" button gives him or her ultimate control.

Both the fig leaf of the IP address, and the legal requirement of the terms of service, have stood in the way of Big Tech's ability to do what the industry organically wants to do, which is to control everything and get all data.

But the pandemic — or rather, the "lockdown," distancing, and masking allowed tech companies to at last achieve what previously had been impossible.

From the tech-world point of view, the genius of COVID restrictions is that they *are* the paywall. The vaccine is the how you swipe your credit card — with recurring payments. And the world itself is the platform.

The ultimate objective for Big Tech was a functionality — or a change in government policy — that would turn Western citizens' online rights and protections into a Chinese-style absence of online rights and protections. For internet companies, such a change would connect all user activity with actual human names and addresses. While such disclosure is standard in closed societies such as China and Iran, that is not the case in the United States and Europe — for now.

Therefore today's alliance of the US government and Big Tech is so terrifyingly dangerous. Though the business goals of a privacy-less internet and the policy goals of a freedom-less West are not identical, at key points they do converge and align.

And in a stroke, the vaccine passport moved digital citizenship in a free society — where data harvesting may be exploitive and tacky, but relatively limited — a giant technological step closer to societies like China or Iran, where private information is readily exposed, putting all at great and immediate risk.

In fact, in the wake of COVID the whole world has become a digitized platform owned by six entities that can be switched on and off at will.

Even as a vaccine passport gives governments vastly greater control over the individual, solving the problem of citizens' freedom of action in a free society, it solves for tech companies the problem of users' privacy online.

As for the leaders who are currently betraying their countries, thinking they will always have a seat at the table with these technological elites, they are badly mistaken. As much as the dissidents who dare challenge this situation, they too can be switched off at the flick of a finger. Machine learning can scan social media and switch off commentators, journalists, physicians, even dissident technologists.

Grids can be switched off. Gone.

Supply chains can be switched off. Gone.

Personalities can be switched off. On September 4, 2021, Candace Owens was told by the facilities director of a COVID test site in Aspen, Colorado, that she could not have a COVID test because of "who you are."[264]

Whole populations can be switched off.

In 2021–22, freedom was lost via vaccine passports in Europe, Canada, Australia, Israel, and many states in the United States without a shot being fired.

As I write, people are being vaccinated in flea-market lots in Lynn, Massachusetts, in buses pulling up to high schools in New Jersey, in walk-in pop-up clinics with unnamed people in gloves and masks injecting folks for free in Grand Central Station and offering them MetroCards. The same is true for PCR tests. At CVS and Walgreens you don't get any thorough documentation of where your test went or any primary records of how your test was done. When I got a PCR test result from a CVS, it was an email with a big green check mark.

Where do those records of tests and vaccinations actually go? I asked the CVS technician where my nasal swab went. He had no idea. I looked at the packaging now enclosing my nasal swab, for a clue. The lettering was in Chinese.

Does your actual test result or actual vaccination confirmation go into the actual passport built by IBM (New York State)[265] or Microsoft and Salesforce?

Who knows?

Have you seen the raw datasets? Is there any law that compels a one-to-one correspondence? Is there any way to check for errors?

No. These databases of both test results and vaccination statuses are compiled by Big Tech companies with no transparency and no accountability. They can switch you on or off at will or mark you as "exposed" to an infectious disease.

There is no way for you to check that your vaccination status is correct as the app records it. Commonly available tests offer no way for you to check that you really are "positive for COVID." (This is why many people who initially have a positive result can get a negative result with a second test from another provider).[266]

If your vaccine passport status goes from green to red, you have no recourse.

The *yes* or *no* about you no longer belongs to you. It can all be whatever the developer says it is.

The "restrictions" then had to be imposed systematically in order to separate the "new normal" isolated and culturally impoverished world from the old, joyful, liberated space on the other side of the paywall — the space and the experiences that until fall of 2020 used to be "the world" and "culture" and "humanity" in the West; a world of human community, freedom of mobility, full access to social goods.

With a vaccine "mandate," whether the actual science supports its use, such troublesome considerations as bodily autonomy, human rights, freedom of association, informed consent, and representative democracy were done away with. At the same time everything people do in the world was monetized. And as life was monetized so it needed to be tracked. And as it was tracked, it was controlled.

These policies served the CCP as much as they served Big Tech: a West "locked down," restricted, masked, and accepting of a society that discriminates based on vaccination status was a West that had forfeited its historical competitive advantage over the CCP — its individualism, its human rights, its egalitarianism, its freedom.

In the 2020–22 world, and the world of masks and distancing forever, the six largest Big Tech companies no longer needed to persuade you or lure you or invite you to abandon real town halls, real classrooms, real athletic teams, real strolls in a funky neighborhood, real chats with the grocer or with the boutique owner who knows your taste and who can compliment you on your new hairstyle, or exclaim with delight when you say that your daughter, whose name she knows, is now in middle school.

Knowing that, the "pandemic" and its masked, distanced aftermath, in which humane spaces can be closed at the edict of any random board of health, has created a world in which a vast hurdle has been overcome: the six largest Big Tech companies no longer need to compete with those spaces or those people or those chats or those smiles, because they have all been ruined.

It is a world in which emojis weigh more than smiles because smiles have been rationed. It is a world in which staying home on Zoom is a lot less miserable than going to the office "IRL." It is a world in which it's suffocating and miserable to be "IRL" with other human beings and liberating and freeing to be online with other human beings. All those new conditions go directly to the truly astonishing inflations in revenues boasted by the top six tech companies during the years of "lockdown," masks, vaccine passports, and distance learning; years that were so disastrous for the rest of us.

CHAPTER FIFTEEN

THEFT

By the summer of 2021, public health agencies were hyper-empowered to reshape society and intervene in capitalist economies in ways they never had been before. In the United States, in Australia, in New Zealand, and in Canada, public health agencies endowed with tyrannical new powers simply bypassed parliaments and Congress. It was the cleverest way to stage a slow-motion coup, one that few would notice, especially as it was being sold as in the public's interest.

On August 3, 2021, the CDC announced its "Eviction Moratorium Order," suspending evictions for a further three months.[267] A group of realtors in Alabama successfully took the CDC to the Supreme Court over this extension, but certain localities maintained protections.[268]

Most rental properties, at least before 2020, belonged to individuals—not institutions. Over 14 million of the nearly 20 million rental properties counted in the Census Bureau's 2018 Rental Housing Finance Survey were held by individual investors. In terms of rental units, while bigger institutions are more likely to own larger properties with hundreds of apartments, individual investors still lay claim to a notable share: over forty percent.[269]

Institutions can weather months without rental income. Individuals with mortgages? Not so much.

Individual investors in communities of color were among the most vulnerable to the CDC's moratoriums. As Matt Murphy, Executive Director of the NYU Furman Center, a real-estate-research institute, had warned in February 2021, the CDC eviction moratorium would destroy the asset ownership of majority-Black communities: "The last thing anyone wants to see is a repeat of the foreclosure crisis with a disproportionate impact on Black and Hispanic landlords."[270]

But for many, that is precisely what happened.

Unsurprisingly, all of this led to a massive transfer of assets from middle class and working people like restaurateurs and event-space owners, to institutional investors.

More than 110,000 eating and drinking establishments closed in 2020, because they were forced to stop transacting.[271] Many restaurant and bar owners own the buildings where they run their businesses. With forced restaurant and bar closures, these property owners, with taxes and insurance to pay, and perhaps mortgages, but with zero or little income, were desperate to sell their buildings by the first quarter of 2021.

In residential real estate, institutions couldn't hide their impact. *Slate* reported that in the first quarter of 2021 corporate investors purchased over fifteen percent of all homes for sale in the United States.[272] So-called "single-family rental" players, like Progress Residential[273] and Blackstone's spinoff company, Invitation Homes, now compete with retail buyers for the same limited housing stock, submitting above-list, all-cash offers sellers can't refuse.[274] And it's not only American companies that are buying American homes. As *The Wall*

Street Journal headline ran in April 2021, "That Suburban Home Buyer Could Be a Foreign Government."[275]

I follow real estate, because I am one of those millions of small landlords who saved up and struggled to pay the mortgage on a rental property so that I would have an otherwise nonexistent retirement income. I watched as the real-estate market in the frozen South Bronx was stopped in its tracks during the pandemic.

I watched Harlem. I watched East Harlem. I watched Chinatown. I watched what was happening upstate.

The "moratorium" via the CDC that forbade small landlords from collecting rent lasted for over six months.[276] No one who is not an institutional investor can afford to wait that long for rent. As Matt Murphy drily notes, "Owners of small properties generally have more fragile finances than larger owners who often boast more diverse portfolios of rental units."[277] For residential properties, the impacts of these CDC edicts are clear — but what about retail properties?

What did the crazy restrictions on weddings and events have to do with real estate? They drove rare and beautiful historic properties into insolvency, and thus onto the market at a discount. In my upstate area, the iconic Taconic Wayside Inn restaurant and bar in Copake Falls folded. It had been built in 1856, and Babe Ruth had sought it out as a watering hole. The owner told me bitterly how he had struggled to stay alive during "lockdown" in the face of a Board of Health that seemed determined to drive him out of business. They forbade dancing — but the establishment was a juke joint. People came there to dance. They forbade seating — he had tried to resort to offering takeout. He closed for three months just to stay alive. The Taconic Wayside Inn was a family enterprise — the owner's father had had the vision, he had bought the place, sealed up the Victorian wooden floors, and put down 1960s linoleum; the son had built the bar with his own hands.

His late wife's name was on the wall in the outdoor seating area. The Taconic Wayfair Inn had been the centerpiece of a little community. The owner showed me the beautifully welded pans hanging from a rack in the kitchen, dating back to his father's overseeing of the business; I marveled at the solidly welded bolts and at the heavy steel surfaces. These were truly heirlooms — and American-made. They did not make pans like that anymore.

Now the premises were ghostly. The owner would have one last summer to serve his friends and neighbors, before some national or global chain bought the family business at a discount and turned it into a focus-grouped Berkshires "experience."

The historic Windflower Inn in Great Barrington also folded and went on the market as a bargain. The owners, a hardworking couple who had moved heaven and earth to make the business prosper, and now had to give it all up, told me that institutional investors were buying up bed-and-breakfast properties and old hotels throughout the Berkshires.

Our mechanic friend at Jim's Auto Body told us that local people had been getting calls from unidentifiable buyers saying that they would pay cash for any properties in the area, no matter what kind.

My former superintendent in the South Bronx said that calls were coming in to owners to buy up their apartment units — in cash.

Which were the most draconian "locked down" and masked cities? San Francisco, Boston, New York, Los Angeles, Chicago: the cities where the real estate is most desirable.

The onerous "COVID" conditions drove people out and landlords suffered and were forced to sell, or residential owners had to sell at a discount in order to move to freer states. So all that beautiful inventory went into the coffers of the likes of BlackRock and other institutional investors.

When I went back into the city in 2020 and 2021, I saw communities in chaos and small businesses increasingly shuttered.

By September 2021, the BBC reported massive closures of small businesses and High Street businesses in Britain as well.[278] The news outlet noted that fifty High Street shops a day had shuttered. As Lisa Hooker, the consumer markets lead at the accounting firm PricewaterhouseCoopers, noted matter-of-factly: "After an acceleration in store closures last year coupled with last minute Christmas tier restrictions and lockdowns extending into 2021, we might have expected a higher number of store closures this year." There was a net decline of over 5,000 outlets.[279]

I've lived in Britain, and I love that country. The culture of patronizing the High Street shops is integral to the culture of that nation. Until 2020, it was a ritual, especially for British women, to wander down the High Street to "the shops": to chat with the butcher, to buy a small bouquet of paperwhites at the florist just when spring appeared, to try on a sweater at a small consignment store, to meet a friend for a cup of tea and a plate of biscuits at a café when shopping was completed. In each visit to each small High Street store, small talk was comfortably, reassuringly exchanged: a joke, gossip, a compliment, a smile.

High Street relationships were the markers of the day or the week, and the interactions between shoppers and shopkeepers formed some of the essential glue of communities nationwide.

It was not just the shops that died, it was the communities. In 2021, department stores, fashion retailers, and restaurants closed. Charity shops and betting shops closed. These may seem like small losses, but charity shops in small British cities were nexuses of volunteerism for retired women and provided affordable clothing and household goods; betting shops were social centers for retired men. Many older folks thus saw their friends in those establishments daily or weekly.

Now those social centers were gone.

These transferred revenues were derived from British women who were now essentially locked in their homes, not permitted to go out to the High Street shops with a friend and try on a date-night dress or a work jacket, get their friend's opinion, and then stop pleasurably to try a new lipstick shade, ending the afternoon with a coffee in a nearby café.

The revenue they were thus forced to spend, alone, looking up from their laptops and sadly out of the window, went instead to e-commerce.

The small stores closed their doors. Graffiti enveloped their store-fronts. Friends who would join you in the past for jaunts to the cafés or excursions to the little consignment stores became email voices and ghostly Zoom links.

But the luxury buildings, waiting for the children of global oligarchs? In London and New York, in Paris and in San Francisco: their towers just kept rising.

———————

On September 9, 2021, *President Biden gave a rage-filled speech railing against the unvaccinated. "Our patience is wearing thin." In my life, I had never heard an American president speak to his constituents in that bullying, aggressive manner. That was not how leaders spoke to citizens in functioning democracies.[280] He announced new vaccine "mandates," as CNN put it, that would compel a hundred million American workers to submit to receiving an mRNA vaccine, whether they wanted one or not.[281] The news outlets did not seem to bother any longer reminding American readers that a "mandate" — a word that had been everywhere, suddenly, since 2020 — was not a thing in our democracy; it was not a law. No one could "mandate" something like this without the consent of Congress.*

Immediately my inbox was flooded with desperate workers, desperate college students' parents, desperate spouses. The messages were heartbreaking. Religious exemptions were being denied routinely. People with serious medical conditions were being forced to comply. Nurses who had served bravely in the COVID "front lines" and young Marines or Air Force pilots who had trained long and hard to serve their country were facing layoffs and loss of retirement security and benefits. The grief was overwhelming.

I could not believe that this was America.

When you are living under emergency measures, by definition you no longer have a functioning democracy. I say these days, "the coup has already taken place."

What is stunning is how few people even now recognize the degree to which the country was living under dictatorial measures.

As the months unfolded, examples of brutality and bizarre terrorization of our children in American and Western schools intensified. Indeed, increasingly we saw the undoing of the social contract of school itself.

The defining of the social contract as it applies to education in the West is a promise of hard work and study in the present in exchange for better outcomes in the future. Indeed, this social contract is the great teacher of Western meritocracy. It establishes our system of education as the single most powerful ideological training ground we have for what it means to be Western and is charged with passing on to upcoming generations the vital lesson that our Western heritage is predicated on fairness, while stressing the inherent relationship between hard work and just reward.

We so take this understanding for granted that we fail to grasp how radical it is and how fortunate we are. In China or Russia, meritocracy is not just an alien concept, but, to those in power, a threatening one, for in encouraging promotion by virtue of talent it inevitably poses a risk to their hegemony. Thus, unless your parents are connected to the CCP, or the ruling oligarchy, how hard you work and how much you achieve educationally are for practical purposes not very relevant. I once cofounded a leadership institute, and I remember being struck, when we were teaching "ethical lead-

ership" skills to a group of college students from Central Europe, how pointless they thought it was, how all rainbows-and-unicorns theoretical. The young adults we were teaching pointed out that the skills we were transmitting were of no use to them, since in Albania and in other former Soviet societies you still had to bribe your teacher to get an "A."

Though the Founding Fathers saw the education of citizens as essential to the sustaining of democracy (and promulgated federal ordinances in 1785 and 1787 making available to states in the new republic land grants for the funding of local schools), well into the nineteenth century, American schools were often miserable, cold, punitive places, rife with rote learning, corporal punishment, and emotional starvation — for those lucky enough to be educated at all.[282] This was true in Britain as well. As the British poet John Addington Symonds wrote, in one of the many memoirs recalling educational institutions of the period, he and his schoolmates were sadistically abused by both older students and administrators.

In fact, the pleasant, emotionally safe, physically non-punitive, and intellectually stimulating quality of modern Western primary and secondary education is a recent achievement, a product of the unflagging efforts of reformers such as Horace Mann, the "father of American education," and Maria Montessori, who developed an educational system that sought to educate the child as a whole.

As a result of these and many other education reformers, American — and Western — schools became places where the social contract was one of basic fairness, intellectual engagement, and safe social interaction: places, in short, to make Western people out of Western children. Children were expected to become adults, with all that *implies, expected to engage in freedom of thought and critical inquiry, expecting to have their own rights and bodily autonomy respected, expecting an essentially free and fair future. Expecting the social contract of the West.*

But in 2020–22 that, too, came to an end. In fact, after March 2020, the effort to destroy this social contract was conscious and systematic, and the time-tested model was replaced through-out the West generally, and in America specifically, with schools, administrators, and teachers willing, and often compelled, to bully, torment, and even physically abuse children. The message of respect and support for parents and kids was everywhere replaced with messaging to parents that they had no say in their children's education or bodily autonomy, and with dicta promoted from on high that appeared intentionally aimed at dissolving the promise of educational meritocracy and making a mockery of fairness.

Inevitably, this revised social contract would be more like those visited on children raised in Communist China or North Korea; it stressed the enforcement of silence, compliance, and the suppres-sion of rebellious independent thought. It would leave children no longer Western in their instincts and expectations, but rather create future adults, the 2049 generation, ever fearful of consequences if they stepped "out of line." These are people who'd always be aware of the possible reimposition of face coverings, or who would do anything to avoid being seated alone in the cold. They would be so generally broken by threats of isolation from their peers that they would readily submit to ongoing mistreatment and control.

Masked classrooms effectively rolled back Western education in its very DNA, recreating the long gone world where fearful children, under the sway of joyless adults, were less seen as individuals and were never heard. In an instant, the rebelliousness and individuality of the Western child, so hard won over so many decades, even centuries, was everywhere stunted, and in too many instances crushed entirely.

A Massachusetts teacher told me that the "gifted and talented" program had been curtailed in her school. It had been assailed — from above — as "racist."

San Francisco's Lowell High School, where I had attended high school, was a selective public high school that had given generations of children (disproportionately the children of immigrants) an impeccable education.

This school board too was seeking to end its selective admissions criteria for being "racist." (This caused a local rebellion).[283]

Harvard University announced that it was ending its requirement that applicants submit scores from tests like the SAT.[284] British students were told that their A-levels, the so-important exams that decide their college futures, might be suspended.[285] As late as 2022, schools in Britain were told they might have to drop subjects such as music because . . . COVID.[286]

All over the West, teens and young adults saw that the social contracts that involved them were being dramatically unwound.

What was the point now?

I had to interview some twentysomethings for an entry-level job. I would ask them where they imagined they would be in five years.

At that question, there would be a stricken silence. Some, both male and female, would be on the verge of tears.

How could they intelligently answer that? The world that had kept its promises with an eye to the future was over, right as they themselves were beginning.

Teachers of young adults began to describe the common experience they were having of a terrible silence that started each masked in-person class, a beat during which the students would simply stare straight ahead of them, immobile, in a sorrow beyond grief.

In late 2021, at the request of some local moms, I went to a school board meeting at a local high school, not far from our Hudson Valley home. One mother had let me know her teenage daughter, a basketball player, had been told by the school that she could not play after-school sports if she did not submit to mRNA vaccination. This talented young athlete would not only be separated from her teammates, but also have an important avenue for college scholarships closed to her.

This edict forcing vaccinations to allow public school students access to after-school activities seemed just bizarre, since at that time New York State did not "mandate" vaccinations for teens to play sports or to do anything else; it seemed, in fact, to be just freelance cruelty on the part of local school administrators.

So I went to the school board meeting, bringing along a cameraman.

As we milled about before the meeting, I noticed the school had removed all the hallway lockers — "because of COVID." What this meant in practice was that the students, whose bodies were still growing and developing, had to carry an entire locker's worth of schoolbooks, seventy-plus pounds worth, in backpacks all day long. Little wonder that one mom said that her twelve-year-old daughter had developed a slipped disk from the relentless weight. But more than just the physical toll it exacted, because kids had been forced to be beasts of burden, this pointless dictate made running around at recess less likely. Out too went spontaneous games of tag or basketball. It meant less free-and-easy social contact — musing on your upcoming test essay on the Progressive Era or savoring the Robert Frost poem you read in your last class. Like the endless stickers every few feet demanding "social distancing," it focused kids' minds on physical struggle and self-surveilling self-control rather than leaving them simply to think creatively or freely.

Understandably, many of the parents were here to ask that this needless and punitive dictate be rescinded.

But once the meeting opened, it was immediately apparent that the parents were being silenced by the way the gathering had been structured. In fact, what was happening was illegal from the get-go, as by law public meetings must be announced publicly in New York State, and this school board had not done so. There was a signup sheet "for speaking," jealously guarded by a school administrator but whisked away after just a few moments, and the audience was told that those who had not signed it had no right to speak. In fact, there is no such rule in New York State. Legally, everyone has the right to speak at public meetings without signing anything. We were also told we had to "mask" in order to attend the meeting. Again, there was no such regulation or law. Moreover, armed police were stationed at the entrance to the auditorium, which itself was intimidating.

Those parents who tried to speak were told by the completely masked school board — facing the audience in a dour semicircle — that each parent had only three minutes to do so. Once more, no such regulation exists in New York State public meetings law. And if the parents dared adjust their masks in order to breathe, as they struggled to express their concern about their children, or objected to any dictum of the school board's at all, the school-board supervisor would shout, in a tone that I had never heard before directed at parents, or any free citizen in America — "Keep your mask on! Put on your mask!" There was no "please." This was an order. It was the tone of the petty tyrant in a closed society.

At one point, a parent demanded answers to the question of what had become of $7.8 million in funding for "COVID measures." Seven point eight million dollars — which would obviously mean unbelievable levels of wealth for those third-party vendors to whom those millions were farmed out by the school boards. What kinds of consulting agreements, or other possible enrichment, might have accrued to the school board members, their spouses, or their adult children? An important question.

But, to my amazement, at this all the school board members rose as one — in unison as if they had practiced — and simply left the auditorium. They filed right out.

It was a CCP-style power play, a dramatic in-your-face shredding of the American social contract, a demonstration to those who had elected them that their obligation for accountability had been superseded and that it was they who were all-powerful.

Sixty parents sat there, stunned. Since the meeting obviously could not continue without the school board, there was nothing they could do. Most filed out, dejectedly.

A handful of us kept waiting. After an hour and a half, the school board re-entered, with no notice to the parents of the resumption of deliberations.

It was almost nine o'clock on a weeknight at this point. The school board resumed the meeting, as they had to by law, but now with only about seven people left to hear them, and with the tired armed cops standing sentry.

By simply ignoring the social contract that made them account-able to citizens, the school board had managed to shake off seventy concerned citizens who'd come looking to protect their children and asking for answers about possible corruption involving the millions of dollars that had been received by the school.

By rewriting the rules of America and substituting the rules of China, the school board had effectively ensured that they would not have to account for that abuse of kids, or for those seven-plus million dollars.

———————

I heard of abuse from so many different sources as 2020 turned into 2021. By now kids were back at school. But the schools that they were attending had been completely transformed into houses of Victorian horrors.

Tiffany Justice, of Moms4Liberty, told me how she had gone with her middle-school son to his school. He had taken off his mask, with her support, and she went with him to the school to make sure he would not be bullied. She said that his teacher immediately ostracized him and told him to sit apart from a circle of his peers. When Ms. Justice objected, a security guard appeared and faced off with her. She was escorted out of the school and accused of causing a disruption. The local newspaper ran a hit piece not much later.

She and her husband finally removed their son from that school. The youth who had gone through that awful experience described it to me — how his teacher made sure he was ostracized by his friends — and his face seemed inexpressibly sad and shocked as he relived the incident.

The only question was how long the damage done to him would endure.

In November of 2021, I was stunned to hear that our local Waldorf school was masking and distancing the children. This treatment was completely alien to Waldorf schools' professed belief in children's need for freedom, free movement, expressiveness, and free play.

In Canada, the message to children was "no mask, no voice."

Across the country, in Portland, Oregon, kindergartners were being forced to sit outside on buckets in near-freezing cold, "distanced" from their friends.[287]

It was the same everywhere, and often worse. A parent on social media told me that he and his wife had taken the masks off their child, but then the other parents told their children not to play with him. Many parents sent me similar emails. A child would "unmask" and then the other children were instructed not to play with that child. The unmasked child would come home in tears.

For lunch, the children in the school of a child I loved were now being given only reheated fast food that could be eaten only with hands. Wraps and pizza. The kids were made to sit in a circle on the gym floor, "distanced," so that they could not easily speak to one another during meals, as they ate this processed, wrapped-up finger food with their little paws, without utensils, like savages.

Sitting up nicely at a table with others, using a knife, fork, and spoon, cutting up meat and vegetables, chewing with one's mouth closed, and having polite conversations with one another during meals is, of course, one of the hallmarks of a developed culture. In our case, it is one of the primary tasks that enables our children to enter civilized Western society. But now these skills, honed over centuries of development of our culture in the West, were deleted from the school experience, and, like so much else, fundamentally compromised.

When the child I loved ate with us, he had all but forgotten how to converse during mealtime. He did not know how to take a beat and listen to others during a meal. He did not know how to tell a story at mealtime.

He did not know to clear his plate, or to offer to help his hostess with clearing others' plates. Instead of the civilized, ordered lunch hour, which had taught generations of Western children of every class and country of origin background to talk to one another, to eat their food politely, and to form community, children were being taught to manage for themselves on the floor like puppies in a kennel.

Why?

Always the same answer. "Because COVID."

But what would soon happen if the skills and habits that enabled our Western children to fend for themselves and prosper in the world were no longer being taught? What if, while our own children's linguistic skills withered and their hands grew less adept at managing even dumbed-down spatial tasks, the children of our global adversaries were being taught how to sit at a table politely, converse with one another, learn spatial skills and form enduring community?

How would that look for us all in 2049?

CHAPTER SIXTEEN

HEROES

In 2021, I interviewed three "dissident doctors" whose views challenging the conventional narrative on both the severity of virus and modes of treatment would be attacked by Big Tech and by the Biden Administration with mounting ferocity as the year unfolded. Even as the skies darkened, this intrepid group — Dr. Harvey Risch of Yale, Dr. Howard Tenenbaum of Mt. Sinai in Toronto, Canada, and Dr. Paul Alexander, formerly of McMaster University, and formerly of the US Department of Health and Human Services, along with such colleagues as Dr. Peter McCullough and Dr. Robert Malone — were proving there were heroes among us. It was abundantly clear by then that all were putting their careers and reputations at risk.

I spoke first with Dr. Risch, starting our conversation with "What is biggest myth about this pandemic? And have you had any blowback as a result of your truth telling?"

Dr. Risch: The biggest myth in the pandemic is that the people are freaking out about the number of cases that are occurring; people have the idea that every case of COVID is bad, we have to get rid of every last one of them until we're 100 percent safe. And this just does not recognize the reality that COVID is a spectrum of responses to a spectrum of organisms. And what we have to do is cope with it the best we can, for as many people as possible.

We've learned quite a bit over the last year. And one of the things we've learned is that the cases don't matter. What matters is what *happens* to the cases. Sure, having a respiratory illness can be unpleasant and difficult. But as long as it's not severe and life-threatening and requires hospitalization, or loss of physical [capacity], or livelihood, then it's manageable, and we get through it, just like everybody gets through all sorts of other illnesses during life. That's just part of life, and we try to manage it the best we can.

All of this freaking out about cases, and more cases, and different cases, and new cases, and new strains, and all this stuff is an anxiety generating panic mechanism to cause people to lose their sense of judgment and reason, because they're panicking about the uncertainty and the perceived risk. What matters is hospitalizations and mortality. And I would just urge people to ignore the cases, as far as their reasoning about how to manage their lives, and look at what's happening. All these data are out there — and what we see is actually good news: the current strain as SARS-CoV-2 has evolved over the last year. We've seen exactly what we expect to see in respiratory viruses, which is that they mutate to become more transmissible, more infectious, and less harmful. And because of that, we see more people getting it and fewer people dying.

We're starting to see evidence even in the United States in a few places that it's starting to go away . . .

And you look at the deaths that are occurring, and it's pretty flat. There's almost no change in the deaths that are occurring from this. So the answer is we should be doing exactly what we're doing right now — letting people who get infected if they're able to cope with it, let them get infected and develop natural immunity, which is very long-lived and very strong. Treat the people who need treatment. We've said it for the last year that we have all these outpatient medications that work very well in treating COVID, and let people just get through it as best they can, which is how normal people get through it without the fear, without the panic, with the success, and that's what works.

Naomi: I've been told this is standard public health knowledge till 2021 — bad respiratory diseases are going to go through a population, they're going to get over time, as you said, more transmissible, but less severe in outcomes. Humans get used to them, they will evolve. That's what the mutations are, or the "variants" that we're being so scared about. It's basically just a natural process, as I understand it, of a virus coexisting with a human population, and we need to get through it and protect the people who are especially immunocompromised, or elderly, or especially at risk, but not freak out. Am I accurately paraphrasing what you just said?

Dr. Risch: Yes, that's exactly right. That's the correct model.

Naomi: Well, this is stunning. And if I've reasonably paraphrased it, it would lead to completely different messaging and policies than the ones we're seeing. For instance, Dr. Fauci keeps showcasing the transmissibility of the Delta variant, but not mentioning that it may be less fatal, and that, as you said, we shouldn't count "cases." He keeps focusing on cases, and on "dynamics," which is a very vague term. And hyping the variant-ness of the disease, as if a variant is a weird, scary thing, that is like a horror movie. And you're saying that . . . Well, it sounds like you're saying that what he's saying is leaving out important data.

Dr. Risch: Correct. And in fact, he's understating the variants. There's been at least four or five thousand variants that people have cataloged so far. Basically, every person who gets the infection produces variants. If you make a trillion viruses, and the enzyme that reproduces the RNA and the virus makes an error in 1 in 100,000 virus particles, you're going to have millions of variants in every person, whether they're vaccinated or not.

Naomi: I want to ask you specifically, what is a case? A relative just got a positive COVID test. She had to test every month for her job. She feels fine. Her son just tested negative. She has no symptoms. Their lives have been uprooted, put on a hold because of this PCR test result. Is that a case? That's what they're counting as cases. That's what Dr. Fauci is freaking out about. But she's basically not sick. So what is a "case"?

Dr. Risch: The CDC addressed this: they did an antibody testing of people — blood donors and other populations. And what they found is that the number of people who had been infected with the virus was about 5.8 times the number of whom they had actually registered through all the PCR testing.

And that's why my measure for looking at what we call herd immunity in the states is to look at the number of cases registered per million. So when a state has 100,000 people per million who've actually been registered as so-called cases, I multiply that by 5.8. So 100,000 per million is 10%, and I multiply that by 5.8. So I say that 58% of that population has had COVID. And that's why you see the states with the highest amounts in the 140,000 per million, because you multiply by 5.8, and that means everybody's had it.

So you can see that most people have had it. So why are we vaccinating everybody? Because most of the people don't need it in the first place.

Naomi: So you're saying almost 60% of the population of the United States is probably immune to COVID? And yet, we're stopping kids from going to school, we're threatening more lockdowns, we're engaging in mandates of federal workers for vaccines, even though it sounds like we're almost at herd immunity from what you're describing?

Dr. Risch: Oh, we're well past herd immunity. Herd immunity was defined by McKendrick in 1927, in modeling about epidemic models that involve susceptibles and infections and recovered people. And herd immunity occurs when the epidemic peaks, when the cases go up, it reaches a peak and starts going down. When the peak starts going down, that is the definition of herd immunity.

What we know is that North Dakota, South Dakota, Tennessee, other states had herd immunity in November, December of last year, well before any of the vaccines were rolled out. By the time vaccines were rolled out, they were well on their way down. Herd immunity, however, shouldn't be taken as proof that the epidemic has gone away. Herd immunity is the beginning of the epidemic going away. We need much more immunity than herd immunity to push it out of the population. But when you have herd immunity, you know that process is happening.

What we're seeing is these bumps that occur in epidemic curves, and then you reach new levels of herd immunity, and they start going back down again. That's what happened in the UK, it's happened in the Netherlands. And that's what we're going to be seeing here over the next three to four weeks.

Naomi: Have you had blowback?

Dr. Risch: Yes, I have, by my colleagues at Yale, who wrote a letter after I published my paper that started this in May of last year on medication usages that work. My colleagues, I disagree with them, but they are free to assert their positions. That's what freedom of speech and freedom of academic thought is about. And we need this in the public domain. This is exactly what makes academic life important and interesting, is the ability to discuss it.

I began my conversation with Dr. Tenenbaum by asking what aspect of this essential conversation he wanted to address first.

Dr. Tenenbaum: So we have a disease that's treatable with early intervention. And so you've got a treatable disease. In fact, it's quite easy to treat. And then you've got this vaccine, which doesn't seem to be very protective, and yet comes with some very significant risks, especially in the younger population, young men in particular. And these people are at risk for developing myocarditis. And every time somebody talks about this from the pro-vaccine side, they say, "Well, it's a mild condition," which is completely untrue. There's no such thing as mild myocarditis. In fact, it's a very dangerous condition.

Even if the individual doesn't pass away from a severe case right away, or from a less severe case, they are still at much higher risk for the development of long-term cardiac diseases, as you know, including cardiomyopathy and things like this. So it's critically important, I think, that we get this message out that the vaccine or the vaccines do not appear to be the answer that we've all been hoping for.

All I can say is that what [the CDC] is telling us is basically 180 degrees away from what we know. But it's completely opposite to what you would logically conclude. Pearson International Airport in Toronto set up lines for vaccinated and unvaccinated individuals. Big signs. It reminds me of something else that happened in the 1930s and 1940s, when you went to the left line or went to the right line.

There are two important messages, that need to get out. That this can be treated relatively easily and managed early. And that the vaccines are not conferring the protection that we thought they would confer.

And the reason I think it's so urgent, is that the vaccine companies, the health agencies are militating to vaccinate children. This to me is criminal. Children have statistically zero risk from dying from COVID-19. They do not pass the disease on to others. And yet, our governments and the pharma companies want to start vaccinating kids even two months old for no reason whatsoever. There's no bio-medical or logical reason that you'd want to do something like that. Can you imagine giving a five-year-old a drug to treat angina? It'd work really well. Never have an angina attack, but he doesn't need it. And the long-term dangers are just not known. I'm not going to say that I know they are long-term dangers, or what they are — but that's the point. We don't know.

For his part, **Dr. Alexander** noted:

Dr. Tenenbaum raised the seriousness about a vaccine, and that is our real problem right now. Because of the way these trials were conducted and the information that has not been shared with the global community, we don't know what are going to be the long-term implications. And that's why when you conduct a trial, when you follow and you conduct the safety part of the trial, you are looking and you follow up for several years, as many years as you can, so that any of the rare signals of harm, you will be able to say, "We followed this vaccine for 10 years, and this is what emerged. This is safe enough to put it out to the population in a mass way," or, "This is not safe enough." But right now, we just don't know.

So I would agree that we are near the end now. We have herd immunity. We have the early treatment, so in case persons get reinfected or infected for the first time, we can offer them treatment that would prevent them from going to hospital, or even worse, going on to death.

And we should do public-service messaging, which would mean employing the CDC, to go over issues around Vitamin D supplementation, issues around a healthier lifestyle, focusing on the issue of obesity, because obesity has emerged as a super-loaded risk factor. Behind age, it is probably the second biggest risk factor in severe COVID.

We should allow the well and the healthy and the young in our society to go about life as naturally as possible, and not deliberately get infected, but as part of their day-to-day living, because they are best able to cope with Delta or any variant that comes along. And they will develop immunity, and thus we inch back closer to herd immunity, and we surpass herd immunity. And we get through this pandemic, and we close it out.

Naomi: I'm getting these heartbreaking emails from parents, in one case a thirty-five-year-old woman, who's two months pregnant. She's weeping because she works for a federal agency, and she's been presented with, "Get a vaccine or lose your job." And this person is saying to me, what would I do? I just want to know your thoughts about this.

Dr. Alexander: Those are two separate questions. We don't give pregnant women anything that isn't absolutely necessary. And we certainly don't give them unknown things that aren't known to be necessary. And the evidence so far is that in the one study that the CDC has published, it didn't follow up the pregnant women long enough to know what happened to the ones who got the vaccine in the beginning, or the first trimester of pregnancy. So we still don't know. And for the CDC to even think that it's safe to use when it's totally unknown about those pregnancy outcomes is irresponsible.

The reality is that FDA in the beginning knew, and the vaccine developers knew, that pregnant women and women of child-bearing age were to be excluded, as they could potentially be harmed. That's why they were excluded, if you look at the protocol, from these [initial] studies. And to then turn around and administrator the vaccines to them, is, to me, a criminal step.

Naomi: I keep thinking about the way the mRNA vaccines are supposed to work. And I keep thinking about the fact that these spike proteins are crossing the blood-brain barrier, and then therefore they're going to also be crossing the placental barrier. And they're also going to be going into the fetus. Is that not correct? And if so, might there not be the same kinds of problems being inflicted on the developing fetus, in terms of interference with the vascular structure, interference possibly with heart issues, or possibly with clotting issues?

Dr. Alexander: Well, we know that the spike proteins are produced. They may be produced up to six months now, according to some data. So they're found in the blood. And we have instances where spike proteins probably were transferred through maternal milk, mother's milk. Because infants die from the very condition associated with vaccination in adults and young adults — this thrombocytopenia. And I mean, one can think of no other explanation. And so, yes, the spike protein is being made in places where it shouldn't be made. And the spike protein is inducing significant damage. We heard from someone from Canada who presented some data who tested patients who've been vaccinated in his practice. He tested them for this marker of clot formation.

He found that sixty percent of the people who had just been vaccinated were demonstrating elevations in this marker, meaning that these people were developing micro-clots, or worse; if it's larger, they really feel ill. So it can range from either not feeling quite too good, because you've developed these micro-clots, to really severe damage, ranging from a heart attack to a stroke. Sixty percent of his patients who had been vaccinated — he had tested them, they're developing clotting.

Naomi: So let me ask one more thing. What happens to the spike protein? Where does it go? How does body get rid of it? Where is it?

Dr. Alexander: Dr. Roger Hodkinson out of Canada — a pathologist — described that he's done a lot of autopsies since this has started on women who have passed away, unfortunately. And he looked at the uterus, because he's a pathologist. And he has determined that the endometrium has the highest expression of the ACE2 receptor. It's highly expressed in places like the placenta, the testes in males. The endometrium.

But he said that is because of that proliferation of the ACE2 receptor, which the spike protein interacts with. And is a cause for concern and needs to be studied, urgently.

And what Dr. Risch said is that when the spike sits on the surface of the cell and protrudes into the blood flow, in that blood are platelets; as the platelets brush up against the spikes, the platelets clump and begins clotting. This is what we're theorizing. And a lot of very smart people like Dr. Hodkinson, Dr. Risch, Dr. Bhakdi, Dr. Malone, are theorizing that that begins that clotting factor. And also, as part of the production of the spike, the metabolic machinery produces some molecular waste, when you produce a foreign protein in the cell. And it places that waste at the door of the cell on the outside. And once your natural killer cells detect that waste, it knows that something apparent is going on in that cell. It's making a foreign protein it should not.

And it begins to attack the cells, and therefore the tissues around the cells.

And that's part of the beginning of the trauma.

———————

The first time I posted an interview with these three physicians and Dr. Peter McCullough, YouTube temporarily froze my account. Why? "Medical misinformation." The second time I posted the above interview, YouTube froze my account altogether.

Nurses were being told that they would be fired for dispensing such "medical misinformation."[288]

One year after YouTube censored the interviews, the micro-clotting that Dr. Bhakdi and his colleagues had hypothesized, and that these doctors had hypothesized as well, and the myocarditis of which they had warned, was abundantly and tragically confirmed. The CDC acknowledged that young men were suffering myocarditis at higher than baseline rates, post-vaccination.[289]

One year after this interview was suppressed, so many young male athletes had collapsed on the athletic field that the event was becoming a ghastly social media meme. Matt Le Tissier, a soccer legend, sounded the alarm on the many sudden deaths of otherwise healthy young athletes.[290]

One year later, a friend, a formerly healthy forty-three-year-old, was in the hospital with post-vaccination blood clots in her lungs.

The news ran headlines of teenage boys and girls dying after COVID shots.[291] "Teen Dies from Blood Clots after Second Jab."[292] A seventeen-year-old girl in Washington State died of a heart attack after her second mRNA vaccination.[293] A thirteen-year-old boy died in his sleep after vaccination.[294] A Michigan teenager died days after getting vaccinated. [295] In Kuala Lumpur, a thirteen-year-old boy collapsed and died eighteen days after receiving his first vaccine.[296]

Model Hailey Baldwin was hospitalized with a clot in her brain.[297] A twenty-six year old relative went to the hospital with a diagnosis of micro-clotting.

I begged a loved one not to get a booster. She looked away — I knew she was under social pressure. Two months later, she was in the ER with aortal collapse. Three months later, she had a heart attack.

One year later VAERS (the Vaccine Adverse Event Reporting System) was reporting thousands of cases of adverse reactions to the vaccine, from thrombotic events (clotting) to severe disruption of womens' menstrual cycles — and, as most reports to VAERS are voluntary,[298] could we even know how many adverse events went unreported?

I'd faced the wrath of Twitter, in April of 2021 for having raised concerns about vaccines and menstrual dysregulation. I was among the first commentators to raise the alarm, based on the accounts women were sharing on social media.

But January 5, 2022, a study funded by the National Institutes of Health confirmed that COVID-19 vaccines cause what they called a "small increase in menstrual cycle length." It was not so "small": "The team found that women who received a COVID-19 vaccine had an average increase in cycle length of nearly one day for each dose."[299] That's potential bleeding for twelve more days a year. How many low-COVID-risk women would opt for that choice, had this been disclosed? And what did that distortion of a menstrual cycle by an average of twenty percent do to the women's fertility? The study did not bother to ask.

Now, nearly a year later, it was common knowledge that women experienced sometimes serious menstrual dysregulations post-mRNA vaccination. Both the NHS and the CDC were pursuing additional studies of menstrual dysregulation. The BBC, which had trolled me relentlessly, now headlined: "Call for Investigation of Menstrual Changes Post COVID Jabs."[300]

But much worse than the hassle that Big Tech censorship had caused in my own life was the fact that millions of women could have had early warning from mainstream media about the risk of menstrual dysregulation and didn't. I was discredited and censored for even raising the issue, and thus many women may have been injured or made less fertile or less healthy as a result of the corruption of news networks and social media.

If YouTube had not censored the dissident doctors for their hypotheses grounded in fact that also turned out to be right, how many people would have sought more information? How many people would, indeed, be healthier or simply be alive?

In those interviews, there were questions I did not ask any of the doctors: In what world does common sense and/or good news become dangerous misinformation?

Who were the real good guys in this scenario and — even more to the point — the real villains?

CHAPTER SEVENTEEN

CRUELTY, CULTS, COERCION

B y the end of 2021, more and more data were arriving to show that the vaccines were not working very well, and that their effects waned over time. A study out of Israel was among the first, but then the studies confirmed one another in droves.[301] As study after study appeared confirming that the vaccines' protective effects degraded over time, and that they did not prevent people from being infected with COVID, I kept naively expecting that their obvious shortcomings would be declared and acknowledged. To my amazement, their deteriorating efficacy became instead an opening for a jolly and rigorous marketing campaign for "boosters." "Boosters" seemed like such an obvious linguistic coverup for "it did not work the first time" that I assumed no one would want to do again and again what had failed on its rollout. But the marketing people were geniuses. Soon well-off people everywhere were showing off their "boosted" status.

Soon, the "Zoom class" was boasting not only about their injections and being "fully vaccinated," but they were also announcing proudly that they were "double-vaxxed and boosted."

A lawyer who sought my business said this to me; so did people I scarcely knew whom I contacted for trivial information; so did a total stranger referred by a colleague, who smugly informed me over the phone that she was "double-vaxxed and boosted."

I always felt an internal grimace at these announcements. I did not want to hear about the birth-control choices, or the prostate treatments, or the hernia operations of the bodies of others. I did not need to see anyone's medicine cabinet. To me, these were incredibly personal decisions and should be private information.

Meanwhile, the side effects of the vaccine began to be impossible to ignore, at least for some of us.

It didn't matter at all to millions, though. A cult of "believing in the vaccine" had taken hold. Along with that belief, a two-tier society had been established in the countries and US states that practiced vaccine discrimination and used vaccine passports.

And along with that two-tier society was launched a thoroughgoing cruelty culture.

Despite the demoralizing data about efficacy, the machine of forced vaccinations ramped up almost hysterically. Nurses quit — and were fired — rather than take the mRNA vaccinations.[302] Firefighters went on strike. Doctors were fired. Hospitals faced a healthcare crisis due to the loss of staffers refusing to get vaccinated — especially bizarre, given that it had now been established that the vaccines were not preventing infection, and that being vaccinated did not stop transmission, and that in any case, tens of millions had natural immunity.

No matter. Verbal attacks on the unvaccinated continued to escalate. Many went so far as to call for denying them medical care.[303]

I invited an old friend over. We had shared an office in DC when we were young idealistic activists. We'd share Thai food with another college friend. And back in our shabby attic office space, "Paul" would make me fall off the furniture with laughter. When a partner left me two decades later, "Paul" would walk beside me through the streets of his quiet suburban neighborhood, listening patiently. He told me about his love life, and I told him about crushes and heartbreaks of my own. We were fast friends. He called me "Wolfie." We always understood each other.

Now he was an important public official.

"I don't sit inside with unvaccinated people," he said.

He said it smugly — as if saying it were gratifying in some way.

Hoping to forgive all craziness in general, and that of my friends and loved ones, I said I would sit outside with him.

On the day we were to meet it rained. I called him. "It's raining," he said with finality, as if the meaning was self-evident.

"Seriously?" I asked. "We can't go have lunch in a restaurant?"

"I don't sit inside with unvaccinated people," he repeated, an ice-cold mission statement. "So our plans won't work."

In forty years of friendship, I had never been subjected to that streak of sheer unmediated meanness in his makeup.

I had even not known it existed.

———————

I received an invitation to a swanky think tank/social club in Manhattan. I'd supported it for years. Luminaries who spoke and were part of the community included New York's elite and global leaders, diplomats and tycoons and media moguls.

"Fully Vaccinated Only," read the invitation.

On September 30, I received an invitation to go birdwatching with the Princeton Alumni Association — an outside event, of course. "Fully vaccinated," it read.

So the world I could no longer enter had their "vaccinated only" parties, and their segregated fashion galas, and their nonprofit-hosted discussions in medically segregated New York City hotels over expensive lunches served by staffers in masks — lunches celebrating luminaries of the civil rights movement or of the LGBTQ rights movement or the immigrant rights movement, or the movement to help girls in Afghanistan get access to schools.

I looked at trips on Travelzoo.com. I found that travel to whole countries now suddenly arrived in search results as only available for the "fully vaccinated." Singapore announced that it was open again "for the vaccinated."[304]

The unvaccinated were being charged over $100 a week for tests. A surcharge on the earnings of unvaccinated workers was part of the discourse.[305] Because she was unvaccinated, a woman was denied a kidney.[306]

By the time I traveled to Oregon in November 2021, the "mask mandate" had been reinstated by Governor Brown, and the coercive powers of her administration were absolute.[307] Since my last visit, things had spiraled psychologically. The van driver who took me from the airport to my hotel could not stop talking. All day long, masked, seeing masks, driving back and forth, same route, and not a single face — his was a life without connection. He could not be silent.

The next day I got into an Uber. Again the driver could not be silent. His ex's ex had substance-abuse problems . . . they'd lost custody of the kids. I always welcomed a good chat, but it was clear that both drivers had been impaired in the same way. They could no longer read emotional cues and could no longer pick up the rhythms of a conversation. And they were starving for human connection.

My elderly, constantly masked relative also could no longer get into the rhythms of human contact.

I went to the local library. I was asked to "mask." There was no accommodation for ADA. The nice librarian referred me to the city attorney. They were following the CDC on masks. What if the CDC was wrong? I asked.

Possible, said the nice librarian.

Were they given any data? I asked. No, he replied.

The rooms where people could study were assigned to "Friends of the Library," so unavailable. All the common spaces where people could ordinarily congregate were closed.

The porch, where you might have gone safely to read in the open air, was being enclosed.

I begged to be allowed to sit somewhere, anywhere, without a mask, as I could not wear one due to my disability. The nice librarian was so sorry. There was nothing he could do.

What if you put me in a distant corner away from any other humans and let me take off my mask?

"The decision from the city is that it is not 'reasonable' in the middle of a pandemic to have someone breathing into collective air."

There it was again — that mystical phrase, "the middle of a pandemic."

But there were so many ways to solve this problem that had not been tried. They could have put disabled people in a separate wing, or on a separate floor. They could have put disabled people on the porch. They could have let people choose what wing they wished to sit in — the masked or the unmasked. But the City of Corvallis had taken it upon itself to make private medical decisions for everyone, and in a way that for some made using the library virtually impossible.

I had written books in libraries and in cafés. You can't write a book wearing a mask. You can barely write an essay.

Were there any cafés in the whole city where I could take my mask off and write?

No, he explained sadly. "You have to put it on between bites." I thought of all the writers and composers who had worked at cafés, and the masterpieces we would never have had if Hemingway had had to put on a mask between sips of wine.

I blurted out: "What will happen to the arts in Corvallis?"

He explained that the security guard all day every day must explain to people that they need to "mask." And, he added, with distaste for the task, "we have to tell people to pull their masks up over their noses."

This library had been turned into a scolding and intrusive overseer. Nice librarians like this one had been turned from society's most magical facilitators to scolds and surveyors of people's intimate relationship to their own breathing.

I thought of a four-year-old girl I'd seen in the library near my home in New York State. She was overjoyed with the delight of being able to take picture books off the shelf and read them. She was delirious with happiness. The poor staff had to chase down the mom and take out brightly colored masks the size of children's faces.

The librarian, in spite of her own more decent inclinations, had to get on the floor next to the protesting child and force her to put a mask on her face. The mother had to ease the child into submission without a struggle. The two adults flanked the tiny girl. The child was shaking her head back and forth and crying.

Now the little girl would associate libraries with trauma, and not with joy.

"Disabled people really can't use this library," I said to the librarian in Oregon.

"That's why we have the home book delivery option," he offered.

"A library is more than just books," I said.

"So it is," he sadly agreed.

———————

November 2021: My husband and I realized we were not invited to a family Thanksgiving. "It's a very small Thanksgiving this year," said our beloved relatives.

I asked my mom if we had not been invited because we were unvaccinated.

"Probably," she said. "People are scared. You can't blame them."

I explained again that vaccines did not affect transmission. "That may be true," she said. "But that is not other people's belief matrix."

We had now left the Enlightenment and entered the world of "belief matrices."

In December, a local community leader entered my screened porch and, without my asking, volunteered that she was "double-vaxxed and boosted." I assured her I did not need to know about her personal medical choices.

When I called to get information about a community event in my area, the neighbor started the conversation by saying he is "double-vaxxed and boosted," as if this was the new Aruba or the new Tesla.

Some weeks later, I invited other neighbors over.

One neighbor told me she was making homemade bread, cream soup, and baked pies. If I am vaccinated, she said, I could come join her and her husband on her screened porch for this delicious feast. If I am unvaccinated, sorry — though she may be willing to walk with me at some point outside.

A new social hierarchy was forming, wherein people allowed fellow vaccinated others into their lives and well lit, festive space. They seemed to relish telling the unvaccinated, "Sorry, maybe you can walk with me outside."

People were enjoying saying the word "distanced": as in "Maybe I can go with you for a distanced walk outside."

The CDC published advice on how to talk to unvaccinated friends and family.[308] I heard the same script from two different relatives and a friend.

"I am so disappointed in you" said two different, formerly non-judgmental friends, independently of one another. "Are you proud of your role in this pandemic?" demanded a third.

"I can't get vaccinated," I explained to them. It was like speaking into a void.

"Are you a medical doctor?" others asked in separate conversations, because they were reading from the same script.

Other acquaintances did come visit but sat outside even as the temperatures dropped to the forties. They were lovely, but when they agreed to be hugged, they involuntarily went rigid with fear.

I called a beloved relative and asked to see him. He didn't let people see him indoors. "That's okay," I assured him, "I'll sit with you outside."

"I don't sit outside with unvaccinated people," he said, in that new, strangely smug and triumphant tone.

He is in his seventies.

I started to tear up, thinking I will never see him again in this lifetime.

———————

December 2021: cruelty and a kind of neo-fascistic sadism was abroad in the world. Rampaging.

Australia was in chains.[309] Austria was locking down the unvaccinated.[310]

On December 17, I was told that as an unvaccinated person I would not be able to be present for the graduation — at a famous, respected university — of someone I love. Again I wept without being able to stanch my tears.

Sometimes I did not recognize the people who were saying these cruel things.

Some were Buddhists. I'd known all of them to be kind, inclusive, tolerant, queer-positive people.

"I don't sit inside with unvaccinated people."

"I don't sit outside with unvaccinated people."

And in this two-tier society, they got to be on top. They got to exclude, to shun, and to feel virtuous doing so.

It almost seemed as if the permission to abuse and discriminate against the unvaccinated rushed into a vacuum that was already there and waiting, as if it had been so uncomfortable to treat all people equally for so long. The right-on progressive community almost seemed to be heaving a sigh of relief at being able to discriminate against us unvaccinated people.

Around the same time, my well-educated, intelligent mother expressed dismay that I was going onto Fox News before coming to see her — though she knew I would be isolating and quarantining.

"Mom, you know I can't infect you if I am not sick," I pointed out.

"It sounds like a superspreader event," she said, with evident disgust.

In yet another mean-spirited, threatening speech in December 2021, President Biden proclaimed: "For unvaccinated, we are looking at a winter of severe illness and death — if you're unvaccinated — for themselves, their families, and the hospitals they'll soon overwhelm."[311]

This was an outright lie, as by now it was abundantly clear vaccination does not stop transmission. Still, the dependent clause terrified everyone we knew.

Christmas 2021: I had booked a family getaway on the Oregon coast. On the very day of President Biden's speech, two relatives canceled our week away. I could not get my deposit back.

Social media attacked those who took Ivermectin: "You are not a horse. You are not a cow. Seriously, y'all. Stop it," tweeted our health agency.[312]

No one seemed to care that even the manufacturers said that vaccination wasn't guaranteed to prevent transmission.[313] No one cared that studies supporting therapeutics were multiplying.[314]

YouTube added to the suspension of content for "medical misinformation," and now also suspended people for being critical of vaccines.[315]

Cruelty became as contagious as any disease.

———————

It was beyond frightening to witness in real time what panic does.

The terror was rampant and beyond irrational. People I knew developed bizarre, ritualistic behavior. One woman did not leave her house for a year and a half. People all around me would fly into a panic if someone maskless approached within six feet, or even eight or twelve.

The collective, settled norms of liberal, civil human society eroded before our eyes.

As many complaints as people may have had with the Western social order, until March 2020 it was understood that one should at least try to empathize with others, try to be inclusive, try to hear an opposing point of view.

But now cruelty and exclusion were visible everywhere around us. People were noticeably harsher in day-to-day communications, especially toward the unvaccinated.

Every day they were being propagandized against empathy. Every day they were being explicitly directed not to empathize with those accused, beyond any semblance of logic, of having "caused" or "perpetuated" the pandemic.

In the United States, citizens were soon being forced to take their second or third experimental injection, the shot being required to go back to school or to keep their jobs as truckers crossing borders, as soldiers and sailors and military pilots and hospital workers.[316] The forcing of injections continued — this, in spite of the fact, that thousands of adverse events were being recorded

*in VAERS, including deaths, shortly after vaccination.[317]
Voices of opposition to tyrannical overreach were being censored
widely. The View, that cozy group of smugly self-certain ladies,
went on about the dangers of Joe Rogan's podcast that had raised
questions about mRNA vaccines.[318] Neil Young, the author of the
song "Rockin' in the Free World," called for the music-streaming
service Spotify to censor Rogan's "misinformation."[319] He was
quickly joined by the former rebel Joni Mitchell and others.[320]
Calls for censorship of opposition echoed across the internet.
Dissident platforms such as Parler were deplatformed by their
hosting services or their payment processors, a digital version of
boycotting businesses.[321]*

*In New York, children as young as two were being forced by the
state's smiling new governor, a woman, to wear facial coverings that
restricted their breathing.[322] Set apart as "other" and falsely derided
as infectious and "unclean," the unvaccinated could not enter
buildings or restaurants in New York City, in Washington, DC, in San
Francisco, or in Los Angeles. Everyone was urged to hate and resent
them, irrationally to blame them for the nation's predicament.[323]
It was a cult, which people joined and to which they offered up
their bodies; if they refused, they were ostracized and denied social
life and professional advancement.*

*Reports proliferated of abusive treatment of the unvaccinated in
hospitals and of therapeutics being withheld from this population.
A vital therapeutic, one consisting of monoclonal antibodies, had
its emergency-use authorization withdrawn by the FDA.[324] The
respected Mayo Clinic was sued for refusing treatment options to a
dying man, despite pleas from his desperate wife.[325]*

As the months passed, it was clear the world was becoming ever more cult-like and insular in its thinking, at least on the progressive side. Friends and colleagues who were highly educated, who had been lifelong critical thinkers — journalists, editors, researchers, doctors, philanthropists, teachers, psychologists — all began to repeat talking points from MSNBC and CNN, overtly refusing to look at any other sources, including peer-reviewed sources in medical journals or even CDC data that challenged those talking points.

It became clear soon enough that if they absorbed information contradictory to the consolidating narrative they risked losing social status, maybe even their jobs; doors would slam shut, opportunities be foreclosed. One well-educated woman told me she did not want to see any unsanctioned information for fear of being disinvited from her bridge group.

Friends and colleagues who had been skeptical their whole adult lives of Big Agriculture — who only shopped at Whole Foods, and would never let their kids eat sugar or processed meat, or ingest a hint of Red Dye No. 2 in candy, or candy itself for that matter, now lined up to inject into their bodies an mRNA injection whose "estimated study completion date" extended into 2024,[326] and then eagerly offer up for injection the bodies of their dependent minor children. These parents proudly announced on social media that they had done this.

In a couple of cases, when I gently advised against this, pointing out that the studies would not end until 2024, they became irate.

This was my people, my tribe, my whole life, the progressive, right-on part of the ideological world — and it became more and more uncritical, less and less able to discuss or reason. Friends and colleagues who their whole adult lives had known the dangers of Big Pharma (and, reflexively wellness-oriented, would only think of using Burt's Bees on their babies' bottoms and sunscreen with no PABAs on themselves) rushed to take the experimental genetic-based therapy; then, like the stone throwers in Shirley Jackson's short story "The Lottery," crowded around to lash out at, shun, punish anyone who raised the slightest question about Big Pharma. Their entire knowledge base about that industry seemed to have magically evaporated into the ether.

It was as if these communities were in the grip of a collective hallucination, like the witch crazes of the sixteenth and seventeenth centuries. Whole understandings and belief systems were abandoned overnight. Intelligent, informed people suddenly saw things that were not there and were unable to see things that were incontrovertibly before their faces.

Feminist health activists, who knew especially well the disastrous results visited upon women by the experimentation of the pharmaceutical and medical industries, likewise lined up to take an injection; never mind that women were reliably reporting that the vaccine was wreaking painful havoc on their menstrual cycles. These formerly reliable custodians of well-informed skepticism and of women's health rights were silent even as such voices as Dr. Paul Alexander warned that spike protein from mRNA vaccines may accumulate in the ovaries (and testes),[327] and as vaccinated women reported hemorrhagic menses, with double-digit percentages in a Norwegian study reporting heavier bleeding.[328] And when mothers reported that their vaccinated twelve-year-olds were suddenly getting their periods and enduring two periods a month? The feminists were silent.

Almost none of the luminaries of feminist health activism, who'd spent decades speaking out on behalf of women's health and women's bodies, now dared peek above the parapet. The two or three of us who did were immediately smeared, libeled, threatened, and silenced.

People who had been up in arms for decades about eating disorders or about the coercive social standards that led to leg shaving were silent about an untested injection that was minting billions for Big Pharma. The Our Bodies Ourselves collective? Nothing on vaccine risks and women's health as a subject category. NARAL? Crickets.

Feminist jurists like Justices Sonia Sotomayor and Elena Kagan were heard debating President Biden's vaccine mandates on January 7, 2022, and it was as if they had never heard of the legal claims for Roe v. Wade: "right to privacy."[329] Indeed, when it came to mandates, Justice Kagan's career-long philosophical view that citizens had a right to physical privacy in medical decision-making — "My body, my choice"; "It is between a woman and her doctor" — vanished, along with her expensive education and all her knowledge of the Constitution.

A part of Justice Sotomayor's reasoning mind seems to have simply shut down at the word "vaccines." Lifelong activists for justice and inclusion, for the Constitution and human rights and the rule of law; friends and colleagues of mine who are LGBTQ-rights activists; constitutional lawyers who teach at all the major universities and run the law reviews; those who argue against excluding anyone from any profession or access based on gender; almost all of them at least on the progressive side of the spectrum were silent as a comprehensive, systematic, cruel, omnipotent discrimination society was erected in a matter of months in places like New York City. States like California adopted systems pretty much like apartheid based on physical characteristics. And yet now these former fighters for human rights and for equal justice under law enthusiastically had endorsed and colluded in the construction of the massive edifice of discrimination.

And even now, these elite justice advocates celebrated their own virtue, and the shared presumption of their superior morality, without seeming to notice that they had become — in less than a year — exactly what they had spent their adult lives professing most to hate.

The vaccine and the virus were mere proximate causes. What had really been accomplished was that now Americans, a formerly proud and independent people, had experienced the submission of their bodies to an intimate and permanent and possibly damaging intrusion that they did not choose. Americans, a formerly kind people, had been transfigured into accepting a culture of cruelty. America, whose equality of treatment of all had been a light for the world, was now, at least in several cities and states, a full-on discrimination society like any other ignorant, unenlightened backwater.

The virus and the vaccine were just the stimuli.

What had really been accomplished was the breaking of America.

CHAPTER EIGHTEEN

PANDEMIC WITHOUT END

By the end of 2021, we were still being spoken of as being "in the middle of a pandemic." All the aberrant, post-humane conditions of "the new normal" were justified by the phrase. But like "conspiracy theory" and "misinformation" it was becoming a phrase without fixed meaning.

In pandemic time, time had ceased to be linear. It was now always pandemic time. "The middle of a pandemic" kept shifting so that it had no actual chronological meaning. It was always the eternal now, the pandemic was always everywhere around us, with no recourse to objective metrics.

When people insisted nonsense be treated as sense, it was always because "we're in the middle of a pandemic."

I was in Corvallis, Oregon, still. And people were losing their minds.

I went to a physical therapist. She showed me the empty dance studio that she had set up in her modest living room. She was a small woman, a caring healer, committed to "body positivity": the idea that people of all shapes and sizes should enjoy their bodies and be healthy. Until the pandemic, she had held dance sessions in this living room. Now by government edict she could have no more than eight people at once — all masked. Of course, the dance classes had migrated to Zoom.

But an in-person class in which women in their various shapes and sizes could celebrate their beauty, enjoy communal dance whatever their weight or ability/disability level, and might later go out for a coffee and stress-, cortisol-, and blood-pressure-lowering conversation — that possibility, so different from dragging oneself from a couch to leap about with ghosts on the screen, was gone.

In Oregon, as elsewhere, obesity rates had skyrocketed "during the pandemic."[330] And of course obesity was one of the primary signals for risk of death from COVID.

Yet closing this healer's dance floor was supposedly a public health measure.

I saw the same harm to public health when I returned to my hotel. A Weight Watchers class was in progress — half empty, of course, and everyone masked. The leader was struggling to make herself heard though her mask. The mask made it difficult to attend the class at all, even to sit still.

For those women, as for so many others, far from contributing to public health, the mandates were a health hazard.

Yet the masks could not be removed, since "we were in the middle of a pandemic."

Would this pandemic ever be declared over?

I learned from Leslie Manookian, of the Health Freedom Defense Fund, that the definition of "pandemic" had been changed. It had been defined as disease and death extending over a large geographical area. That was no longer the case.

Manookian explained that only the WHO — largely funded by the Bill & Melinda Gates Foundation — now had the power to declare the start of a pandemic. Or the end of a pandemic. As the second-largest contributor to the WHO, as of September 2021, the Bill & Melinda Gates Foundation had invested $780 million in the organization.[331]

Nearly two years after "two weeks to flatten the curve," we were, for a very great many, still "in the middle of a pandemic." Though the focus of legacy-media messaging had turned from the "highly infectious Delta variant" to "the much more easily communicated Omicron variant," millions had been so thoroughly traumatized they would never be able to grasp or credit the only metrics ever of true significance: hospitalizations and deaths. Some were vowing, and not facetiously, that they would never surrender their masks.

In mathematics, an "asymptote" is a line that a curve approaches but never touches. It comes closer and closer but never connects. "The middle of a pandemic" could be a conceptual asymptote.

I do not doubt that we had been "in the middle of a pandemic" — certainly this was true in the spring of 2020. But a year and a half later, as the claims of the dissident researchers and physicians were increasingly borne out by reality, it was clear the pandemic would be endemic.

Like most others, I did not know what the word meant when I first heard it. But I quickly came to understand it was a concept on which our very future depends.

It means the pandemic is over — as over as it can be, anyway — with a wiser and more enlightened humanity coexisting with the fact of respiratory virus.

Yet like the "war on terror," the "middle of the pandemic" theoretically might never end, not completely. The war on terror effectively redefined the "battlefield" as everywhere — your airport, your schools, your home. It generated a welter of "war-footing" rules invoked by the unelected ranging from federal department heads to TSA officers. And by every objective measure it has been a disaster. Yet the rules are still in place and, at its height (and even afterward), it, too, generated untold billions in profits for those positioned to exploit it.[332] The outbreak of disease of 2020–21 was a misfortune in human history — but also not for everyone. And that same small, privileged group at the very center of power has a keen interest in ensuring that it, too, keeps us forever on at least a semi-war footing — and keeps the pesky rules of free peaceful Western nations safely in abeyance.

Two years on, much of what had been America was dead.

By now the eradication of Western cultural wealth was largely complete. By now it was generally accepted that people could fully police others' behavior, and other people's bodies.

And that meant the end of the Western tradition of the sovereign individual with free will, who decides for him or herself but also understands that his or her will cannot be imposed on others who are not directly harming him or her. It heads squarely into the collectivist assumption in which third parties' bodies are legitimately policed.

Close to where we live, Olana, the majestic nineteenth-century home of one of the great Hudson River School painters of the America panorama, Frederic Edwin Church, was still closed. Parts of the National Shrine of the Divine Mercy in Stockbridge, Massachusetts, were closed "pending the end of COVID protocols." The park in Millerton, where generations of local American children learned to swim and enjoyed summer camp, was closed. The refreshments stand in Rudd Pond state park, down Route 22, was closed. Clermont State Historic Site, the seat of early America's prominent Livingston Family, was closed. There are brief descriptions of people and events outside in the gardens, but they are patchy and incomplete in telling the story. Schoolchildren in New York State could no longer enter the home of Robert Livingston, who helped draft the Declaration of Independence.

The reason for all these closures? The driver of this erasure of our history as Americans, an erasure that suits both Big Tech and the

CCP, an erasure that plays into the hands of the World Economic Forum with its hostility to nationalism and to national identities?

Still: "COVID-19."

I joined a Zoom conference of beloved elders. They were so frail. So much color had drained from their faces, they were almost white. There were hollows around their eyes. Without grandchildren, without Thanksgiving, without Hanukah, without Christmas, without dinner parties, without banquets, without christenings, without hugs, their socializing now was reduced to a Zoom protocol — a meeting, an agenda. They were so very, very alone.

CHAPTER NINETEEN

EVIL BEYOND HUMAN
IMAGINATION

I had come to believe there was more afoot here than just human vanity, or culpability, or even conventional evil. Here was an infection of the soul, endured by so many in 2020–22. There was the helter-skelter desertion of classical liberalism's — modern civilization's — most cherished post-war ideals; the sudden abandonment of post-Enlightenment norms of critical thinking; the dilution of parents' sense of protectiveness over the bodies and futures of their minor children; the acceptance of a world in which people can't gather to worship. We were faced with the suddenly manifested structures and their drivers, who erected this demonic world in less than two years and imposed it on everyone else; these heads of state and heads of the medical boards and heads of school boards and these teachers; these heads of unions and these national leaders and the state-level leaders and the town hall-level functionaries; all the way down to the men or women who disinvite relatives from Thanksgiving due to social pressure, because of a medical status which is no one's business and which affects no one.

This massive edifice of evil, was too complex and really, too elegant, to assign to just human awfulness and human inventiveness. It suggested a spiritual dimension of evil.

This evil was like a gigantic cultural spacecraft that landed on Earth, with a technology to unfold and almost at once set loose upon the egalitarian, post-Enlightenment West a global dystopia run on cruelty and cognitive dissonance.

How could otherwise nice people have come to do such evil?

How could they have allowed the suppression of young children's respiration or consigned friends and colleagues to eat in the street like outcasts? How could it have happened, in "enlightened" New York City, that cops would have been sent to arrest a woman with a terrified nine-year-old child for trying to visit the Museum of Natural History without "papers"?[333]

We detained those exposed to a "contagious disease" in forcible quarantine, without charge or trial, and cast people from their jobs, stigmatizing them as threats to health and decency. All of this happened — indeed, continues to happen even as this is written — in America, a land where, since the Civil Rights Act of 1964, the principle of equality governing human relations has been a matter of law, and where laws against the abuse of or corporal punishment of children in public schools are on the books in virtually every state.

Some commentators — including myself — have been comparing these years, 2020–22, in the West and in Australia, to the early years of Nazi leadership. It is easy to take that as a cheap and overwrought comparison, as evocations of Nazism usually are, and so to dismiss it out of hand as hyperbolic. And, indeed, certainly no one with a shred of decency would compare the evils wrought by the pandemic to the unspeakable horrors of the Nazi death camps.

Yet there is a comparison to be made to the years long preceding those horrors, when within Germany the psychological ground was laid for what would follow. This is when many vicious new norms and policies were set in place, often culturally policed. It was a culture of casual, escalating cruelty, a culture of mounting degradation of the "othered," an ever more rigid two-tier society, all of it by degrees transforming what had been a modern civil society into one capable of committing hitherto unimaginable evil, an evil that would be countenanced and even endorsed by doctors, medical associations, journalists, famous composers and filmmakers, universities, teachers, shopkeepers, and neighbors.

This is what we must recognize.

Indeed, it was a short slide from creating a two-tier society to embracing eugenics to identifying "life unworthy of life" to using the language of "hygiene" and public safety to set up the first Nazi euthanasia programs.

Anodyne language and medical authority and bureaucratization concealed the true nature of what was a visible, nauseating, daily-spreading evil.

*Early on in the pandemic, I asked a renowned medical-freedom
activist how he stayed strong in his mission as his name was
besmirched and he faced career attacks and social ostracism. He
replied with Ephesians 6:12: "For we wrestle not against flesh and
blood, but against principalities, against powers, against the rulers
of the darkness of this world, against spiritual wickedness in high
places."*

*I thought of that a lot over the intervening months. It made more
and more sense to me.*

*After many years of thinking that my spiritual life was not that
important, I started to pray again. I'd once have thought that
was very personal, almost embarrassingly so, and thus it was not
something I should mention in public. But now, at a gathering in
the woods with the health-freedom community, I told the group
that I was now willing to speak about God publicly. Why? Because
I had looked at what had descended on us from every angle, using
my normal critical training yet found that it was so elaborate in
its construction and so cruel, with an almost superhuman, flam-
boyant, baroque imagination made from the essence of cruelty
itself, that I could not conceive that it had been accomplished by
mere humans working on the bumbling human level in the dumb
political space.*

*In the magnitude of the evil around us; in its awe-inspiring level
of darkness and inhumanity; in the policies aimed at killing children's joy, restricting their breath, speech, and laughter; at killing
ties between families and extended families; at killing churches*

and synagogues and mosques; and, from the highest levels, from the president's own bully pulpit, demanding people to collude in excluding, rejecting, dismissing, shunning, hating their neighbors and loved ones and friends: in all of this the presence of such rampant, elemental evil I felt a darkness beyond anything human. I don't think humans are smart or powerful enough to have come up with this horror all alone.

So I told the group in the woods that the very impressiveness of evil all around us in all of its awful majesty was leading me to believe in a newly literal and immediate way in the presence, the possibility, the necessity of a countervailing force — that of God.

As a classical liberal writer in a post-war world that was a huge leap for me to take — and to say it out loud.

Grounded postmodern intellectuals are not supposed to talk about or believe in spiritual matters, certainly not in public. We are supposed to be shy about referencing God Himself, and definitely not talk about evil or the forces of darkness. As a Jew I come from a tradition in which Hell (or "Gehenom") is not the Miltonic hell of the later Western imagination, but rather a quieter interim spiritual place. "The Satan" exists in our literature (in Job for example) but neither is this the Miltonic Satan, that rock star, but a figure more modestly known as "the accuser."

We Jews, though, do have a history and literature that lets us talk about spiritual battle between the forces of God and negative forces that debase, that profane, that seek to ensnare our souls. We have seen this drama before, and not that long ago.

Other traditions of course also have ways to discuss and understand the spiritual battle taking place through humans, and through human leaders, and here on earth.

Of course, if you know intellectual history, you understand it was not always eccentric for intellectuals to talk in public about God, and even about God's adversary, and to worry in public about the fate of human souls. Mind and soul are not in fact at odds, and the body is not in fact at odds with either. Indeed, this acceptance of our three-part, integrated nature is part of our Western heritage. This is a truth only recently obscured or forgotten, a memory of our integrity as human beings that is only for the last seventy years or so, under attack.

The object of this spiritual battle?

It seemed to be for nothing short of the human soul.

One side, though, is wrestling for the human soul by targeting the human body that houses it, a body made in God's likeness: the temple of God.

CHAPTER TWENTY

THE NEW AUTHORITARIANS VS. THE INDIVIDUAL

Abruptly, in early 2022, came the turn.

In January there were massive anti-mandate protests[334] in The Netherlands, Switzerland, France, Spain, Italy, and in the United Kingdom, Boris Johnson dropped COVID restrictions.[335]

By January and into mid-February 2022, many other nations and US states had also retreated from the worst of the tyranny. They retreated in "lockstep." I could not think of another time in history in which systematic aggressions had been imposed on many nations' populations all at once, and then had been rolled back, all at once.

Denmark "Ease[d] COVID Restrictions" in January.[336] Italy loosened theirs in February.[337] Israel, the petri dish of "restrictions," dropped its "Green Pass" in February.[338]

It was hard not to suspect the retreat was related to the decision by a US court that Pfizer would not, as they had desperately sought, be able to conceal their internal documents for seventy-five years. They had to be disclosed now, thousands at a time.[339]

The Moderna CEO, for his part, sold his shares[340] and shut down his Twitter account.[341]

The news came in, day by day. Not only did the vaccine not work against new variants — as the Pfizer CEO Albert Bourla astonishingly told the business press, it offered "little protection"[342] — but now some countries were reporting higher rates of COVID-19 among the vaccinated.[343]

The former cheerleaders of "lockdowns," masks, and mRNA vaccinations were now laying down their paper trails and talking to their lawyers. Many people I knew, who just months before had reveled in their vaccinated status, fell quiet and somber. Dr. Walensky told a sympathetic interviewer at her alma mater that people had asked for CDC guidance as if they were asking her if they should have fries at Shake Shack.[344] Gone was any acknowledgment of her coercive declarations that broke thousands of small-property owners.

Those few governments, from Sweden to Florida, that had faced up to the storm of savage mockery and abuse, stood vindicated.

I took no pleasure in this. People were still dropping dead. People were still being harmed. Stroke, ministroke, heart disease, muscle aches, cognitive impairment, high cholesterol, migraines, neurological problems. So many people were ill.

But this sad and terrible story was far from over. Some leaders were so addicted to control over the citizenry they heedlessly, arrogantly continued to resist the data. France passed a vaccine passport.[345] In Washington, DC, proof of vaccination was still required to enter restaurants and gyms.[346]

When in January 2022 the Supreme Court ruled against President's Biden's vaccine mandate for all but the military and healthcare workers,[347] and a federal court struck down his mandate that federal workers be vaccinated,[348] the Biden Justice Department immediately appealed, and the administration mobilized the private sector to compel vaccinations.[349]

But what bode most frighteningly ill going forward were the events in Ottawa, Canada, where Prime Minister Justin Trudeau's response to three weeks of peaceful, even joyous, demonstrations by truckers seeking an end to the abusive and nonsensical mandates threatening their livelihood was the invocation of the rarely used Emergency Powers Act, enabling authorities not just to arrest and remove the protesters — which was done with needless violence — but to locate and seize their (and their supporters') financial assets via cooperation by banks, investment firms, credit unions, loan companies, insurance companies, and fundraising platforms.[350] It was left to my old acquaintance Chrystia Freeland, the Deputy Prime Minister and Minister of Finance, to announce this naked assault on democracy in jaw-droppingly Orwellian terms. "Team Canada has stood together over the past two years," she said. "We have trusted one another. We've leaned on one another. What we are facing today is a threat to our democratic institutions, to our economy, and to peace, order, and good government in Canada. It cannot stand and it will not stand."[351]

Here was proof, for those still seeking it, that in less than two years, the West, with its troublesome freedom and democracy, was over.

Still, even in this, there was a whisper of hope. Beaten down though they were, the Canadian truckers inspired similar grassroots actions around the globe. In Israel, Belgium, The Netherlands, France, Italy, and the United States, flags were raised with the words, "Freedom," "Liberté," "La Libertà."

And although the truckers weren't always given credit, by coincidence Quebec, Ontario, and Manitoba soon joined their fellow provinces of Alberta, Saskatchewan and Prince Edward Island in dropping Canada's COVID-19 passport system.[352]

Above all, in the face of the globalist-aligned elites' overwhelming power, and the certainty that they will continue their vicious rearguard action, the truckers reaffirmed what is most vital: the power of the individual to refuse to submit.

———————

I recently attended a gathering for medical freedom advocates in a little community center in the Hudson River Valley. Over the years of the pandemic, I had come to cherish this group of activists, who had steadfastly continued to gather through the depths of the "lockdown," that evil time in history — which is still not yet behind us. Joining their relaxed pot-luck dinners around delicious salads and chewy homemade breads helped me remember what it meant to be part of a sane human community. It helped keep me sane.

Now, again, at this gathering, children frolicked, just like normal, speaking and laughing and breathing freely, not suffocating in masks like little zombies or being warned by terrified adults to keep from touching other human children. Dogs were petted. Neighbors spoke to one another at normal ranges, without fear or phobias. Bands played much-loved folk songs or cool little indie-rock numbers they had written themselves, and no one, graceful or awkward, feared dancing. People sat on the house's steps shoulder to shoulder, in human warmth, and chatted over glasses of wine or homemade cider. No one asked anyone personal medical questions.

It was just a party — that simple thing — a party in the woods.

Children were dancing and playing with gongs.

A guitarist stood up with a ballad. A dad offered a funny song.

A beautiful older teenage girl with dark hair picked out notes on a piano.

Children curled up against their parents, people began to dance and flirt. Older folks chatted gently in corners by a fireplace. I felt the deeply soothing feeling of being in a big room full of humans who had no problem with me, who represented no threat to me, who wanted to share food and camaraderie. This was a deep peace as old as our first ancestors finding fellowship with other hominids around a fire, their kids safe, the predators far away beyond the shadows. No one was alone.

Outside the night deepened and darkened, quenching the deep green of the trees. The darkness outside was immeasurable.

It grew and grew.

Inside, in the fragile light, all you could hear were the thin sounds of human voices, a sound halfway between scared and hopeful.

It was the sound of human voices coming together, in spite of the darkness.

Human voices lifted up, and together — singing.

CONCLUSION

RESISTANCE

I n early March 2022, I interviewed Edward Dowd, a former portfolio manager at BlackRock who has been warning the world about what he called "Pfizer's data fraud." Appearing on the scene at the start of 2022, he was cautioning his peers in the investment community that betting on the Pfizers of the world is a bet against freedom forever. The charts he shared of CDC data showed, he warned, that boomers had died after vaccination at the same scale of deaths from "the Vietnam War." He expected that fraud investigations would sink Pfizer stock and drive Moderna into bankruptcy.[353]

I asked him where he got his personal courage.

He replied with something like, "I will keep going until we either win our freedoms back, or I am in a Gulag."

I understood. This is truly a time in history for the hammering out of heroes and heroines in the forge of crisis. And so it is also a time of cowardice, when those who choose collusion, when they know better, are allowing their souls to shrivel in that same heat.

For a year and a half, once it became clear that this crisis was never about "the virus" but rather about a global bid to kill off our free world and suppress all of our freedoms — I'd been getting DMs from people I know socially or professionally, people from journalism, from politics, from medicine, from science, saying variations on: "Naomi, I really respect you and totally agree with what you are saying. But, of course, I can't say anything publicly because [fill in the nonsensical, craven reason, such as 'My boss will get mad at me']."

I was initially baffled by these messages. What do these people want? Why do they think I need their excuses?

So I asked other, braver people what this was. They laughed and said, "They want you to tell them that it is OK."

But it is *not* OK.

The DMs insist that I am "brave." But I am not "brave"; they're just cowards.

I am beyond exasperated by those who stay in the shadows, agreeing with the risk-taking of others. It casts those who do take risks for the wellbeing of others as being somehow naturally better-fitted for this difficult job. It's a form of guiltlessly offloading personal responsibility. But there is no room left to equivocate; there is no room left to moon about in the middle.

At this point, there is no middle.

In the past two years, I have seen the bravest men and women of our time forced to hurtle into battle.

I watched Dr. Paul Alexander race into the thick of a peaceful trucker protest in Canada that was being targeted by Canadian authorities and send back defiant — peaceful — dispatches from the front.

I watched Dr. Martin Kulldorff, Dr. Sunetra Gupta, and Jeffrey Tucker, along with Dr. Jay Bhattacharya, early on tell the truth about "lockdowns" in the face of continual whirlwinds of institutional and media blowback.

Dr. Harvey Risch dared to say that we had attained herd immunity at a time when people were being professionally ostracized for doing so. The reporters who had showed courage I can count on two hands. Steven K. Bannon kept producing reports on attacks on liberty in the face of government legal scrutiny. Natalie Winters and *The National Pulse* team reported on government malfeasance regarding COVID when the president was saber-rattling scarily against purveyors of "misinformation."

Meanwhile, non-reporters were doing the job of AWOL or cowering reporters. Dr. Henry Ealy and the two Oregon state senators, Dennis Linthicum and Kim Thatcher, broke the massive story, mentioned above, of CDC malfeasance regarding government data.

I watched Jenin Younes of NCRA speaking up publicly against unlawful "lockdowns," knowing she would endure professional opposition. Leslie Manookian of HFDF early on sued coercive governors and governments, and she won. Lori Roman, of the ACRU, responded to every single email I forwarded from a desperate parent trying to protect a young-adult daughter or son, often a soldier, or a pregnant government employee, or a student, from forced mRNA vaccination.

I saw Stephanie Locricchio and Aimee Villella of Children's Health Defense rally thousands of moms and dads to confront their abusive governors and the cruel, forced-masking, forced-vaccinating schools. I saw these parents put their bodies between middle schoolers and the vans parked in the schoolyards where minors were to be injected against their parents' wishes with an experimental product, the serious harms of which had been scrupulously concealed.

But, of course, the real question is not, "What drives such parents to put their bodies between the van and the kids?" Rather, it is "Where the heck are all the other parents?"

Such heroes and heroines, and other less-known peaceful warriors aligned with liberties, would rather have been almost anywhere else, at work or enjoying their families, free of the need to face down bullies and stand up to security guards. But unlike most others, they understood that they were called to rise to this moment.

The thing is, we all are called. For this is a time when we all need to be at least somewhat brave.

The fact is, I don't know anyone heroic who likes the current battle. But what separates the heroic from the rest is knowing, in a moment when obvious right and wrong have not been so clear since 1941, that they could not live with themselves if they simply walked away.

You always hear heroes saying, "I had no choice" or "I was just doing my job." Heroes and heroines are right. They are just doing their jobs. They are doing their jobs *as human beings* with responsibilities to others. Dr. Patrick Phillips — the Canadian ER doctor who had spoken out early against the harms of "lockdowns" when many fellow doctors were silent — said something like, "I realized that many of my peers were silent because they were worried about their careers. But I also realized that if I didn't speak out, soon I would have no career worth saving."

Dr. Jay Bhattacharya said something like: "If I did not speak out, what was the point of my career in public health?" Dr. Peter McCullough, in the middle of fighting for everyone, and facing the erasure of the professional credentials after his name, went on television and said something like, "They can arrest me for saying this. Just don't give these mRNA vaccines to your child."

Watching these brave people made me braver than I would have been myself.

I was in New York City one day and found myself no longer able to bear it. My hotel, the Walker Hotel in Tribeca, had a café and a restaurant in the lobby with signs stating that these facilities were for "vaccinated only."

So on day three of my stay, I politely informed the staff at the Blue Bottle Coffee shop that I was unvaccinated and that I would now take my small coffee and my overnight oats to the forbidden lunch counter, and I would sit there peacefully, but that I would not comply with the NYC directive for the café to discriminate against me. The staff strenuously informed me — doing their job — that my doing so was against NYC "mandates." I said that I understood, but that I was nonetheless choosing not to comply. They warned that they would call the manager. I said that I understood. I then sat down at the illegal lunch counter, texted my lawyer to be on standby, posted publicly to Governor Kathy Hochul and to Mayor Eric Adams that I was currently intentionally violating the discriminatory NYC mandate that prevented unvaccinated people from being seated in cafés and restaurants and that I was at the Walker Hotel café lunch counter at that very moment if they wished to arrest me. Then I waited for an hour, heart pounding, to be arrested.

Do you know what happened?

Nothing.

Later that day I was at Grand Central Station. Almost all of the lower-level food court was roped off for the vaccinated, and there was nowhere for an unvaccinated New Yorker to sit down, let alone to eat lunch. At the entrance to the restricted seating area, a heavyset bouncer in a mask was demanding people's digital vaccinated cards along with — unprecedented in my experience — their IDs.

I explained that I wished to enter, and that I was unvaccinated and had no "Key to NYC" pass.

Two cops appeared at once. They nicely indicated the other seating area (over there, far away) saved for the unvaccinated. I explained that the strength of New York City, and of America for that matter, was its diversity and its equal treatment of all, and that if people had refused to comply with other forms of discrimination and forced separate accommodations, discriminatory rules would have ended sooner. For the second time that day, I stated I intended peacefully not to comply.

A third police officer, their senior, appeared. He explained that I would be given a summons for trespassing.

The cop with the notebook with the summons form took as long as he possibly could to write it out. No one wanted to arrest me or even give me a summons.

Finally the three cops surrounded me and firmly escorted me to the upper level. I was quite scared, but I told myself not to give in. On the upper level, I waited to be arrested. I was braced for the handcuffs. Once again my heart was racing. I have been arrested before in NYC, and it is frightening and uncomfortable.

But when I asked if I could now walk away and take my train — no one stopped me.

The takeaway? When I refused to comply with these unlawful "mandates" that had burnt out the soul of a once-great city, nothing happened.

The bullies, Governor Kathy Hochul and Mayor Eric Adams, who put these scary-sounding, Dear Leader-esque "edicts" in place and like petty tyrants forced free people to act against their wishes, were, like the Great and Powerful Oz, all bluster. There was nothing there.

But it took those awful, frightening moments of pressing against those terrifying-sounding "mandates" to prove, at least to myself, that they were meaningless.

The heroes and heroines whom I knew had that day given me the courage to prove something I believed was important enough to take a personal risk to demonstrate. I would not have known how to be brave without having witnessed their greater bravery.

Who are those now standing up, speaking out and taking risks against encroaching tyranny?

Overwhelmingly, it is not the "Zoom class," for all their virtue-signaling about social justice.

It is working people. It is truckers, moms, firefighters, and cops. When I spoke at a rally against forcing injections on first responders in NYC, the audience was made up mostly of working people. The people who march for every other cause in NYC — my affluent, liberal "tribe" — sat that one out.

It was the first responders who put their bodies in harm's way for the safety of my colleagues and acquaintances. But when it came to it, when it came to protecting the bodies of first responders from coercion and harm, the "Zoom class" failed utterly to reciprocate with courage of their own. To say the least, in this time of testing, we have not all been equally brave.

For the duration of the pandemic an old friend — an affluent, educated man who works at the Pasteur Institute — harangued me continually on social media, assailing me for my warnings about harms from mRNA vaccines.

Since reports questioning the data integrity of Pfizer's vaccine trials emerged,[354] his trolling abruptly ceased.

Then, on Facebook, he sent me news of his admittedly very pretty golden retriever.

In the run-up to the First World War, women handed out white feathers to healthy young men who had not enlisted in the war effort, a metaphor for their cowardice.

If there is a white feather to be given these days, it is to those who now try to change the subject from the mounting evidence of the damage done by their "side" to the bodies of children to the charm of their golden retrievers.

I hope and trust that all people will rethink our remaining silences — we all have them — and look at ourselves, in this moment, before it is too late.

In this moment when freedom itself is in the balance, when the alternative is servitude forever, this decision on whether to speak up makes all the difference. Tyrannies only fall when there is mass resistance. History is clear on this. When it is just a few, well, they are marginalized, silenced, smeared, or, when things go far enough, arrested. What matters most is that enough people stand up and resist all at once.

One of my favorite quotations is this, from the late poet Audre Lorde: "My silences had not protected me. Your silence will not protect you." It is truer now more than ever.

This is a dangerous moment indeed.

But it could also become a moment of profound blessing.

Danger, if we meet it, also gives each of us a God-given opportunity to serve our kind. In the process we become immeasurably more than we had been before.

Maybe in the course of forcing ourselves to act bravely, we actually do become brave.

———————

Someday all our kids and grandkids will ask each of us directly: "Why did you stand by? Why did you not help me?" "I could not breathe." Or, God forbid: "Now I have these health problems."

Or else they will say: "Thank you so much for speaking for me when I was too little to speak."

"Dad, Mom, Grandma, Grandpa," they will ask: "What did you do?"

So let me leave you with this question:

What *did* you do?

ENDNOTES

Introduction

1 Chrystia Freeland, "Remarks by the Deputy Prime Minister and Minister of Finance regarding the Emergencies Act," February 14, 2022, https://deputypm.canada.ca/en/news/speeches/2022/02/14/remarks-deputy-prime-minister-and-minister-finance-regarding-emergencies.

2 Rich Calder, "Canadian police arrest over 100 people in trucker protests," *The New York Post*, February 19, 2022, https://nypost.com/2022/02/19/canadian-police-arrest-over-100-people-in-trucker-protests/.

3 "Chrystia Freeland," World Economic Forum, https://www.weforum.org/people/chrystia-freeland.

4 "We Are a Nonprofit Fighting Poverty, Disease and Inequity Around the World," Bill & Melinda Gates Foundation, https://www.gatesfoundation.org; "Who Stands between YOU and the Next Pandemic?" EcoHealth Alliance, https://www.ecohealthalliance.org; "Using the Power of Epidemiology to Fight the Spread of COVID-19," Council of State and Territorial Epidemiologists, https://www.cste.org.

5 Klaus Schwab, "Time for a Great Reset," ProjectSyndicate.org, June 3, 2020, https://www.project-syndicate.org/commentary/great-reset-capitalism-covid19-crisis-by-klaus-schwab-2020-06?barrier=accesspaylog.

6 Hans van Leeuen, "When Will Things Get Back to Normal? Never, Says Davos Founder," *Financial Review*, July 22, 2020, https://www.afr.com/world/europe/when-will-things-get-back-to-normal-never-says-davos-founder-20200714-p55br2.

7 "WEF Founder: We Must Prepare for an Angrier World." July 14, 2020, YouTube, CNBC International TV, https://www.youtube.com/watch?v=LJTnkzl3K64.

8 Ibid.

9 World Economic Forum, "Davos Agenda: What Can We Expect of 2022? Highlights and Key Takeaways," *The European Sting*, January 24, 2022, https://europeansting.com/2022/01/24/davos-agenda-what-can-we-expect-of-2022-highlights-and-key-takeaways/.

10 Karen Matthews, ""Disrespectful" of Thousands to Attend Secret Orthodox Wedding in Brooklyn," NBCNewYork.com, November 22, 2020, https://www.nbcnewyork.com/news/coronavirus/cuomo-disrespectful-of-thousands-to-attend-secret-orthodox-wedding-in-brooklyn/2739905/.

11 Amy Howe, "Divided Court Allows Indoor Worship Services to Resume in California," SCOTUS Blog, February 6, 2021, https://www.scotusblog.com/2021/02/divided-court-allows-indoor-worship-services-to-resume-in-california/.

12 The Martha's Vineyard Hebrew Center, "The Martha's Vineyard Hebrew Center is Now Zoom Only . . . Out of an abundance of caution, and after consultation with health professionals, the Trustees of the Hebrew Center have decided to close the sanctuary for the immediate future until further notice. Commencing Friday 12/24 all Hebrew Center events will be exclusively via Zoom. In addition, the school also remains closed and all classes will continue on Zoom. The Omicron variant has added a new level of uncertainty in the pandemic. The health and safety of our congregation and community continue to be our primary concern and responsibility. We regret

this seeming step back, but we have come far since the start of the pandemic and hopefully will be moving forward again in the future. Hoping all a happy, healthy and safe secular new year. Robert W. Herman DMD, President, MVHC Board of Trustees"; "*The building is closed for services and events. The office will be staffed remotely and also on site, one person at a time with full precautions*," https://www.mvhc.us.

13   John Malcolm, "Are Parents Being Tagged as "Domestic Terrorists" by the FBI? Justice Department Needs to Show Its Cards," November 18, 2021, The Heritage Foundation, https://www.heritage.org/crime-and-justice/commentary/are-parents-being-tagged-domestic-terrorists-the-fbi-justice.

14   AIER Staff, "Lockdowns Did Not Control the Coronavirus: The Evidence," December 19, 2020, https://www.aier.org/article/lockdowns-do-not-control-the-coronavirus-the-evidence/.

15   David Adam, "Special Report: The Simulations Driving the World's Response to COVID-19," April 20, 2020, Nature.com, https://www.nature.com/articles/d41586-020-01003-6.

16   Tiana Herring, Prison Policy Initiative, "The Research is Clear: Solitary Confinement Causes Long-Lasting Harm," December 8, 2020, https://www.prisonpolicy.org/blog/2020/12/08/solitary_symposium/.

17   Ibid.

18   Ibid.

19   "Specifically, it has been demonstrated that situations of severe solitary or group confinement . . . are associated with an increase of psychotic symptoms, paranoia and hallucination experiences in healthy populations, who were especially selected and trained to survive in extreme conditions (Cochrane and Freeman, 1989; Gunderson and Nelson, 1963; Strange and Klein, 1973). Similarly, some patients isolated . . . also develop a psychotic syndrome including visual hallucinations and paranoid delusion, unrelated to their neurological condition (Granberg-Axèll et al., 2001)." Louise Morales-Brown, "What Does it Mean to be "Touch Starved"?" January 19, 2021, Medical News Today, https://www.medicalnewstoday.com/articles/touch-starved#what-it-means.

20   Jacques Launay, "Choir Singing Improves Health, Happiness — and is the Perfect Icebreaker." The Conversation, University of Oxford Research, https://www.ox.ac.uk/research/choir-singing-improves-health-happiness-—-and-perfect-icebreaker.

21   Harvard Kennedy School, "Collaboration in a Fractured World: Klaus Schwab MC/MPA Speaks at Harvard Kennedy School," October 2, 2017, https://www.hks.harvard.edu/more/alumni/alumni-stories/collaboration-fractured-world-klaus-schwab-mcmpa-speaks-harvard-kennedy.

22   Jessica Dickler, "Krispy Kreme doubles its free doughnut incentive for vaccinations," *CNBC*, August 30, 2021, https://www.cnbc.com/2021/08/30/krispy-kreme-doubles-its-free-doughnut-incentive-for-vaccinations.html.

23   "McDonald's offers COVID-19 vaccines, free food at select Bay Area locations," *ABC7 News*, June 21, 2021, https://abc7news.com/mcdonalds-free-food-covid-19-vaccine-covid-vaccinations-stuff/10816998/.

24   "The Great Barrington Declaration," October 4, 2020, https://gbdeclaration.org/.

25   The Editorial Board, "Lockdowns Didn't Stop Covid," *The Wall Street Journal*, May 9, 2021,

https://www.wsj.com/articles/lockdowns-didnt-stop-covid-11620596906.

26   Hanke, Steve H., Jonas Herby and Lars Jonung. 2022. "A Literature Review and Meta-Analysis of the Effects of Lockdowns on COVID-19 Mortality." Studies in Applied Economics No. 200, https://sites.krieger.jhu.edu/iae/files/2022/01/A-Literature-Review-and-Meta-Analysis-of-the-Effects-of-Lockdowns-on-COVID-19-Mortality.pdf.

27   Sahil Kapur, "Democrats turn against mask mandates as Covid landscape and voter attitudes shift," *NBC News,* March 1, 2022, https://www.nbcnews.com/politics/politics-news/democrats-turn-against-mask-mandates-covid-landscape-voter-attitudes-shift-rcna18043.

28   "Federal Judge Tells FDA it Must Make Public 55,000 Pages a Month of Pfizer Vaccine Data," *FDA News,* January 10, 2022. https://www.fdanews.com/articles/206113-federal-judge-tells-fda-it-must-make-public-55000-pages-a-month-of-pfizer-vaccine-data.

Chapter One: March 2020: "Lockdown"

29   Heloise Wood, "Naomi Wolf and Sandi Toksvig to Headline Women of the World Festival," *The Bookseller,* November 29, 2019, https://www.thebookseller.com/news/news/naomi-wolf-and-sandi-toksvig-headline-10th-women-world-festival-2020-1122451.

30   "TO ALL FREE MEN OF OUR KINGDOM we have also granted, for us and our heirs for ever, all the liberties written out below, to have and to keep for them and their heirs, of us and our heirs:" "English Translation of Magna Carta", British Library, https://www.bl.uk/magna-carta/articles/magna-carta-english-translation

31   Lisa Schnirring, "Italy Expand COVID-19 Lockdown to Whole Country," *Center for Infectious Diseases Research and Policy,* March 9, 2020. https://www.cidrap.umn.edu/news-perspective/2020/03/italy-expands-covid-19-lockdown-whole-country.

32   "About Health Disparity," The Institute for Family Health, https://institute.org/bronx-health-reach/about/about-health-disparity/.

33   Michael Paulson, "Broadway, Symbol of New York Resilience, Shuts Down Amid Virus Threat," *The New York Times,* March 12, 2020, https://www.nytimes.com/2020/03/12/theater/coronavirus-broadway-shutdown.html.

Chapter Two: "Uniform Safety for Everyone"

34   "Governor Cuomo Announces New York Ending COVID-19 State Disaster Emergency on June 24," June 23, 2021, https://www.governor.ny.gov/news/governor-cuomo-announces-new-york-ending-covid-19-state-disaster-emergency-june-24.

35   New York State, "Governor Cuomo Signs the New York State "On Pause" Executive Order," March 20, 2020, https://www.governor.ny.gov/news/governor-cuomo-signs-new-york-state-pause-executive-order.

36   Israel Ministry of Foreign Affairs, "Victims of Mahane Yehuda Bombing," https://mfa.gov.il/mfa/mfa-archive/1998/pages/victims%20of%20mahane%20yehuda%20bombing.aspx.

37   Staff and Agencies, "Jerusalem Suicide Bomber Kills Six," *The Guardian,* April 12, 2002, https://

www.theguardian.com/world/2002/apr/12/israel4.

38 New York State, "Governor Cuomo Announces New York Ending COVID-19 State Disaster Emergency on June 24", June 23 2021, https://www.governor.ny.gov/news/governor-cuomo-announces-new-york-ending-covid-19-state-disaster-emergency-june-24.

39 New York State, "Governor Cuomo Signs the New York State "On Pause" Executive Order," March 20, 2020, https://www.governor.ny.gov/news/governor-cuomo-signs-new-york-state-pause-executive-order.

40 New York State Assembly, 11-16 PUBLIC HEARING ON ADAPTATION AND RECOVERY OF LIBRARIES THROUGHOUT THE COVID-19 PANDEMIC, November 16, 2021, https://nystateassembly.granicus.com/MediaPlayer.php?view_id=9&clip_id=6437.

41 Staff and Agencies, "New York Arts Institutions Closed Because of Coronavirus, *The New York Times,* March 12, 2020, https://www.nytimes.com/2020/03/12/arts/ny-events-cancellations-coronavirus.html?action=click&module=RelatedLinks&pgtype=Article.

42 Sam Levin, "Revealed: Amazon Told Workers Paid Sick Leave Law Doesn't Cover Warehouses," *The Guardian,* May 7, 2020, https://www.theguardian.com/technology/2020/may/07/amazon-warehouse-workers-coronavirus-time-off-california.

43 Luis de Leon, "How the COVID-19 pandemic has impacted bookstores," *KVUE ABC,* December 3, 2020, https://www.kvue.com/article/news/health/coronavirus/adjusting-to-the-pandemic-how-bookstores-continue-to-stay-open/269-d4060f39-810f-487b-9a55-8cec6ec72ed5.

44 Kelly Tyko, "Are liquor stores open during coronavirus? New York says liquor stores are 'essential,' can stay open," *USA Today,* March 20, 2020, https://www.usatoday.com/story/money/2020/03/20/coronavirus-new-york-liquor-stores-essential/2887048001/.

45 Dan Levin, "Is Marijuana an 'Essential' Like Milk or Bread? Some States Say Yes," *The New York Times,* April 10, 2020, https://www.nytimes.com/article/coronavirus-weed-marijuana.html.

46 Government of the United Kingdom, "Staying at home and away from others (social distancing)," Cabinet Office, March 23, 2020, https://www.gov.uk/government/publications/full-guidance-on-staying-at-home-and-away-from-others.

47 California Department of Parks and Recreation, "State Parks COVID-19 Resource Center," https://www.parks.ca.gov/?page_id=30350.

48 "COVID-19 State of Emergency," https://www.mass.gov/info-details/covid-19-state-of-emergency.

49 "Coronavirus Act 2020," March 25, 2020, https://bills.parliament.uk/bills/2731.

50 "The CARES Act," March 27, 2020, https://www.congress.gov/bill/116th-congress/house-bill/748.

51 "The HEROES Act," May 15, 2020, https://www.congress.gov/bill/116th-congress/house-bill/6800/text?r=48.

52 "The American Rescue Plan," March 11, 2021, https://www.congress.gov/bill/117th-congress/house-bill/1319/text.

53 Nathaniel Weixel, "Treasury threatens to claw back COVID-19 funds because of Arizona school anti-mask rules," *The Hill,* January 14, 2022, https://thehill.com/policy/healthcare/589785-trea-

sury-threatens-to-claw-back-covid-funds-because-of-arizona-school-anti.

54   Jay Cameron, Interview by Dr. Naomi Wolf, *DailyClout,* March 8, 2022, https://dailyclout.io/
jay-cameron-explains-canadas-emergency-act/.

Chapter Three: Understanding the Criminals

55   Grace Ashford, "Noncitizens' Right to Vote Becomes Law in New York City," *The New York*
Times, January 9, 2022, https://www.nytimes.com/2022/01/09/nyregion/noncitizens-nyc-voting-
rights.html.

56   Kight, Stef W., and Jonathan Swan, "Scoop: Biden officials fear 'mass migration event' if COVID
policies end," *Axios,* March 17, 2022, https://www.axios.com/biden-border-mexico-migrants-title-
42-a91b6441-2197-463f-ab1f-2435824a9566.html.

57   Gregorio Billikopf Encina, "Milgram's Experiment on Obedience to Authority," University of
California at Berkeley, November 15, 2004, https://nature.berkeley.edu/ucce50/ag-labor/7article/
article35.htm.

58   Ibid.

59   Mark Lowen, "Greek Debt Crisis: What Was the Point of the Referendum?," BBC News, July 11,
2015, https://www.bbc.com/news/world-europe-33492387/.

60   Ian Johnston, Nathalie Savaricas, Leo Cendrowicz, "Greece referendum: Greeks say 'No' to austerity and plunge Europe into crisis," *The Independent,* July 6, 2015, https://www.independent.co.uk/
news/world/europe/greece-referendum-results-live-greeks-say-no-to-austerity-and-plunge-the-eu-
into-crisis-10367617.html.

61   Daniela Vincenti and Sarantis Michalopoulos, "Monti: Ignoring the Greek referendum was a
violation of democracy," October 23, 2015, Euractiv.com, https://www.euractiv.com/section/euro-
finance/news/monti-ignoring-the-greek-referendum-was-a-violation-of-democracy/.

62   Larry Getlen, "China's Secret Plan to Topple the US as the World's Superpower," *The New York*
Post, February 8, 2015, https://nypost.com/2015/02/08/chinas-secret-plan-to-topple-the-us-as-the-
worlds-superpower/.

63   US-China Economic And Security Review Commission, "Hearing: China's Propaganda and Influence Operations, Its Intelligence Activities that Target the United States, and the Resulting Impacts
on US National Security," April 30, 2009, https://www.uscc.gov/hearings/hearing-chinas-propa-
ganda-and-influence-operations-its-intelligence-activities-target; Transcript: https://www.uscc.gov/
files/000249.

64   Sarah Cook, Senior Research Analyst for East Asia, Freedom House, testimony before the "US-
China Economic and Security Review Commission Hearing on China's Information Controls,
Global Media Influence, and Cyber Warfare Strategy": "Chinese Government Influence on the
US Media Landscape," May 4, 2017, https://www.uscc.gov/sites/default/files/Sarah%20Cook%20
May%204th%202017%20USCC%20testimony.pdf.

65   Freedom House, "Chinese Communist Party's Media Influence Expands Worldwide," January
14, 2020, https://freedomhouse.org/article/chinese-communist-partys-media-influence-expands-

worldwide.

66   International Federation of Journalists, "The China Story: Reshaping the World's Media," June 2020, https://www.ifj.org/fileadmin/user_upload/IFJ_ChinaReport_2020.pdf.

67   Rick Hess, "Microsoft Education Exec. On Ed. Tech During Coronavirus," *EdWeek,* April 30, 2020, https://www.edweek.org/education/opinion-microsoft-education-exec-on-ed-tech-during-coronavirus/2020/04.

Chapter Four: "Standing Together by Staying Apart"

68   Felisher, Or, Gabriel Gianordoli, Yuliya Parshina-Kottas, Karthik Patanjali and Bedel Saget, "This 3-D Simulation Shows Why Social Distancing is So Important," *The New York Times,* April 14, 2020, https://www.nytimes.com/interactive/2020/04/14/science/coronavirus-transmission-cough-6-feet-ar-ul.html.

69   Gorman, James, Michael Levenson and Tara Parker-Pope, "What We Know About Your Chances of Catching the Virus Outdoors," *The New York Times,* May 15, 2020, https://www.nytimes.com/2020/05/15/us/coronavirus-what-to-do-outside.html.

70   Thomas Mann, *The Magic Mountain,* Vintage Books (New York, 1996): 222–23.

71   Staff and agencies, "Historical Guide to Yellow Fever," *PBS: American Experience,* https://www.pbs.org/wgbh/americanexperience/features/fever-historical-guide-yellow-fever/.

72   Elizabeth Fenn, "The Great Smallpox Epidemic," *History Today,* August 8, 2003, https://www.historytoday.com/archive/great-smallpox-epidemic.

73   Charles E. Rosenberg, *The Cholera Years: The United States in 1832, 1849, and 1866,* (Chicago: The University of Chicago Press, 1987), 4.

74   NIH US National Library of Medicine, "Visual Culture and Public Health Posters: Tuberculosis," https://www.nlm.nih.gov/exhibition/visualculture/tuberculosis.html.

75   Marta K. D. Cobb, "Public Health In Jane Eyre and the Victorian Era," *The Victorian Web,* May 1994, https://victorianweb.org/authors/bronte/cbronte/jane1.html.

76   American Psychological Association, "Resilience in a Time of War: Tips for Parents and Teachers of Elementary School Children," 2011, https://www.apa.org/topics/resilience/kids-war.

77   Benjamin Rush, *Observations upon the Origin of the Malignant Bilious, or Yellow Fever in Philadelphia, and upon the Means of Preventing it: addressed to the Citizens of Philadelphia,* (Philadelphia: Budd and Bartram, 1799), 12, https://nrs.lib.harvard.edu/urn-3:hms.count:1115396?n=12.

78   Library of Congress, "First Bank of the United States, 120 South Third Street, Philadelphia, Philadelphia County, PA," https://www.loc.gov/item/pa0850/.

79   Reynolds-Finley Historical Library, The University of Alabama at Birmingham, "The Life of Florence Nightingale," https://library.uab.edu/locations/reynolds/collections/florence-nightingale/life.

80   Felice Batlan, "Law and the Fabric of the Everyday: The Settlement Houses, Sociological Jurisprudence, And the Gendering of Urban Legal Culture," *Southern California Interdisciplinary Law Journal,* Volume 15 (2006), 264, https://gould.usc.edu/why/students/orgs/ilj/assets/docs/15-2%20Batlan.pdf.

81   Laura Bliss, "How the Battle for Sunlight Shaped New York City," *Bloomberg CityLab,* December 18, 2016, https://www.bloomberg.com/news/articles/2016-12-18/new-york-city-zoning-and-the-fight-for-sunlight.

82   Janice M. Leone, "Bethlehem House, Nashville," *Tennessee Encyclopedia,* October 8, 2017, https://tennesseeencyclopedia.net/entries/bethlehem-house/.

83   Wade, Louise C. "The Heritage from Chicago's Early Settlement Houses." *Journal of the Illinois State Historical Society (1908-1984)* 60, no. 4 (1967): 411–41. http://www.jstor.org/stable/40190170.

84   Rony Caryn Rabin, "Alcohol-Related Deaths Spiked During the Pandemic, a Study Shows," *The New York Times,* March 22, 2022, https://www.nytimes.com/2022/03/22/health/alcohol-deaths-covid.html.

85   Angela Buckley, "Oscar Wilde Comes to Reading Gaol — 120 Years On," BerkshireLive.com, November 22, 2017, https://www.getreading.co.uk/news/berkshire-history/oscar-wilde-comes-reading-gaol-10472787.

86   The Iona and Peter Opie Archive, British Academy Research Project, Digital Humanities Institute, https://www.opiearchive.org.

Chapter Five: The "New Normal"

87   Jordan Novet, "Zoom Provides Disappointing Revenue Forecast for First Quarter and Full Year," CNBC.com, February 28, 2022, https://www.cnbc.com/2022/02/28/zoom-zm-earnings-q4-2022.html.

88   Megan Gearhardt, "Coronavirus and Zoom Have Marked a Generation," NBCnews.com, June 7, 2020, https://www.nbcnews.com/think/opinion/coronavirus-zoom-have-marked-generation-let-s-call-them-zoomers-ncna1226241.

89   Tara Parker-Pope, "What's the Risk of Catching Coronavirus from a Surface? Touching Contaminated Objects and then Infecting Ourselves with the Germs is Not Typically How the Virus Spreads. But it Can Happen." *The New York Times,* May 28, 2020, https://www.nytimes.com/2020/05/28/well/live/whats-the-risk-of-catching-coronavirus-from-a-surface.html.

90   "COVID-19 mistakes and myths," *UC Davis Health,* August 5, 2021, https://health.ucdavis.edu/coronavirus/covid-19-information/coronavirus-mistakes.

91   Ozer, Nicole and Jay Stanley, "Diners Beware: That Meal May Cost You Your Privacy and Security," *ACLU,* July 27, 2021, https://www.aclu.org/news/privacy-technology/diners-beware-that-meal-may-cost-you-your-privacy-and-security/.

92   Jordan Crook. "HelloFresh Cooks Up $50 Million Series D From Insight Venture Partners," TechCrunch, June 18, 2014, https://techcrunch.com/2014/06/18/hellofresh-cooks-up-50-million-series-d-from-insight-venture-partners/?guccounter=1&guce_referrer=aHR0cHM6Ly93d3cuZ29vZ2xlLmNvbS8&guce_referrer_sig=AQAAAFX9ssOqAFN21SL8Vfxc7auIPBOgeZb8DbLd2GAzzf4vecxiEHzN1Q.

93   Burt Helm. "The World's Most Ruthless Food Startup: The Inside Story of How HelloFresh

Clawed Its Way to the Top," *Inc.,* June 27, 2018, https://www.inc.com/magazine/201808/burt-helm/hellofresh.html.

94   "Annual Report 2018." *HelloFresh SE, 2019,* https://ir.hellofreshgroup.com/download/compa-nies/hellofresh/Annual%20Reports/DE000A161408-JA-2018-EQ-E-00.pdf., "Annual Report 2019." *HelloFresh SE, 2020,* https://ir.hellofreshgroup.com/download/companies/hellofresh/Annual%20Reports/DE000A161408-JA-2019-EQ-E-01.pdf, "Annual Report 2020." *HelloFresh SE, 2021,* https://ir.hellofreshgroup.com/download/companies/hellofresh/Annual%20Reports/DE000A161408-JA-2020-EQ-E-00.pdf., "Annual Report 2021." *HelloFresh SE, 2022,* https://ir.hellofreshgroup.com/download/companies/hellofresh/Annual%20Reports/DE000A161408-JA-2021-PN-EQ-E-00.pdf

95   Oxford COVID-19 Government Response Tracker, https://covidtracker.bsg.ox.ac.uk/.

96   Harris, Rich and Lauren Leatherby, "States That Imposed Few Restrictions Now Have the Worst Outbreaks," *The New York Times,* November 18, 2020, https://www.nytimes.com/interactive/2020/11/18/us/covid-state-restrictions.html.

97   AIER Staff, "Lockdowns Do Not Control the Coronavirus: The Evidence," December 19, 2020, https://www.aier.org/article/lockdowns-do-not-control-the-coronavirus-the-evidence/.

98   Len Blavatnik – "Industrialist," http://lenblavatnik.com/industrialist/technology-ventures/. Accessed March 23, 2022.

99   Ibid.

100 Zhihu Inc. – "Corporate Profile," https://ir.zhihu.com/Company-Profile. Accessed March 23, 2022.

101 Access Technology Ventures, AccessTechnologyVentures.com. Accessed March 23, 2022.

102 Blavatnik School of Government – Research – Research Programmes – "Pathways for Prosperity," https://www.bsg.ox.ac.uk/research/research-programmes/pathways-prosperity. Accessed March 23, 2022.

103 Alan Feuer and Andrea Salcedo, "New York City Deploys 45 Mobile Morgues as Virus Strains Funeral Home," *The New York Times,* April 2, 2020, https://www.nytimes.com/2020/04/02/nyregion/coronavirus-new-york-bodies.html.

104 Ibid.

105 The Hart Island Project, "The History," https://www.hartisland.net/history.

106 The Hart Island Project, https://www.hartisland.net.

107 "Coronavirus: New York ramps up mass burials amid outbreaks," *BBC,* April 10, 2020, *https://*www.bbc.com/news/world-us-canada-52241221.

108 J. D. Simkins, "Hospital Ship Comfort Departs NYC, Having Treated Fewer than 200 Patients," NavyTimes.com, April 30, 2020.

109 Caroline Linton, "Field Hospital That Treated Coronavirus Patients in Central Park to Close," CBSnews.com, May 2, 2020, https://www.cbsnews.com/news/field-hospital-that-treated-coronavirus-patients-in-central-park-to-close/.

110 Brian M. Rosenthal, "This Hospital Cost $52 Million. It Treated 79 Virus Patients.," *The New York Times,* July 21, 2020, https://www.nytimes.com/2020/07/21/nyregion/coronavirus-hospital-usta-queens.html.

111 Michelle Andrews, "Is Cuomo Directive to Blame for Nursing Home Deaths, As US Official Claims?," KHN.org News, August 24, 2020, https://khn.org/news/is-cuomo-directive-to-blame-for-nursing-home-covid-deaths-as-us-official-claims/.

112 Caroline Linton, "Field Hospital That Treated Coronavirus Patients in Central Park to Close," CBSnews.com, May 2, 2020, https://www.cbsnews.com/news/field-hospital-that-treated-coronavirus-patients-in-central-park-to-close/.

113 "Coronavirus Field Hospital in Central Park Shutting Down On Monday," newyork.cbslocal.com, May 2, 2020, https://newyork.cbslocal.com/2020/05/02/coronavirus-field-hospital-in-central-park-shutting-down-on-monday.

114 "Coronavirus Field Hospital in Central Park Shutting Down On Monday," newyork.cbslocal.com, May 2, 2020, https://newyork.cbslocal.com/2020/05/02/coronavirus-field-hospital-in-central-park-shutting-down-on-monday.

115 "COVID-19 Deaths per 100K," *US News & World Report,* March 20, 2022, https://www.usnews.com/news/best-states/coronavirus-data/covid-death-rate?active[]=12&chart_type=map, accessed March 23, 2022.

116 "Amtrak Requires facial Coverings as Added Measure of Protection," May 7, 2020. https://media.amtrak.com/2020/05/amtrak-requires-facial-coverings-as-added-measure-of-protection/.

Chapter Six: How Emergency Policy is Made

117 Jacqueline Maley, The political art of not wasting a crisis, or getting wasted by it," *Sydney Morning Herald,* May 17, 2020, https://www.smh.com.au/politics/federal/the-political-art-of-not-wasting-a-crisis-or-getting-wasted-by-it-20200515-p54tej.html.

118 Nathan J. Robinson, "Bill Clinton's Act of Terrorism," *Jacobin,* Oct 12, 2016, https://www.jacobinmag.com/2016/10/bill-clinton-al-shifa-sudan-bombing-khartoum/.

119 Ibid

120 Ibid.

121 Ibid.

122 Scott Peterson, "Sudanese factory destroyed by US now a shrine," *The Christian Science Monitor,* August 7, 2012, https://www.csmonitor.com/World/Africa/2012/0807/Sudanese-factory-destroyed-by-US-now-a-shrine.

123 Andrew Jacobs, "Now the US Has Lots of Ventilators, But Too Few Specialists to Operate Them," *The New York Times,* November 22, 2020, https://www.nytimes.com/2020/11/22/health/Covid-ventilators-stockpile.html.

124 Lina Zeldovich, "Some Signs of Recovery from Severe COVID-19 Lung Damage," *The New York Times,* October 18, 2020, https://www.nytimes.com/2020/10/18/health/Covid-lung-damage-recovery.html.

125 Pidd, Helen and Peter Walker, "'Don't kill granny' message for Preston youth aims to slow spread of Covid-19," *The Guardian,* August 8, 2020, https://www.theguardian.com/world/2020/aug/07/preston-added-to-areas-with-bans-on-households-mixing-due-to-covid-19.

126 The Rt Hon Priti Patel MP and Home Office, "Rule of six comes into effect to tackle coronavirus," September 14 2020, https://www.gov.uk/government/news/rule-of-six-comes-into-effect-to-tackle-coronavirus.

127 Boris Johnson, UK Parliament, "Covid-19: Winter Plan," November 23, 2020, https://hansard.parliament.uk/commons/2020-11-23/debates/81549EE3-DAFC-43CB-B8E6-C4F2C32393C8/Covid-19WinterPlan.

128 Anissa Gardizy, "Watch: COVID-19 commercials," *The Boston Globe,* May 7, 2020, https://www.bostonglobe.com/2020/05/07/business/watch-covid-19-commercials/.

129 Chris Smyth and Rosemary Bennett, "'Don't Kill Granny with Coronavirus,' Warns Matt Hancock," September 8, 2020, *The Times,* https://www.thetimes.co.uk/article/affluent-youth-are-catching-coronavirus-most-says-matt-hancock-qvbpxw2nk.

130 Ramesh Thakur, "Who Killed Granny? Shameless Emotional Manipulation has Shaped Too Much of Global COVID Policy, Disastrously," *The Times of India,* February 12, 2021, https://timesofindia.indiatimes.com/blogs/toi-edit-page/who-killed-granny-shameless-emotional-manipulation-has-shapedr-too-much-of-global-covid-policy-disastrously/.

131 Laura Dodsworth, *A State of Fear: How the UK Government Weaponized Fear During the COVID-19 Pandemic* (London: Pinter & Martin), 2021.

132 Thompson CN, Baumgartner J, Pichardo C, et al. COVID-19 Outbreak — New York City, February 29–June 1, 2020. MMWR Morb Mortal Wkly Rep 2020;69:1725–1729. DOI: http://dx.doi.org/10.15585/mmwr.mm6946a2

Chapter Seven: The Unverifiable Pandemic

133 Staff and agencies, "Coronavirus in the US: Latest Map and Case Count," *The New York Times,* https://www.nytimes.com/interactive/2021/us/covid-cases.html, accessed March 22, 2022.

134 "Our World in Data," https://ourworldindata.org/explorers/coronavirus-data-explorer.

135 Johns Hopkins University and Medicine Coronavirus Resource Center, https://coronavirus.jhu.edu.

136 Apoorva Mandavilli, "Your Coronavirus Test Is Positive. Maybe It Shouldn't Be.," *The New York Times,* August 29, 2021, https://www.nytimes.com/2020/08/29/health/coronavirus-testing.html

137 Henry Ealy, Michael McEvoy, Daniel Chong, John Nowicki, Monica Sava, Sandeep Gupta, David White, James Jordan, Daniel Simon, Paul Anderson, "COVID-19 Data Collection, Comorbidity & Federal Law: A Historical Retrospective" *Science, Public Health Policy, and The Law,* Volume 2:4-22, October 12, 2020, (https://www.researchgate.net/publication/344753727_COVID-19_Data_Collection_Comorbidity_Federal_Law_A_Historical_Retrospective).

138 "Oregon Senators Kim Thatcher and Dennis Linthicum File Grand Jury Petition Alleging CDC, FDA Violated Federal Law by Inflating COVID Death Data," September 19, 2021, https://

or.childrenshealthdefense.org/news/oregon-senators-kim-thatcher-and-dennis-linthicum-file-grand-jury-petition-alleging-cdc-fda-violated-federal-law-by-inflating-covid-death-data/.

139 https://dockets.justia.com/docket/oregon/ordce/3:2022cv00356/165733, *Ealy et al v. Redfield et al*, JUSTIA Dockets Filings, March 4, 2022.

140 "Oregon Senators Kim Thatcher and Dennis Linthicum File Grand Jury Petition Alleging CDC, FDA Violated Federal Law by Inflating COVID Death Data," September 19, 2021, https://or.childrenshealthdefense.org/news/oregon-senators-kim-thatcher-and-dennis-linthicum-file-grand-jury-petition-alleging-cdc-fda-violated-federal-law-by-inflating-covid-death-data/.

141 Henry Ealy, Michael McEvoy, Daniel Chong, John Nowicki, Monica Sava, Sandeep Gupta, David White, James Jordan, Daniel Simon, Paul Anderson, "COVID-19 Data Collection, Comorbidity & Federal Law: A Historical Retrospective" *Science, Public Health Policy, and The Law*, Volume 2:4-22, October 12, 2020, (https://www.researchgate.net/publication/344753727_COVID-19_Data_Collection_Comorbidity_Federal_Law_A_Historical_Retrospective)

142 Reuters, "CDC reports fewer COVID-19 pediatric deaths after data correction." *Reuters*, March 18, 2022, https://www.reuters.com/business/healthcare-pharmaceuticals/cdc-reports-fewer-covid-19-pediatric-deaths-after-data-correction-2022-03-18/.

143 Melody Schreiber, "CDC coding error led to overcount of 72,000 Covid deaths," *The Guardian*, March 24, 2022, https://www.theguardian.com/world/2022/mar/24/cdc-coding-error-overcount-covid-deaths.

144 Ibid.

145 Johns Hopkins Coronavirus Resource Center: https://coronavirus.jhu.edu/map.html; COVID19Tracking.com; Worldometers.info, https://www.worldometers.info/coronavirus/; *The New York Times*, Track Coronavirus Cases in Places Important to You: https://www.nytimes.com/interactive/2021/us/covid-cases-deaths-tracker.html; "COVID-19: Track Coronavirus Cases": https://coronavirus.data.gov.uk; Office for National Statistics: Coronavirus—COVID19 — Latest Statistics": https://www.ons.gov.uk/peoplepopulationandcommunity/healthandsocialcare/conditionsanddiseases/articles/coronaviruscovid19/latestinsights.

146 The COVID Tracking Project, https://covidtracking.com.

147 Brad Schmidt, "November Officially Oregon's Deadliest Month of Coronavirus Pandemic as State Reports 20 More Fatalities, 1,189 Cases," *The Oregonian*, November 25, 2020, https://www.oregonlive.com/coronavirus/2020/11/november-officially-oregons-deadliest-month-of-coronavirus-pandemic-as-state-reports-20-more-fatalities-1189-cases.html.

148 Dirk VanderHart, "Freeze, Oregon: Gov. Brown Restricts Businesses Again as COVID-19 Cases Surge," OPB, November 13, 2020, https://www.opb.org/article/2020/11/13/oregon-governor-kate-brown-covid-19-restrictions/.

149 Oregon coronavirus cases and deaths," USA Facts,. https://usafacts.org/visualizations/coronavirus-covid-19-spread-map/state/oregon.

150 United States Census Bureau, "Oregon Population 4.2 Million in 2020, Up 10.6% From 2010," August 25, 2021, https://www.census.gov/library/stories/state-by-state/oregon-population-change-between-census-decade.html.

151 Oregon coronavirus cases and deaths," USA Facts,. https://usafacts.org/visualizations/coronavirus-covid-19-spread-map/state/oregon.

152 "What Are the Odds of Dying in a Car Crash?" July 15, 2021, ERInjuryAttorneys.com, https://erinjuryattorneys.com/odds-of-dying-in-a-car-crash/.

153 Benton County, Oregon, "Benton County COVID-19 (Coronavirus) Information," updated March 21, 2022, https://www.co.benton.or.us/covid19.

154 Oregon Health Authority, "2020 Benton County resident deaths," https://visual-data.dhsoha.state.or.us/t/OHA/views/CountyDash/CountyDash_cause?%3Adisplay_count=n&%3Aembed=y&%3AisGuestRedirectFromVizportal=y&%3Aorigin=viz_share_link&%3AshowAppBanner=false&%3AshowVizHome=n, accessed March, 27 2022.

155 Oregon Health Authority, "2020 resident deaths," https://visual-data.dhsoha.state.or.us/t/OHA/views/CountyDash/CountyDash_cause?%3Adisplay_count=n&%3Aembed=y&%3AisGuestRedirectFromVizportal=y&%3Aorigin=viz_share_link&%3AshowAppBanner=false&%3AshowVizHome=n, accessed March, 27 2022.

156 Bill & Melinda Gates Foundation – About – Committed grants – "The Atlantic," https://www.gatesfoundation.org/about/committed-grants/2019/04/inv000891.

157 Sydney Ember, "Laurene Powell Jobs's Organization to Take Major Stake in The Atlantic," *The New York Times,* July 28, 2017, https://www.nytimes.com/2017/07/28/business/media/atlantic-media-emerson-collective-majority-stake.html.

158 Emerson Collective – "Priorities," https://www.emersoncollective.com/

159 Gillian B White, "Emerson Collective Acquires Majority Stake in The Atlantic," July 28, 2017, https://www.theatlantic.com/business/archive/2017/07/emerson-collective-atlantic-coalition/535215/

160 Joan Michelson, "Steve Ballmer Combats Government Misinformation with USA Facts – COVID-19, Race, Jobs, Environment," *Forbes,* June 24, 2020, https://www.forbes.com/sites/joanmichelson2/2020/06/24/steve-ballmer-combats-government-misinformation--with-usa-facts----covid-19-race-jobs-environment/?sh=3e8034f875f1.

161 "COVID-19 Dashboard by the Center for Systems Science and Engineering (CSSE) at Johns Hopkins University," *Johns Hopkins University of Medicine Coronavirus Resource Center,* https://coronavirus.jhu.edu/map.html.

162 "The Event 201 scenario," https://www.centerforhealthsecurity.org/event201/scenario.html.

163 "Event 201," https://www.centerforhealthsecurity.org/event201/.

164 World Economic Forum – About – "Leadership and Governance," https://www.weforum.org/about/leadership-and-governance.

165 Sam Shead, "Microsoft, Salesforce and Oracle Back Plan to Develop a Digital COVID Vaccination Passport," CNBC.com, January 14, 2021, https://www.cnbc.com/2021/01/14/microsoft-salesforce-and-oracle-working-on-covid-vaccination-passport.html.

166 Project Baseline – COVID-19 FAQs – "What is Verily?" https://www.projectbaseline.com/covid-support/.

167 Project Baseline – COVID-19 Testing FAQs – "How is Rite Aid involved?" https://www.project-baseline.com/studies/covid-19/.

168 Project Baseline – COVID-19 Testing FAQs – "Why am I being asked to sign an authorization form?" https://www.projectbaseline.com/studies/covid-19/.

169 "Alphabet, Inc. Form 10-K for Fiscal Year Ended December 31, 2019." *EDGAR*. Securities and Exchange
    Commission, 2020, https://www.sec.gov/Archives/edgar/data/1652044/000165204420000008/goog10-k2019.htm.

170 "Alphabet, Inc. Form 10-K for Fiscal Year Ended December 31, 2021." *EDGAR*. Securities and Exchange
    Commission, 2022, https://www.sec.gov/Archives/edgar/data/0001652044/000165204422000019/goog-20211231.htm.

171 Apoorva Mandavilli, "The Coronavirus is Mutating. What Does That Mean for Us?," *The New York Times,* December 20, 2020, https://www.nytimes.com/2020/12/20/health/coronavirus-britain-variant.html.

172 BBC News, "Coronavirus: "Double Mutant" COVID Variant Found in India," March 5, 2021, https://www.bbc.com/news/world-asia-india-56507988.

Chapter Eight: "Lockdown" is not "Quarantine": What "Restrictions" Really Achieve

173 Christopher Hobson, *The Rise of Democracy: Revolution, War and Transformations in International Politics Since 1776* (Edinburgh: Edinburgh University Press, 2015), 75.

174 United Nations, Universal Declaration of Human Rights, December 10, 1948, https://www.un.org/en/about-us/universal-declaration-of-human-rights.

175 **Chapter Eight: "Lockdown" is not a "Quarantine": What "Restrictions" Really Achieve**

Andreas Fulda, "In China, there's no freedom of movement, even between country and city," *City Monitor,* January 10, 2017, https://www.citymetric.com/politics/china-theres-no-freedom-movement-even-between-country-and-city-2697.

176 In-hua Kim, "Ask a North Korean: How restricted is movement in North Korea?," *NK News,* July 24, 2020, https://www.nknews.org/2020/07/ask-a-north-korean-how-restricted-is-movement-in-north-korea/.

177 British Library, "Anti-Jewish decrees," https://www.bl.uk/learning/histcitizen/voices/info/decrees/decrees.html.

178 Holocaust Encyclopedia, "German Jews During the Holocaust," https://encyclopedia.ushmm.org/content/en/article/german-jews-during-the-holocaust.

179 *Webster's New International Dictionary of the English Language, 1913,* s.v. "quarantine," accessed March 27, 2022, https://www.websters1913.com/words/Quarantine.

180 Leviticus 13:45.

181 "What Does the Bible Say About Quarantine?" P. J. Grisar, *The Forward,* March 9, 2020, https://forward.com/culture/441195/what-does-the-bible-say-about-quarantine/.

182 Conti, A.A, "Quarantine Through History," *International Encyclopedia of Public Health* (2008): 454–462.

183 Richard Aspin, "The Trouble with Madeira," *History Today*, July 14, 2021, https://www.historytoday.com/miscellanies/trouble-madeira.

184 Caroline Fraser, *Prairie Fires: The American Dreams of Laura Ingalls Wilder* (New York: Picador, 2017), 49.

185 Robert E. Wright, *Financial Exclusion: How Competition Can Fix a Broken System* (Great Barrington: The American Institute for Economic Research, 2019), 103.

186 Jaclyn Lopez Witmer, "Holiday Stress: How to Cope During the Coronavirus Pandemic," W Therapy, November 16, 2020, https://withtherapy.com/therapist-insights/holiday-stress-how-to-cope-during-the-coronavirus-pandemic.

187 Tara Parker-Pope, "How Do I Make Thanksgiving Grocery Shopping Safer?," *The New York Times*, November 19, 2020, https://www.nytimes.com/2020/11/19/well/live/thanksgiving-grocery-shopping-supermarket-safety.html.

188 Shainna Ali, "When Holiday and Pandemic Stress Collide," *Psychology Today*, November 19, 2020, https://www.psychologytoday.com ›modern-mentality.

189 Vicky Hallett, "Everything's different this year — why not holiday stress?," *National Geographic*, November 24, 2020, https://www.nationalgeographic.com/family/article/everything-is-different-this-year-so-why-not-holiday-stress-coronavirus.

190 The Brownstone Institute, "Lockdowns Fail: They Do Not Control the Virus," July 15, 2021, https://brownstone.org/articles/lockdowns-fail-they-do-not-control-the-virus/.

191 Vinay Prasad, "At a Time When the US Needed COVID-19 Dialogue Between Scientists, Francis Collins Moved to Shut it Down," *STAT*, Dec 23, 2021, https://www.statnews.com/2021/12/23/at-a-time-when-the-u-s-needed-covid-19-dialogue-between-scientists-francis-collins-moved-to-shut-it-down/.

192 Burki, T., 2020. *Herd immunity for COVID-19*. Available at: <https://doi.org/10.1016/S2213-2600(20)30555-5>

193 Ibid.

194 Vinay Prasad, "At a Time When the US Needed COVID-19 Dialogue Between Scientists, Francis Collins Moved to Shut it Down," *STAT*, Dec 23, 2021, https://www.statnews.com/2021/12/23/at-a-time-when-the-u-s-needed-covid-19-dialogue-between-scientists-francis-collins-moved-to-shut-it-down/.

195 Toby Young, "Why Can't We Talk About the Great Barrington Declaration?," *The Spectator*, October 17, 2020, https://www.spectator.co.uk/article/why-cant-we-talk-about-the-great-barrington-declaration.

Chapter Nine: Frozen with Fear: A Cult Takes Shape

196 Gorman, James, Michael Levenson and Taa Parker Pope, "What We Know About Your Chances of Catching the Virus Outdoors," *The New York Times*, May 15, 2020, https://www.nytimes.

com/2020/05/15/us/coronavirus-what-to-do-outside.html.

197 Ville Vuorinen, Mia Aarnio, Mikko Alava, Ville Alopaeus, Nina Atanasova, Mikko Auvinen, Nallannan Balasubramanian, Hadi Bordbar, Panu Erästö, Rafael Grande, Nick Hayward, Antti Hellsten, Simo Hostikka, Jyrki Hokkanen, Ossi Kaario, Aku Karvinen, Ilkka Kivistö, Marko Korhonen, Risto Kosonen, Janne Kuusela, Sami Lestinen, Erkki Laurila, Heikki J. Nieminen, Petteri Peltonen, Juho Pokki, Antti Puisto, Peter Råback, Henri Salmenjoki, Tarja Sironen, Monika Österberg, "Modelling aerosol transport and virus exposure with numerical simulations in relation to SARS-CoV-2 transmission by inhalation indoors," *Safety Science*, Volume 130, 2020, 104866, ISSN 0925-7535,https://doi.org/10.1016/j.ssci.2020.104866. (https://www.sciencedirect.com/science/article/pii/S0925753520302630).

198 COVID-19 Response Reporting – COVID-19 Interactive Dashboard – "COVID-19 Deaths," https://www.mass.gov/info-details/covid-19-response-reporting#covid-19-interactive-data-dashboard-

199 Kenneth Chang, "How Coronavirus Infected Some, but Not All, in a Restaurant," *The New York Times,* April 20, 2020, https://www.nytimes.com/2020/04/20/health/airflow-coronavirus-restaurants.html.

200 Lu J., Gu J., Li K., Xu C., Su W., Lai Z., et al. "COVID-19 Outbreak Associated with Air Conditioning in Restaurant, Guangzhou, China, 2020." *Emerging Infectious Diseases* 2020, 26 (7):1628–31, https://doi.org/10.3201/eid2607.200764.

201 Kenneth Chang, "How Coronavirus Infected Some, but Not All, in a Restaurant," *The New York Times,* April 20, 2020, https://www.nytimes.com/2020/04/20/health/airflow-coronavirus-restaurants.html.

202 G.P. Guy, Jr., F.C. Lee, G. Sunshine, et al. "Association of State-Issued Mask Mandates and Allowing On-Premises Restaurant Dining with County-Level COVID-19 Case and Death Growth Rates — United States, March 1–December 31, 2020." *Morbidity and Mortality Weekly Report*, March 12, 2021, 70(10): 350–54, http://dx.doi.org/10.15585/mmwr.mm7010e3.

203 Roni Carin Rabin, "The Virus Spread Where Restaurants Reopened or Mask Mandates Were Absent," *The New York Times,* March 5, 2021, https://www.nytimes.com/2021/03/05/health/coronavirus-restaurant-dining-masks.html.

204 Zachary J. Madewell, PhD; Yang Yang, PhD; Ira M. Longini Jr, PhD; et al., M. Elizabeth Halloran, MD, DSc; Natalie E. Dean, PhD,"Household Transmission of SARS-CoV-2 A Systematic Review and Meta-analysis," *Journal of the American Medical Association*, December 14, 2020, *JAMA Netw Open.* 2020;3(12):e2031756. doi:10.1001/jamanetworkopen.2020.31756, https://jamanetwork.com/journals/jamanetworkopen/fullarticle/2774102

205 Rob Hackford, "New York State: Restaurants, Bars Accounted for 1.43% of COVID-19 Cases Over the Last 3 Months," WGRZ.com, December 11, 2020, https://www.wgrz.com/article/news/health/coronavirus/new-york-state-restaurants-bars-accounted-for-143-of-covid-19-cases-over-last-3-months/71-02e600f3-ae63-4f87-90e8-f80b6f6bd304.

206 Dr. Naomi Wolf, Opinion: "Dr Naomi Wolf and Academic Whistleblower Dr. Simon Goddek Discuss the One-Day Peer Review for COVID Test Research Paper and the Academic Persecution Faced by Scientists," Daily Clout, January 12, 2021, https://dailyclout.io/opinion-dr-naomi-wolf-

and-academic-whistleblower-dr-simon-goddek-discuss-the-one-day-peer-review-for-covid-test-research-paper-and-the-academic-persecution-faced-by-scientists/.

207 Dr. Vatsal Thakkar, https://vatsalthakkar.com.

208 Naomi Wolf, Kevin McKernan, and Bobby Malhotra, Science Whistle-blowers Kevin McKernan & Bobby Malhotra Explain Why Covid Pcr Tests Are 'Garbage,'" ThePlatform.ie, April 1, 2021, https://theplatform.ie/whistle-blowers-kevin-mckernan-bobby-malhotra-explain-why-covid-pcr-tests-are-garbage/.

209 Corman-Drosten Review Report, "Eurosurveillance Response," last updated 12, 28, 2021, https://cormandrostenreview.com/eurosurveillance-response/.

210 Professor Jay Bhattacharya, "Prof Jay Bhattacharya, Signatory of Gt Barrington Declaration: Why 'Lockdown' Will Kill Millions," YouTube/Daily Clout, February 10, 2021, https://www.youtube.com/watch?v=YZKncweeOvY&t=123s.

211 Dr. Patrick Phillips, "Dr. Naomi Wolf and Courageous ER Physician Dr. Patrick Phillips on 'Lockdown' Public Health Policies," YouTube/Daily Clout, January 12, 2021, https://www.youtube.com/watch?v=hoeAo00KdLI&t=266s.

212 "Governor Announces Wedding Receptions and Catered Events Can Now Resume Statewide," March 15, 2021, https://www.governor.ny.gov/NEWS/GOVERNOR-CUOMO-ANNOUNCES-WEDDING-RECEPTIONS-AND-CATERED-EVENTS-CAN-NOW-RESUME-STATE-WIDE.

213 Bill & Melinda Gates Foundation, "CNN," https://www.gatesfoundation.org/about/committed-grants?q=CNN#committed_grants

Chapter Ten: "The Software of Life"

214 Chris Pandolfo, "Exclusive: The Federal Government Paid Hundreds of Media Companies to Advertise the COVID-19 Vaccines While Those Same Outlets Provided Positive Coverage of the Vaccines," TheBlaze.com March 3 2022, https://www.theblaze.com/news/review-the-federal-government-paid-media-companies-to-advertise-for-the-vaccines.

215 Ibid.

216 John Frank, "Colorado is Paying Social Media Influencers to Tout COVID-19 Vaccines", AXIOS.com, July 23, 2021, https://www.axios.com/local/denver/2021/07/23/colorado-paying-social-media-influencers-covid-vaccine.

217 Staff and agencies, "Pfizer, Unions, Others Donated $61.8 Million for Biden's Inaugural," US News & World Report, April 21, 2021, https://www.usnews.com/news/top-news/articles/2021-04-21/pfizer-unions-others-donated-618-million-for-bidens-inaugural.

218 Ahmed Sule, "The 'COVID-industrial complex'— a web of Big Pharma, Big Tech, and politicians –are profiting off the pandemic at the expense of the public," Business Insider, March 28, 2021, https://www.businessinsider.com/case-against-covid-industrial-complex-pandemic-pharma-politicians-tech-profiting-2021-3.

219 Staff and agencies, "YouTube blocks all anti-vaccine content," Reuters, September 29, 2021,

https://www.reuters.com/technology/youtube-blocks-all-anti-vaccine-content-2021-09-29/.

220 Moderna – mRNA Technology – Our mRNA Platform – "mRNA Platform: Enabling Drug Discovery & Development," https://www.modernatx.com/mrna-technology/mrna-platform-enabling-drug-discovery-development.

221 Scioli Montoto Sebastián, Muraca Giuliana, and Ruiz María Esperanza, "Solid Lipid Nanoparticles for Drug Delivery: Pharmacological and Biopharmaceutical Aspects," *Frontiers in Molecular Biosciences* 7 (2020), https://www.frontiersin.org/article/10.3389/fmolb.2020.

222 Stephen Buranyi, "The MRNA Vaccine Revolution is Just Beginning," March 6, 2021, Wired, https://www.wired.com/article/mrna-vaccine-revolution-katalin-kariko.

223 "Open letter from Doctors and Scientists to the European Medicines Agency regarding COVID-19 vaccine safety concerns," WhatDoTheyKnow.com, March 17, 2021, https://www.whatdotheyknow.com/en/request/open_letter_from_doctors_and_sci?unfold=1.

224 Mark Walker and Jack Healy, "A Motorcycle Rally in a Pandemic? 'We Kind of Knew What Was Going to Happen'" *The New York Times*, November 7, 2020, https://www.nytimes.com/2020/11/06/us/sturgis-coronavirus-cases.html.

Chapter Eleven: How Masks Suppress the Human Advantage

225 Paul E. Alexander, "The Dangers of Masks," *American Institute for Economic Research,* April 9, 2021, https://www.aier.org/article/the-dangers-of-masks/.

226 34 CFR 300.114, https://www.govregs.com/regulations/title34_chapterIII_part300_subpartB_subjgrp40_section300.114FR 300.114 - LRE requirements. (govregs.com).

227 Chris Frith, "Role of Facial Expressions in Social Interactions," *Phil. Trans. R. Soc. B* 364 (2009): 3453–58 http://doi.org/10.1098/rstb.2009.0142.

Chapter Twelve: The Tech Bubble: Vast Wealth via Killing Human Competition

228 Natalie Glover, "Children born during pandemic have lower IQs, US study finds," *The Guardian,* August 12, 2021, https://www.theguardian.com/world/2021/aug/12/children-born-during-pandemic-have-lower-iqs-us-study-finds.

229 Sean C. L. Deoni, Jennifer Beauchemin, Alexandra Volpe, Viren D'Sa, and the RESONANCE Consortium, "The COVID-19 Pandemic and Child Cognitive Development: Initial Findings in a Longitudinal Observational Study of Child Health," August 11, 2021, *medRxiv* 2021.08.10.21261846 (preprint), https://doi.org/10.1101/2021.08.10.21261846.

230 Rae Hodge, "Zoom privacy risks: The video chat app could be sharing more information than you think," *CNET News,* January 14, 2022, https://www.cnet.com/news/privacy/zoom-privacy-risks-the-video-chat-app-could-be-sharing-more-information-than-you-think/.

231 Steven Waterhouse Interview by Dr. Naomi Wolf, January 10, 2021, https://www.youtube.com/watch?v=hEmbgpvik0k.

232 Eric Spitznagel, "How a business conference turned into the world's most exclusive party," *New*

York Post, January 29, 2022, https://nypost.com/2022/01/29/how-the-world-economic-forum-became-the-most-exclusive-party-ever/.

233 Klaus Schwab, "Strengthening Collaboration in a Fractured World,"2017 Malcolm H. Wiener Lecture on International Political Economy, Harvard Kennedy School, 2017, https://iop.harvard.edu/forum/strengthening-collaboration-fractured-world-featuring-special-guest-yo-yo-ma.

234 Young Global Leaders, "Jacinda Adern," https://www.younggloballeaders.org/community?utf8=☒&q=jacinda&.

235 "Annual Report." *Amazon.com,Inc., (*2013->2021), https://ir.aboutamazon.com/sec-filings/default.aspx.

236 Matthew Johnston, "Biggest Companies in the World by Market Cap," *Investopedia,* March 4, 2022, https://www.investopedia.com/biggest-companies-in-the-world-by-market-cap-5212784.

237 Samantha Subin, "Etsy Jumps After Earnings Show Continued Sales Growth, Even After Pandemic-Era Mask Boom," CNBC.com, November 4, 2021, https://www.cnbc.com/2021/11/04/etsy-stock-up-on-q3-2021-earnings-beat.html.

238 "Annual Report." *Etsy,Inc., (*2013->2020), https://investors.etsy.com/financials/sec-filings/default.aspx.

239 Thomas Alsop, "Nintendo's Net Sales from Fiscal 2008 to 2021," *Statista,* February 8, 2022, https://www.statista.com/statistics/216622/net-sales-of-nintendo-since-2008/.

240 "Annual Report 2010." *Nintendo Co. Ltd., 2010,* https://www.nintendo.co.jp/ir/pdf/2010/annual1003e.pdf;
"Annual Report 2011." *Nintendo Co. Ltd., 2011,* https://www.nintendo.co.jp/ir/pdf/2011/annual1103e.pdf;
"Annual Report 2012." *Nintendo Co. Ltd., 2012,* https://www.nintendo.co.jp/ir/pdf/2012/annual1203e.pdf;
"Annual Report 2013." *Nintendo Co. Ltd., 2013,* https://www.nintendo.co.jp/ir/pdf/2013/annual1303e.pdf;
"Annual Report 2014." *Nintendo Co. Ltd., 2014,* https://www.nintendo.co.jp/ir/pdf/2014/annual1403e.pdf;
"Annual Report 2015." *Nintendo Co. Ltd., 2015,* https://www.nintendo.co.jp/ir/pdf/2015/annual1503e.pdf;
"Annual Report 2016." *Nintendo Co. Ltd., 2016,* https://www.nintendo.co.jp/ir/pdf/2016/annual1603e.pdf;
"Annual Report 2017." *Nintendo Co. Ltd., 2017,* https://www.nintendo.co.jp/ir/pdf/2017/annual1703e.pdf;
"Annual Report 2018." *Nintendo Co. Ltd., 2018,* https://www.nintendo.co.jp/ir/pdf/2018/annual1803e.pdf;
"Annual Report 2019." *Nintendo Co. Ltd., 2019,* https://www.nintendo.co.jp/ir/pdf/2019/annual1903e.pdf;
"Annual Report 2020." *Nintendo Co. Ltd., 2020,* https://www.nintendo.co.jp/ir/pdf/2020/annual2003e.pdf;
"Annual Report 2021." *Nintendo Co. Ltd., 2021,* https://www.nintendo.co.jp/ir/pdf/2021/annual2103e.pdf

241 "Quarterly Report." *Apple Inc., (*2019->2022), https://investor.apple.com/sec-filings/default.aspx; "Annual Report." *Apple Inc., (*2019->2021), https://investor.apple.com/sec-filings/default.aspx

242 Nicholas Vega "Microsoft's market cap grew more than $800 billion in 2021— here's how it compares to the most valuable companies in the world," CNBC.com, December 27, 2021, https://www.cnbc.com/2021/12/27/how-much-the-biggest-companies-grew-in-2021.html#:

243 "Microsoft Education Webinar Series," Microsoft, https://info.microsoft.com/AU-WWEDU-CATALOG-FY19-06Jun-03-MicrosoftEducationWebinarSeries-SRDEM2463_CatalogDisplay-Page.html.

244 "Annual Filings." *Microsoft Corporation, (*2013->2021), https://investor.apple.com/sec-filings/de-fault.aspx

245 Project Baseline – COVID-19 Testing FAQs – "Why am I asked to create an account?" https://www.projectbaseline.com/studies/covid-19/.

246 "Google, Inc. Form 10-K for Fiscal Year Ended December 31, 2013." *EDGAR.* Securities and Exchange

Commission, 2014, https://www.sec.gov/Archives/edgar/data/1288776/000128877614000020/goog2013123110-k.htm;

"Google, Inc. Form 10-K for Fiscal Year Ended December 31, 2014." *EDGAR.* Securities and Exchange

Commission, 2015, https://www.sec.gov/Archives/edgar/data/1288776/000128877615000008/goog2014123110-k.htm;

"Google, Inc. Form 10-K for Fiscal Year Ended December 31, 2015." *EDGAR.* Securities and Exchange

Commission, 2016, https://www.sec.gov/Archives/edgar/data/1288776/000165204416000012/goog10-k2015.htm;

"Alphabet, Inc. Form 10-K for Fiscal Year Ended December 31, 2016." *EDGAR.* Securities and Exchange

Commission, 2017, https://www.sec.gov/Archives/edgar/data/1652044/000165204417000008/goog10-kq42016.htm;

"Alphabet, Inc. Form 10-K for Fiscal Year Ended December 31, 2016." *EDGAR.* Securities and Exchange

Commission, 2017, https://www.sec.gov/Archives/edgar/data/1652044/000165204417000008/goog10-kq42016.htm;

"Alphabet, Inc. Form 10-K for Fiscal Year Ended December 31, 2017." *EDGAR.* Securities and Exchange

Commission, 2018, https://www.sec.gov/Archives/edgar/data/1652044/000165204418000007/goog10-kq42017.htm;

"Alphabet, Inc. Form 10-K for Fiscal Year Ended December 31, 2018." *EDGAR.* Securities and Exchange

Commission, 2019, https://www.sec.gov/Archives/edgar/data/1652044/000165204419000004/goog10-kq42018.htm;

"Alphabet, Inc. Form 10-K for Fiscal Year Ended December 31, 2019." *EDGAR.* Securities and Exchange

Commission, 2020, https://www.sec.gov/Archives/edgar/data/1652044/000165204420000008/

goog10-k2019.htm;

"Alphabet, Inc. Form 10-K for Fiscal Year Ended December 31, 2020." *EDGAR*. Securities and Exchange

Commission, 2021, https://www.sec.gov/Archives/edgar/data/1652044/000165204421000010/goog-20201231.htm;

"Alphabet, Inc. Form 10-K for Fiscal Year Ended December 31, 2021." *EDGAR*. Securities and Exchange

Commission, 2022, https://www.sec.gov/Archives/edgar/data/0001652044/000165204422000019/goog-20211231.htm

247 Tony Wan, "Coursera's Filing Shows Growing Revenue and Loss During a Pandemic," EdSurge.com, March 5, 2021, https://www.edsurge.com/news/2021-03-05-coursera-s-ipo-filing-shows-growing-revenue-and-loss-during-a-pandemic.

248 Susan Adams, "Online Education Provider Coursera Is Worth $& Billion After Going Public", April 1, 2021, *Forbes.com,* https://www.forbes.com/sites/susanadams/2021/04/01/online-education-provider-coursera-is-worth-7-billion-after-going-public/?sh=32ff50dd15ec.

249 Riley de Leon, "Coursera closes up 36%, topping $5.9 billion market cap in Wall Street debut," *CNBC,* March 31, 2021, https://www.cnbc.com/2021/03/31/coursera-ipo-cour-begins-trading-on-the-nyse.html.

250 Susan Adams, "Online Education Provider Coursera Is Worth $& Billion After Going Public," April 1, 2021, Forbes.com, https://www.forbes.com/sites/susanadams/2021/04/01/online-education-provider-coursera-is-worth-7-billion-after-going-public/?sh=32ff50dd15ec.

251 Dhawal Shah, "Analyzing Coursera's IPO Filing, $293.5 million revenue. $281 million paid to partners, 12k Degree Students," "The Report" by ClassCentral.com, March 9, 2021, https://www.classcentral.com/report/coursera-s1-analysis/.

252 Nicholas Vega, "Microsoft's Market Cap Grew More than $800 Billion in 2021 — Here's How It Compares to the Most Valuable Companies in the World," December 27, 2021, https://www.cnbc.com/2021/12/27/how-much-the-biggest-companies-grew-in-2021.html.

253 "Ben Shapiro SLAMS MSM's Denial of Deplatforming Conservatives," YouTube/Glenn Beck, February 18, 2021, https://www.youtube.com/watch?v=2H8-6E9SBLc.

254 Martin Kulldorff, Twitter, October 4, 2021, https://twitter.com/martinkulldorff/status/1445190760635289604.

255 Tim Schwab, "Journalism's Gates keepers," *Columbia Journalism Review*, August 21, 2020, https://www.cjr.org/criticism/gates-foundation-journalism-funding.php.

256 Dorn, Sara and Mary Kay Linge, "Schumer got $50K in donations from Facebook – and his daughter got a job," *New York Post,* November 17, 2018, https://nypost.com/2018/11/17/schumer-got-50k-in-donations-and-a-job-for-his-daughter-from-facebook/.

Chapter Thirteen: "Vaccine Passports" and the End of Human Liberty

257 Isabel Kershner, "As Israel Reopens, 'Whoever Does Not Get Vaccinated Will Be Left Behind'," *The New York Times,* February 18, 2021, https://www.nytimes.com/2021/02/18/world/middleeast/

israel-covid-vaccine-reopen.html.

258 Sam Shead, "Microsoft, Salesforce and Oracle Back Plan to Develop a Digital COVID Vaccina-
     tion Passport", *CNBC.com,* January 14, 2021, https://www.cnbc.com/2021/01/14/microsoft-
     salesforce-and-oracle-working-on-covid-vaccination-passport.html.

259 Atlantic Council – "Central Bank Digital Currency Tracker," https://www.atlanticcouncil.org/
     cbdctracker/.

260 New York State, "Governor Cuomo Announces Launch of Excelsior Pass to Help Fast-Track
     Reopening of Businesses and Entertainment Venues Statewide," March 26, 2021, https://www.
     governor.ny.gov/news/governor-cuomo-announces-launch-excelsior-pass-help-fast-track-reopening-
     businesses-and., State of California, "Digital COVID-19 Vaccine Record," https://myvaccinere-
     cord.cdph.ca.gov/.

261 European Union, "Coronavirus: Commission proposes a Digital Green Certificate," March 17,
     2021, https://ec.europa.eu/commission/presscorner/detail/en/ip_21_1181.

262 Allison Fox, "France to Require Proof of Vaccination for Restaurants, Cafés, Trains, and more
     Public Places," *Travel + Leisure,* January 18, 2022, https://www.travelandleisure.com/travel-news/
     france-vaccine-requirements-for-restaurants.

263 Patrick Kingsley, "In Israel, people over 60 and medical workers will receive fourth vaccine doses.,"
     The New York Times, December 21, 2021, https://www.nytimes.com/2021/12/22/world/middlee-
     ast/vaccine-booster-israel-covid.html.

Chapter Fourteen: Switching You Off

264 Brendan Cole, "Candace Owens Says She Was Refused COVID Test Because of Her Anti-
     Vaccination Stance," *Newsweek,* September 2, 2021, https://www.newsweek.com/candace-owens-
     colorado-vaccination-covid-refused-test-aspen-1625289.

265 Mark Wilson, "Designing for uncertainty: How IBM created a vaccine passport," *FastCompany,*
     April 13, 2021, https://www.fastcompany.com/90624276/designing-for-uncertainty-how-ibm-
     created-a-vaccine-passport.

266 Linda Geddes, "Covid tests: how can people be positive on lateral flow and negative on PCRs?"
     The Guardian, February 16, 2022, https://www.theguardian.com/world/2022/feb/16/covid-tests-
     how-can-people-be-positive-on-lateral-flow-and-negative-on-pcrs.

Chapter Fifteen: Theft

267 Rappeport, Alan, Michael D. Shear and Glenn Thrush, "The Biden administration issues a new
     eviction moratorium as the virus surges," *The New York Times,* August 3, 2021,

268 NOLO, "The US Supreme Court Has Ended the CDC's Eviction Ban," August 26, 2021, https://
     www.nolo.com/legal-updates/the-u-s-supreme-court-has-ended-the-cdc-s-eviction-ban.html.

269 Drew Desilver, "As national eviction ban expires, a look at who rents and who owns in the US,"
     Pew Research Center, August 2, 2021, https://www.pewresearch.org/fact-tank/2021/08/02/as-
     national-eviction-ban-expires-a-look-at-who-rents-and-who-owns-in-the-u-s/.

270 Greg David, "NYC's Small Landlords of Color Among Those Battling for Survival Amid Rent Moratorium," TheCity.nyc, February 7, 2021, https://www.thecity.nyc/2021/2/7/22271280/nyc-small-landlords-tenants-rent-moratorium-black-hispanic.

271 Rachel King, "More than 110,000 Eating and Drinking Establishments Closed in 2020," Forbes.com, January 26, 2021, https://fortune.com/2021/01/26/restaurants-bars-closed-2020-jobs-lost-how-many-have-closed-us-covid-pandemic-stimulus-unemployment/.

272 Elena Botella, "Investment Firms Aren't Buying all the Houses. But They are Buying the Most Important Ones." June 19, 2021, Slate.com https://slate.com/business/2021/06/blackrock-invitation-houses-investment-firms-real-estate.html

273 Gibbs, Margot, Peter Whoriskey and Spencer Woodman, "This Block Used To Be For First-Time Homebuyers. Then Global Investors Bought In," *The Washington Post,* December 15, 2021, https://www.washingtonpost.com/business/interactive/2021/investors-rental-foreclosure/.

274 Aly J. Yale, "Why Investors Are Scooping up So Much Real Estate – and How Regular Homebuyers Can Compete," *Nasdaq,* February 3, 2022, https://www.nasdaq.com/articles/why-investors-are-scooping-up-so-much-real-estate-and-how-regular-homebuyers-can-compete.

275 Konrad Putzier, "That Suburban Home Buyer Could Be a Foreign Government," *The Wall Street Journal,* April 13, 2021, https://www.wsj.com/articles/that-suburban-home-buyer-could-be-a-foreign-government-11618306380.

276 Anna Bahney, "CDC extends eviction moratorium until June 30," *CNN,* March 29, 2021, https://www.cnn.com/2021/03/29/success/cdc-eviction-order-extended/index.html.

277 Greg David, "NYC's Small Landlords of Color Among Those Battling for Survival Amid Rent Moratorium," TheCity.nyc, February 7, 2021, https://www.thecity.nyc/2021/2/7/22271280/nyc-small-landlords-tenants-rent-moratorium-black-hispanic.

278 Emma Simpson, "Almost 50 Shops a Day Disappear from High Streets," September 5, 2021, BBC.com, https://www.bbc.com/news/business-58433461.

279 Jasper Jolly, "More than 8,700 chain stores have closed in 2021, analysis shows," *The Guardian,* September 5, 2021, https://www.theguardian.com/business/2021/sep/05/more-than-8700-chain-stores-close-in-2021-analysis-shows.

280 "Biden to the Unvaccinated: Our Patience is Wearing Thin," CNN.com, https://www.cnn.com/videos/politics/2021/09/09/biden-message-unvaccinated-americans-patience-sot-lead-vpx.cnn

281 Kevin Liptak and Kaitlan Collins, ""Biden Announces New Vaccine Mandates That Could Cover 100 Million Americans," cnn.com, September 9, 2021, https://www.cnn.com/2021/09/09/politics/joe-biden-covid-speech/index.html

282 Center on Education Policy, "History and Evolution of Public Education in the US," 2020, https://files.eric.ed.gov/fulltext/ED606970.pdf.

283 Ida Mojadad, "School Board Aims to Change Lowell's Culure, End Selective Admissions," *The San Francisco Examiner*, February 3, 2021, https://www.sfexaminer.com/news/school-board-aims-to-take-on-lowells-culture-of-racism-end-selective-admissions/.

284 Natalie Wexler, "Harvard Dropped its SAT Requirement, But Don't Expect More Diversity,"

Forbes.com, December 29, 2021, https://www.forbes.com/sites/nataliewexler/2021/12/29/harvard-has-dropped-its-sat-requirement-but-dont-expect-more-diversity/?sh=6d1d3778c26b.

285 Billy Camden, "GCSE and A-level 2021 exams cancelled," *FE Week,* January 4, 2021, https://feweek.co.uk/gcse-and-a-level-2021-exams-cancelled/.

286 Sally Weale, "Schools in England May Suspend Certain Subjects to Cope with COVID," *The Guardian,* January 4, 2022, , https://www.theguardian.com/education/2022/jan/04/schools-in-england-may-suspend-certain-subjects-to-cope-with-covid.

287 Paul Joseph Watson, "Video Shows Kindergarten Students Forced to Sit Outside on Buckets in Freezing Weather," Yournews.com, December 9, 2021, https://yournews.com/2021/12/09/2263998/video-shows-kindergarten-students-forced-to-sit-outside-on-buckets/.

Chapter Sixteen: Heroes

288 Carol Davis, "Spreading COVID-19 Misinformation Could Cost Nurses Their Job," *HealthLeaders Media,* November 23, 2021, https://www.healthleadersmedia.com/nursing/spreading-covid-19-misinformation-could-cost-nurses-their-job.

289 Centers for Disease Control and Prevention, "Clinical Considerations: Myocarditis and Pericarditis after Receipt of mRNA COVID-19 Vaccines Among Adolescents and Young Adults," page last reviewed November 9, 2021, https://www.cdc.gov/vaccines/covid-19/clinical-considerations/myocarditis.html.

290 Justus R Hope MD, "Matt Le Tissier sounds the alarm on sudden soccer deaths," *The Deseret Review,* February 7, 2022, https://www.thedesertreview.com/opinion/columnists/matt-le-tissier-sounds-the-alarm-on-sudden-soccer-deaths/article_9595fc68-883a-11ec-bec7-e7ed577bc660.html.

291 John Woolfolk, "Teen boy dies a few days after receiving second COVID vaccine," *The Mercury News,* June 25, 2021, https://www.mercurynews.com/2021/06/25/teen-boy-dies-a-few-days-after-receiving-second-covid-vaccine-shot/.

292 "Teen Dies from Blood Clots After Second Jab," *Bangkok* Post, November 6, 2021 https://www.bangkokpost.com/thailand/general/2210515/teen-dies-from-blood-clots-after-second-jab.

293 John Ley, "Seventeen-year-old Washington Female dies from Heart Attack weeks after Receiving Second Pfizer Vaccination," Clark County Today, November 15, 2021, https://www.clarkcountytoday.com/news/seventeen-year-old-washington-female-dies-from-heart-attack-weeks-after-receiving-second-pfizer-vaccination/.

294 Dave Bondy, "Teen Dies in His Sleep After Receiving Pfizer COVID Vaccine; CDC Investigating," WEYI Staff, July 3, 2021 https://wset.com/news/nation-world/teen-dies-in-sleep-after-receiving-pfizer-covid-vaccine-cdc-investigating-michigan-saginaw-jacob-clynick-second-dose-vaers/

295 Addy Bink, "Teen Dies Days After Getting COVID-19 Vaccine, Officials Investigating," ABC4.com, July 6, 2021, https://www.abc4.com/coronavirus/teens-death-days-after-getting-covid-19-vaccine-under-investigation.

296 Kalbana Perimbanayagam, "MOH probing case of teen who died 18 days after first vaccine dose," *New Straits Times,* February 21, 2022, https://www.nst.com.my/news/nation/2022/02/773362/

moh-probing-case-teen-who-died-18-days-after-first-vaccine-dose.

297 Eileen Reslen, "Justin Bieber Speaks Out on Hailey Baldwin's "Really Scary" Medical Emergency,"
PageSix.com, March 17, 2022, https://pagesix.com/2022/03/17/justin-bieber-calls-hailey-bald-
wins-blood-clot-scary//

298 VAERS — VAERS Data —"Disclaimer," https://vaers.hhs.gov/data.html.

299 A. Edelman, E.R. Boniface, E. Benhar, L. Han, K.A. Matteson, C. Favaro, J.T. Pearson,
B.G. Darney, "Association Between Menstrual Cycle Length and Coronavirus Disease 2019
(COVID-19) Vaccination: A US Cohort, *Obstet Gynecol*, January 5, 2022, doi: 10.1097/
AOG.0000000000004695, Online ahead of print, PMID: 34991109.

300 BBC News, "Call for Investigation of Menstrual Changes After COVID Jabs," September 16,
2021 https://www.bbc.com/news/health-58573593.

Chapter Seventeen: Cruelty, Cults, Coercion

301 Carl Zimmer, "Israeli Data Suggest Possible Waning of Effectiveness of Pfizer Vaccine," *The New
York Times*, July 23, 2021, https://www.nytimes.com/2021/07/23/science/covid-vaccine-israel-
pfizer.html.

302 Marlene Lenthang, "Hundreds of hospital staffers fired or suspended for refusing COVID-19 vaccine mandate," *ABC News*, September 30, 2021, https://abcnews.go.com/US/hundreds-hospital-
staffers-fired-suspended-refusing-covid-19/story?id=80303408.

303 Ed Yong, "It's a Terrible Idea to Deny Medical Care to Unvaccinated People," *The Atlantic*, January
20, 2022, https://www.theatlantic.com/health/archive/2022/01/unvaccinated-medical-care-hospi-
tals-omicron/621299/.

304 Newsdesk, "Singapore to open to Vaccinated US and Canadian Travelers," *Travel Agent Central*,
October 12, 2021, https://www.travelagentcentral.com/destinations/singapore-open-vaccinated-us-
and-canadian-travelers.

305 Bruce Japsen "Coming Soon For The Unvaccinated: A $50 Monthly Paycheck Deduction From
Your Employer," *Forbes*, August 8, 2021, https://www.forbes.com/sites/brucejapsen/2021/08/08/
coming-soon-for-the-unvaccinated-a-50-monthly-paycheck-deduction-from-your-
employer/?sh=6336fb8147ae.

306 Nieberg, Patty, Thomas Peipert and Colleen Slevin, "Colorado Woman Who Won't Get Vaccinated Denied Transplant," *US News & World Report*, October 8, 2021, https://www.usnews.
com/news/health-news/articles/2021-10-07/colorado-woman-who-wont-get-vaccinated-denied-
transplant.

307 State of Oregon, "Governor Brown reinstates statewide masking mandate," August 11, 2021,
https://covidblog.oregon.gov/governor-brown-reinstates-statewide-masking-mandate/.

308 Centers for Disease Control and Prevention, "How to talk about COVID-19 vaccines with friends
and family," April 27, 2021, https://www.cdc.gov/coronavirus/2019-ncov/vaccines/talk-about-
vaccines.html.

309 Agencies and staff, "Howard Springs: Australia police arrest quarantine escapees," *BBC News,* December 1, 2021, https://www.bbc.com/news/world-australia-59486285.

310 Agencies and staff, "Covid: Austria introduces lockdown for unvaccinated," *BBC News,* November 15, 2021, https://www.bbc.com/news/world-europe-59283128.

311 Allie Malloy and Maegan Vasquez, "Biden Warns of Winter of "Severe Illness and Death" for Unvaccinated Due to Omicron," CNN.com, December 16, 2021, https://www.cnn.com/2021/12/16/politics/joe-biden-warning-winter/index.html.

312 US FDA, Twitter post, August 21, 2021, 7:57 AM, https://twitter.com/us_fda/status/1429050070243192839?lang=en.

313 Joseph Choi, "Pfizer chairman: We're not sure if someone can transmit virus after vaccination," *The Hill,* December 3, 2021, https://thehill.com/news-by-subject/healthcare/528619-pfizer-chairman-were-not-sure-if-someone-can-transmit-virus-after.

314 Zimmer, Carl, Katherine J. Wu, Jonathan Corum and Matthew Kristoffersen, "Coronavirus Drug and Treatment Tracker," *The New York Times,* March 20 2022, https://www.nytimes.com/interactive/2020/science/coronavirus-drugs-treatments.html.

315 "YouTube blocks all anti-vaccine content," *Reuters,* September 29, 2021, https://www.reuters.com/technology/youtube-blocks-all-anti-vaccine-content-2021-09-29/

316 Jim Gamarone, "Service Members Must be Vaccinated or Face Consequences, DOD Official Says," Defense.gov, December 21 2021, https://www.defense.gov/News/News-Stories/Article/Article/2881481/service-members-must-be-vaccinated-or-face-consequences-dod-official-says/.

317 Vaccine Adverse Event Reporting System, https://vaers.hhs.gov.

318 The View, "Joe Rogan Responds to Spotify Controversy," The View, January 31, 2022, YouTube video, 6:26, https://www.youtube.com/watch?v=BUwh6q6-Og8.

319 Anne Steele, "Spotify Takes Down Neil Young's Music After His Joe Rogan Ultimatum," *The Wall Street Journal,* January 26, 2022, https://www.wsj.com/articles/neil-youngs-music-is-being-taken-down-by-spotify-after-ultimatum-over-joe-rogan-11643230104.

320 Ben Sisario, "Joni Mitchell Plans to Follow Neil Young Off Spotify, Citing 'Lies,' *The New York Times,* January 28, 2022, https://www.nytimes.com/2022/01/28/arts/music/joni-mitchell-neil-young-spotify.html.

321 Robert Hart, "Parler Sues Amazon Again in Wake of Deplatforming," Forbes.com, March 3 2021, https://www.forbes.com/sites/roberthart/2021/03/03/parler-sues-amazon-again-in-wake-of-deplatforming/?sh=58e2c725166d.

322 State of New York, "Vaccination and Mask Requirements for Child Care Programs," December 6, 2021, https://www1.nyc.gov/assets/doh/downloads/pdf/covid/providers/covid-19-vaccination-mask-requirements-child-care.pdf.

323 Charles M. Blow, "I'm Furious at the Unvaccinated," *The New York Times,* December 8, 2021, https://www.nytimes.com/2021/12/08/opinion/unvaccinated-people-anti-vaxxers.html.

324 https://www.fda.gov/news-events/press-announcements/coronavirus-covid-19-update-fda-revokes-emergency-use-authorization-monoclonal-antibody-bamlanivimab

325 Katherine Lewin, Lawsuit to allow Ivermectin to be administered to Jacksonville man moves to 1st District Court," *Florida Times-Union*, January 14, 2022, https://www.jacksonville.com/story/news/2022/01/14/mayo-clinic-lawsuit-to-allow-ivermectin-as-a-treatment-moves-out-of-duval/9120594002/.

326 National Library of Medicine (US). (2020, April -). Study to Describe the Safety, Tolerability, Immunogenicity, and Efficacy of RNA Vaccine Candidates Against COVID-19 in Healthy Individuals. Identifier NCT04368728. https://clinicaltrials.gov/ct2/show/NCT04368728?term=NCT04368728&draw=2&rank=1

327 John Ley, "Pfizer COVID-19 vaccine delivers less long-term protection from hospitalization after four months," *Clark County Today*, September 21, 2021, https://www.clarkcountytoday.com/news/pfizer-covid-19-vaccine-delivers-less-long-term-protection-from-hospitalization-after-four-months/.

328 Norwegian Institute of Public Health, "Menstrual changes following COVID-19 vaccination," December 21, 2021, https://www.fhi.no/en/news/2022/menstrual-changes-following-covid-19-vaccination/?fbclid=IwAR1cpKbtZV_HSkcQAk7AVCL4PH_jBWqzssJl6fWIjVOX-IT6F-nMwKwg6XTA.

329 "Roe v. Wade (1973)." Legal Information Institute. Cornell Law School. https://www.law.cornell.edu/wex/roe_v_wade_%281973%29.

Chapter Eighteen: Pandemic Without End

330 Kaia Hubbard, "The Pandemic Has Worsened the US Obesity Epidemic," *US News and World Report*, September 15, 2021, The Pandemic Has Worsened America's Obesity Epidemic, Report Finds | Best States | US News.

331 Annalisa Merelli, "The WHO Has a Worrisome Reliance on the Bill & Melinda Gates Foundation," December 16, 2021, *Quartz*, https://qz.com/2102889/the-who-is-too-dependent-on-gates-foundation-donations/.

332 Farah Stockman, "The War on Terror Was Corrupt From the Start," *The New York Times*, September 13, 2021, https://www.nytimes.com/2021/09/13/opinion/afghanistan-war-economy.html.

Chapter Nineteen: Evil Beyond Human Imagination

333 Snejana Farberov, "Girl, 9, and five adults arrested at NYC museum for refusing to show COVID vaccine cards," *Daily Mail*, January 21, 2022, https://www.dailymail.co.uk/news/article-10427451/Girl-9-five-adults-arrested-NYC-museum-refusing-COVID-vaccine-cards.html.

Chapter Twenty: The New Authoritarians vs. The Individual

334 "Anti-vaccine protesters rally in France, Germany, Austria, Italy," *Aljazeera*, January 9, 2022, https://www.aljazeera.com/news/2022/1/9/more-than-100000-rally-in-france-against-covid-vaccine-rules.

335 "UK PM Johnson drops COVID-19 restrictions," *Reuters*, January 19, 2022, https://www.reuters.com/world/uk/uk-pm-johnson-drops-covid-19-restrictions-2022-01-19/.

336 Reuters, Denmark Eases Coronavirus Restrictions, As Cases Hit New Record," reuters.com, January 17, 2022, https://www.reuters.com/world/europe/denmark-eases-coronavirus-restrictions-cases-hit-new-record-2022-01-17/.

337 Reuters, "Italy to Ease COVID Restrictions, Draghi Says," Reuters.com, February 2, 2022, https://www.reuters.com/world/europe/italy-set-ease-covid-restrictions-draghi-says-2022-02-02/.

338 Al Jazeera, "Israel PM Announces End of Vaccine 'Green Pass,' February 17, 2022, AlJazeera.com, https://www.aljazeera.com/news/2022/2/17/israel-pm-announces-end-of-vaccine-green-pass

339 Amanda D'Ambrosia, "FDA Begins Releasing COVID Vax Documents," Medpage Today, March 7, 2022, https://www.medpagetoday.com/special-reports/exclusives/97544.

340 Spencer Kimball, "Moderna CEO Stephane Bancel has sold more than $400 million of company stock during the pandemic," *CNBC*, March 17, 2022, https://www.cnbc.com/2022/03/17/moderna-ceo-stephane-bancel-has-sold-more-than-400-million-of-company-stock-during-the-pandemic.html.

341 Stephanie Dube Dwilson, "Moderna CEO Stephane Bancel Deletes Twitter Account," *Heavy*, February 13, 2022, https://heavy.com/news/moderna-ceo-deletes-twitter-account-stephane-bancel/.

342 Reuters Fact Check, "Fact Check-Pfizer CEO's comments on limited COVID-19 vaccine protection refer to the Omicron variant," *Reuters*, January 13, 2022, https://www.reuters.com/article/factcheck-bourla-omicronprotection/fact-check-pfizer-ceos-comments-on-limited-covid-19-vaccine-protection-refer-to-the-omicron-variant-idUSL1N2TT29Z.

343 Daniel Funke, "Fact check: Unvaccinated more likely to get omicron than fully vaccinated, boosted," *USA Today*, January 28, 2022, https://www.usatoday.com/story/news/factcheck/2022/01/28/fact-check-omicron-variant-isnt-more-likely-infect-vaccinated/9191880002/.

344 Washington University School of Medicine, "CDC director Rochelle Walensky visits #WashUMed," Washington University School of Medicine, March 3, 2022, YouTube video, 56:00, https://www.youtube.com/watch?v=I_hYgIpxM4A.

345 "French parliament approves more restrictive vaccine pass," *France 24*, January 16, 2022, https://www.france24.com/en/europe/20220116-french-parliament-approves-more-restrictive-vaccine-pass.

346 Kayla Benjamin, "DC's Vaccine Mandate is Over—but Many Restaurants, Gyms, and Entertainment Venues Still Require Vax Proof," *Washingtonian*, February 16, 2022, https://www.washingtonian.com/2022/02/16/dc-vaccine-mandate-owner-which-indoor-venues-still-require-vax-proof/.

347 Nina Totenberg, "Supreme Court blocks Biden's vaccine-or-test mandate for large private companies," *NPR*, January 13, 2022, https://www.npr.org/2022/01/13/1072165393/supreme-court-blocks-bidens-vaccine-or-test-mandate-for-large-private-companies.

348 Nick Niedzwiadek, "Biden administration makes case to save vaccination mandate for federal employees," *Politico*, March 8, 2022, https://www.politico.com/news/2022/03/08/biden-administration-vaccination-mandate-federal-employees-00015181.

349 The White House Briefing Room, "Statement by President Joe Biden on the US Supreme Court Decision on Vaccine Requirements," January 13, 2022, https://www.whitehouse.gov/briefingroom/statements-releases/2022/01/13/statement-by-president-joe-biden-on-the-u-s-supreme-

courts-decision-on-vaccine-requirements/.

350 Austen, Ian and Dan Bilefsky, "Trudeau Declares Rare Public Emergency to Quell Protests," *The New York Times,* February 14, 2022, https://www.nytimes.com/2022/02/14/world/americas/justin-trudeau-emergencies-act-canada.html.

351 Freeland, "Remarks by the Deputy Prime Minister and Minister of Finance regarding the Emergencies Act," February 14, 2022, https://deputypm.canada.ca/en/news/speeches/2022/02/14/remarks-deputy-prime-minister-and-minister-finance-regarding-emergencies.

352 Sophia Harris, "Several provinces are dropping vaccine passports, but some businesses aren't on board, *CBC,* February 17, 2022, https://www.cbc.ca/news/business/provincial-vaccine-mandate-business-1.6354502.

Conclusion: Resistance

353 Edward Dowd, Interview by Dr. Naomi Wolf, *DailyClout,* March 7, 2022, https://dailyclout.io/edward-dowd-explains-bombshell-fraud-charge-re-pfizer-hiding-deaths-data/.

354 Thacker PD. Covid-19: Researcher blows the whistle on data integrity issues in Pfizer's vaccine trial. BMJ. 2021 Nov 2;375:n2635. doi: 10.1136/bmj.n2635. PMID: 34728500. https://www.bmj.com/content/375/bmj.n2635